TROUBLED TIMES: Macclesfield 1790-1870

Keith Austin

CHURNET VALLEY BOOKS
1 King Street, Leek, Staffordshire. 01538 399033
email: picture.book@virgin.net web: freespace.virgin.net/c.hinton/

© Keith Austin and Churnet Valley Books 2001

ISBN 1 897949 71 5

Printed in Malta by Interprint Limited

In memory of Jill Norris, 1949-1985,
whose enthusiasm for the history of Macclesfield's
silk workers inspired my original research.

Acknowledgements

To a large extent this book is the result of the research that I did for the Macclesfield Silk Heritage Project (now the Macclesfield Museums Trust) during 1983-4, when, under the leadership of the late Jill Norris, several researchers pieced together the story of Macclesfield's silk industry. Now, together with additional material gleaned over the years, I have finally produced this book. It would not have been possible without the help of others and I would like to thank the following:

Macclesfield Public Library, Macclesfield Registrar of Births and Deaths, Manchester Central Library and Southampton City Council Archives, all for access to their records.

Macclesfield Museums Trust, Cheshire Record Office, the Science Museum, the British Museum, Macclesfield Environmental Services, Mrs J. Leach, David Broadhurst and Doug Pickford, all for their generosity in providing illustrations.

I would also like to thank Christine Pemberton for processing many of the illustrations.

Lastly, a special thanks to my wife Joyce for understanding my 'obsession' with 19th century Macclesfield and its working people.

Contents

Sources

I have acknowledged sources of illustrations wherever I have been able. The following abbreviations are used:

MMT: Macclesfield Museums Trust
BM: The British Museum
CRO: Cheshire Record Office
SM: The Science Museum
MES: Macclesfield Environmental Services

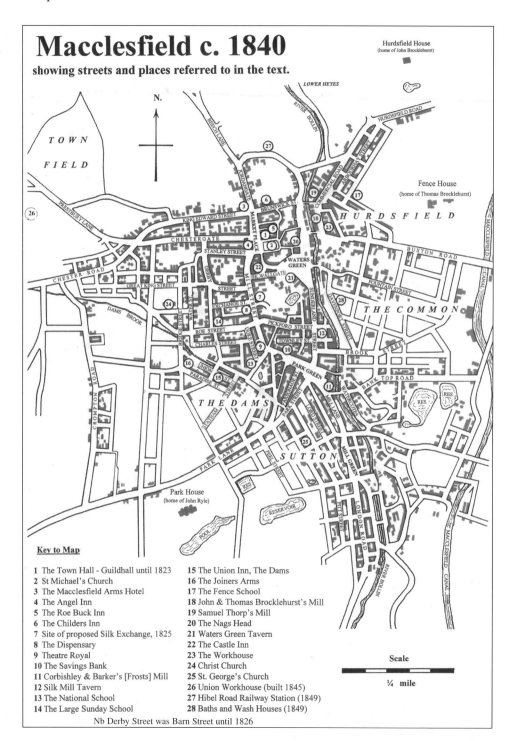

Macclesfield c. 1840
showing streets and places referred to in the text.

Key to Map

1 The Town Hall - Guildhall until 1823
2 St Michael's Church
3 The Macclesfield Arms Hotel
4 The Angel Inn
5 The Roe Buck Inn
6 The Childers Inn
7 Site of proposed Silk Exchange, 1825
8 The Dispensary
9 Theatre Royal
10 The Savings Bank
11 Corbishley & Barker's [Frosts] Mill
12 Silk Mill Tavern
13 The National School
14 The Large Sunday School
15 The Union Inn, The Dams
16 The Joiners Arms
17 The Fence School
18 John & Thomas Brocklehurst's Mill
19 Samuel Thorp's Mill
20 The Nags Head
21 Waters Green Tavern
22 The Castle Inn
23 The Workhouse
24 Christ Church
25 St. George's Church
26 Union Workhouse (built 1845)
27 Hibel Road Railway Station (1849)
28 Baths and Wash Houses (1849)

Nb Derby Street was Barn Street until 1826

Introduction

The period from 1790 to 1870 saw some of the most troubled times in Macclesfield's industrial history. During these years the Town's silk industry alternately thrived and declined - even boomed explosively then slumped with cataclysmic results over one very brief period.

There were the good times, when a silk worker's wage was sufficient for him to raise a family in modest comfort. Then there were bad times, when unemployment would blast through their humble homes, leaving hearthstones cold, cupboards bare and their families dressed in rags and tatters. Throughout, long hours and poor pay bred resentment and led to strikes - and a labour dispute often resulted in workers being imprisoned under an Act of 1767 that made it a criminal offence to leave work unfinished.

Yet despite such trials and although they were largely uneducated, many silk workers, particularly hand loom silk weavers, campaigned tirelessly to improve their lot. Hundreds - sometimes thousands - attended meetings concerning trade or politics. Many took prominent local parts in the nationwide issues of their times: political reform, the Factory Acts, the New Poor Law, free trade, trades unionism, Owenism or co-operation - all had their protagonists or antagonists from among their ranks.

"Troubled Times" is told largely from the perspective of the hand loom silk weavers, quite often in their own words. This is largely due to the local newspaper, *the Macclesfield Courier*, which documented their activities and meetings in some detail from the mid 1820s onwards. Consequently, the story tends towards a one-sided view of what happened. However, if the weavers' accounts of events were contradicted by their employers, little survives. Although the employers therefore often appear mean and harsh, they were no better nor worse than most employers in any industry of their time. Some were good, even benevolent, while others were penny-pinching in the extreme. But business rather than philanthropy was their main concern, and to ignore market forces and fail to keep abreast with competitors was, as nowadays, an invitation to decline and bankruptcy - which several did suffer.

Nevertheless, there was a certain attitude that permeated many an employer's dealings with his operatives. It was an attitude not unusual in an era when the terms 'master' and 'servant' were still much used, and had some bearing in a court of law. At its very worst it was summarised by the following statement from a Macclesfield employer when writing to a working class newspaper, *the Trades Journal*, on 16th April 1841.

"Armed as I am with the laws of my country, I shall never submit to the insulting dictates of a perverse and headstrong class of men: never shall I employ an unionist; never shall I have in my employment any man save him who will submit to my orders, and advance to my rules. What do ye want but your wages? What have poor men to do with notions of rights and privileges?"

Macclesfield's hand loom silk weavers and their fellow silk workers did aim to get fair wages; but they also had strong ideas about rights and privileges as well. The writer, Thomas Adolphus Trollope, characterised such men:

"factory workers themselves, but had by various circumstances, native talent, industry and energy or favouring fortune - more likely all together - managed to raise themselves out of the slough of despond in which their fellows were overwhelmed."

It is from the struggles of Macclesfield men of this calibre, and others like them elsewhere, that we have inherited many of our rights and privileges. Their story and that of the times they lived in is told, to the best of my ability, within the pages of this book.

Keith Austin, Buglawton, July 2000

Old Macclesfield, the 108 steps looking from the Waters Green area. *(MMT)*

Chapter 1. The Spitalfields Inheritance

Macclesfield's association with the manufacture of silk goods was almost two centuries old by the 1790s. As early as 1617 silk buttons had been made there, but the industry declined due to an Act of Parliament of 1722 which forbade the wearing of buttons made from woven stuffs. Replacing it in importance were two other silk operations; the throwing of silk twist for weaving and to a lesser extent the actual weaving of narrow silk ribbons by townswomen. The silk throwing industry flourished and in 1744 Charles Roe, an entrepreneur from Derbyshire, established the first water-powered throwing mill at Park Green. Soon, other throwsters had multi-story mills built nearby, powered by the River Bollin or the Dams Brook which flowed into it.

In these early years the thrown silk was mostly woven elsewhere, often at Spitalfields in London where silk weaving was long established. The craft had been brought to the area in the late 17th and early 18th centuries by Huguenots - Protestant refugees from Catholic France. By the latter half of the 18th century Spitalfields weavers were well organised and militant; and after serious riots in 1773 the Government was forced to pass an Act of Parliament which guaranteed fixed prices for their labour, these so high that the weavers became a sort of 'aristocracy' among wage earners. Spitalfields manufacturers, who wished to avoid the high wages demanded by their own weavers, began sending work out into the provinces. Silk, probably from this source, was being woven on broad-looms in Macclesfield by 1780.

Silk-weavers' Windows, Spitalfields.

Spitalfields in the eighteenth century. (*MMT*)

An Act similar to the Spitalfields Act had been enforced in Dublin at around this time, with the same consequence. As the silk weaving work migrated out into provincial towns so too did some of the silk weavers themselves. Many went to Manchester from London or Dublin and some came on into Macclesfield in their search to ply their trade. There they set themselves up as 'undertakers' - weaving silk on a sub-contract basis from local manufacturers; or else working directly for the undertakers as journeymen.

Such men brought with them the organisational traditions of their trade. By 1796 they were sufficiently unified to form a committee of weavers and draw up a new list of prices for woven silk, replacing the Manchester list which had been in use for the previous ten years. Manufacturers had no choice but to accede to their demands. However, at this date the relations between manufacturers and this weavers' committee was relatively amicable, for trade was good and the social divide between them not too extreme, two or three manufacturers having themselves once been weavers.

The town itself was expanding rapidly under the influx of the newcomers and the numbers of its dwellings almost doubled. Many of the newly built houses were small in size, two up and two downstairs rooms only, and were ranged in rows or around courtyards, often adjacent to the mills clustered about the River Bollin and Dams brook. Others had a third story, a garret with a long window extending to almost the whole of the house width which would provide daylight enough for long hours of work. These were to be the 'loom-shops' of the hand-loom silk weavers of Macclesfield.

During the late 1790s a family named Prout came to Macclesfield. They most likely originated in London, particularly its east side where silk weaving was the predominant trade and the name Prout relatively common. This itself may even have been the Anglicisation of the French 'Prouteaux,' the surname of several Spitalfields families from about 1714 onwards. If the Prout's were themselves silk weavers, then they probably migrated to Macclesfield via other towns as did other itinerant weavers. They brought with them their son John, born at Nailsworth, Gloucestershire, in 1794. Another son, William, was born at Macclesfield in 1800.

Young John Prout was set to work by his parents as soon as he was of an age when it was considered reasonable for a child to do so - at four years old. This was not uncommon, for the children of poor parents were expected to make some contribution towards their keep as soon as they were capable of managing simple tasks, either at home or in work outside from which money could be earned. And there was plenty of work for children to do in Macclesfield's silk mills. Visiting the town in 1787, the evangelist John Wesley had noted in his journal, *"Took a view of Mr Ryle's silk mill which keeps 250 children in perpetual employment."* John Ryle's mill was just one of several such establishments

Many of these children were 'poor law apprentices,' either orphans or the offspring of destitute parents. Overseers of parish poorhouses apprenticed children to the owners of throwing mills for terms of three years. In most cases the wages were paid directly to the poorhouse where the child resided, but occasionally the mill owner would provide board and lodgings - with a corresponding reduction in the wage. Working parents could also see the advantages of having their children apprenticed to a silk throwster. While adult male workers in silk throwing earned around eight shillings per week and women about half that, a child's wages, depending on age and proficiency, could add from 2s. to as much as 4s. per week to the family budget. Mill hours were long, eleven per day plus two compulsory 'overhours,' adding up to 76 hours for a six day week; but parents would probably have subscribed to John Wesley's view that such work for children was a means of *"diverting them from the temptations of idleness."*

Work for children in silk mills consisted largely of 'piecing' - mending broken strands of silk - or bobbin winding. The youngest children were usually employed as piecers, for their small and nimble fingers were considered to be most suitable to the delicate nature of the operation. Apart from the mills, there was work for children to do in weavers' garrets, the youngest as 'quill winders' - winding silk onto small bobbins for a shuttle -

Silk weaver's apprenticeship certificate, 1819. *(MMT)*

while older children were often employed as weavers of plain goods. Many children were employed by their own parents in the long-windowed loom-shop above where they lived. Some, whose parents were in other trades, were also found work with weavers; for the possibility of progressing on to plain weaving by the age of eight or nine could be followed by an apprenticeship to the trade. This, as opposed to the three year 'apprenticeships' in name only offered by silk throwsters, was a real apprenticeship during which the child learned a skilled trade. A skilled weaver was someone with status above that of the ordinary silk worker, enjoying not only better remuneration for his or her labour but also a degree of independence and dignity unknown by those who worked in a factory.

John Prout started weaving when aged thirteen, from which it might be inferred that his earlier working years were with a weaver, possibly his own father. Weavers' apprentices were bound by legally stamped indentures for seven years to a master of the trade, usually before the age of sixteen. There were two types of apprenticeship in operation in Macclesfield: 'domestic apprentices' received bed and board only within the masters home, while 'half-pay apprentices' lived in their own homes and received half of what their labour earned. Because of limited accommodation in weavers' homes, the half-pay apprentice was the most common arrangement. Apprenticeships were strictly administered by the weavers' committee, mainly in order to retain some control of the labour market. Only master weavers who were 'undertakers' - that is those who undertook to do weaving jobs on a sub-contract arrangement with silk manufacturers - were allowed to take them on and then at a maximum of two, depending on how many of their own children were 'in the loom.' One prerogative enjoyed by an undertaker's eldest son was that he could practice the craft without the necessity of serving an apprenticeship.

Having served their time as an apprentice, the next stage was that of journeyman weaver. Journeymen wove on looms provided by the undertaker in his loom shop, for which they paid him 'loom-rent' [or 'loom standing'] and other small sums of money for such things as coals, candles and quill winding. Some would aspire to becoming an undertaker, and providing they could raise sufficient capital might in time become one, with a loom shop of their own and journeymen, apprentices and quill winders working under them. Undertakers obtained warps for weaving from a manufacturer's warehouseman, returning them once they were completed and paying the full price they received, less deductions, to their journeymen. They could usually recoup the capital outlay for a loom in twelve months; the loom rents then forming the major part of their

Draw-loom weaving. *(MMT)*

income supplemented by weaving done by themselves or the members of their own, often large, families.

The early years of John Prout's working life were later looked back upon by him and others as a period of comparative plenty. With the weavers' committee regulating the trade in their interests the work was plentiful and their wages were at a similar level to those of other skilled tradesmen. During the 1790s and early 1800s they earned on average from 15s. to just over a pound per week whereas bricklayers and carpenters could earn 18s. This compared very well with the 8s. paid to unskilled male workers in silk mills, the 'millman' or 'silk steward.' From their earnings they would pay around 1s. per week in rent, while best beef was fourpence per pound and butter between 5d. and 9d. per pound.

At this time, war with France meant there were often food shortages, while that which was available was either expensive or of poor quality. The price of wheat, 48s. 11d. per quarter locally when war began in 1793, reached 94s. 6d. in 1811 and was up to 108s. 9d. by 1813. Serious riots occurred in the Market Place in March 1800, during which meal and flour was taken by force from stallholders, and a similar riot there had to be suppressed by the militia in the April of 1812. In 1796 the Town's council had tried to intervene at the market

Waters Green 1810. *(MMT)*

place on the behalf of local inhabitants, encouraging farmers bringing their produce to town to sell at a "fair price." Yet silk workers apparently took the best available at any price, for Mayor Michael Daintry was to bemoan the fact: "Fine wheaten bread.......is chiefly consumed by people who work in the manufactories and who in general pay little regard to economy or to the interests of the community."[1]

In spite of attempts by the Government and other interests to drive working people away from a wheaten diet and towards the cheaper potato, Macclesfield's workers would insist on their white loaf. Local historian John Corry, writing in 1817 of the war period, echoed Mayor Daintry's sentiments in a more scathing tone:

"Nothing was thought too good for the industrious weaver.....Nothing that the market could afford was too good for them."[2]

The weavers themselves saw their own living standards in a more modest light. Of conditions in 1807, the year that John Prout started weaving, he later claimed:

"the condition of the weavers was one of comparative competency, though the trade had never risen to the heights of some mechanical operations; they then had the means of obtaining every necessity. They had rules and regulations in the trade which promoted stability, secured wages, and tended to promote uniformity and a kindred feeling between masters and workmen."[3]

This *"kindred feeling"* had united not just manufacturers and weavers, but other silk workers and townsfolk generally in a common cause during 1803. Incensed by a Government Bill aiming to allow the import of silk handkerchiefs from India, a committee of seven men, mostly weavers, was set up, subscriptions were raised from manufacturers and local shopkeepers, and two paid agents were delegated to conduct the opposition. Fortunately for Macclesfield the Bill was lost, for the activities of their chosen delegates had not in any way contributed to victory. Most of the money collected subsidised several sessions of eating, drinking and smoking at a liquor dealer's establishment and the two men were later charged with embezzlement and misappropriation of funds. Yet the whole episode did show that both silk manufacturers and their workers shared a sense of unity.

This situation was to change drastically when the war came to a close; indeed the cracks were showing even by 1805.

The Revolution in France and the war that followed had instilled in the British Government such a fear of Jacobins [French Revolution sympathisers] and other radicals, even religious dissenters, that any organisation of working people was viewed with suspicion. Acting on reports from parts of industrial Britain where discontented workers were forming themselves into unions, the Government passed the Combination Acts in 1799 and 1800. These were ostensibly aimed at suppressing any combination of masters or workmen who might unite to further their own interests in the workplace: in effect they were used mostly to suppress working people.

Macclesfield's working people were largely defiant of the new Acts. As the first few years of the nineteenth century proceeded, local manufacturers complained that in every branch of manufacture workmen had at different times turned out for an advance in wages and while on strike they had been supported by subscriptions raised among other workers. A strike by millmen resisting wage reductions at Critchley and Brinsley's silk throwing mill in 1805 was the first to result in the ringleaders being prosecuted under the terms of the Combination Acts. Five men aged between 15 and 36 were charged with conspiring *"with divers persons to quit service and raise the wages of themselves and other servants."* Secret meetings on Macclesfield Common and collections among other workers were organised for their support, and the men were ultimately acquitted.

Less fortunate were the seven leaders of Macclesfield's artisan hatters, a trade whose national association was legitimised by charter from Charles II in 1667. After their new list of prices was rejected by employers in March 1806, Macclesfield hatters held a mass meeting on Danes Moss and called a strike that was accompanied by some intimidation of those who remained at work. Their seven leaders were indicted as *"servants"* - a term which they objected to as they saw themselves as craftsmen - who were *"unjustly and corruptly"* conspiring not to work for their accustomed wages. Found guilty they were each sentenced to 12 months imprisonment at Chester Castle.

During the early 1800s the weavers' committee flourished unchecked by law, even though their very existence contravened the Combination Acts. But apart from a short-lived slump in 1808, trade was improving and the manufacturers themselves had little reason to bring down the heavy hand of Government on the weavers. In fact, during 1810 trade was so good that some manufacturers began to pay more than the prices for woven goods listed in 1796. When the weavers' committee got to hear of this they called a meeting with manufacturers to revise all prices; those still paying the old prices were made to pay more while others, overpaying by too much, were made to pay less, conforming to the new list. Three years later, with trade still expanding, the 1810 list was revised upwards for every silk article that was made.

However, there was growing resentment on the part of some silk manufacturers. Although a few had once been silk weavers themselves, the social gulf between them and their weavers had widened and they had less and less direct personal contact with the weavers' committee. The fact that they took no part in choosing the committee or of fixing prices rankled with them. Any newly designed silk article was taken first to the weavers' committee for a price to be determined by them; and even if manufacturers were consulted it was the committee's decision that invariably prevailed. This was said to have acted as a deterrent to the introduction of new designs, when demand for 'fancy trade' articles was growing. Increasingly the manufacturers viewed the weavers' committee as an illegal combination - a combination that ought to be broken.

This had already happened in Manchester, where in 1812 silk manufacturers had refused to abide by the list prices and had totally disrupted the organisation of their silk weavers. With silk being woven more cheaply there, Macclesfield's manufacturers lost trade to them and were eager to follow the Manchester example. In 1814, when the Elizabethan Statute of Artificers [1562] which gave legal status to the seven year apprenticeship was repealed by Government, Macclesfield's silk manufacturers were provided with a lever with which to achieve their aims. The apprenticeship system was being undermined already, for in 1807 *"fugitive boys and girls"* were working without indentures in the town. The weavers had tried to deal with abuses: in 1810 they ended the non-apprenticeship prerogative enjoyed by a master weaver's eldest son and insisted that a weaver's child served his or her time with someone other than their father. But after 1814, anyone could work as a weaver, with or without papers.

In the aftermath of the Battle of Waterloo and a final conclusion to the Revolutionary and Napoleonic era, a post-war slump coupled with the return of ex-soldiers and militia men on to the labour market offered Macclesfield's silk manufacturers their opportunity. In November 1815 they demanded a 25 to 30% reduction in the list of prices. This was rejected by the weavers' committee, but a compromise reduction of one penny per square yard was offered in return. When this was refused they called a strike from November 4th which was to last for up to sixteen weeks. During it about 1,000-1,400 looms stood idle.

The first reaction of manufacturers was to compel their weavers to complete the work already in their looms. This was achieved by making examples of those who had not by prosecuting them. By leaving work unfinished these weavers were deemed to have broken their contracts under the Master and Servant Act of 1767 - a criminal offence for a servant but only a civil offence for a master. Local magistrates sentenced several strikers to terms of imprisonment.

Next, the manufacturers advertised in the *Macclesfield Courier*, stating that as their *"liberal and reasonable propositions"* had been rejected by the weavers they would henceforth regulate the trade under new principles. An extract from the recent Act of Parliament repealing the Statute of Artificers followed, after which it continued:

"The Masters are determined to avail themselves of the remedy to which the Law of the Land presents them for the removal of the existing evil and are resolved to throw the trade open to the employment of any who are able and willing to engage in it. The Masters will never henceforth treat with the Weavers as a body."[4]

They were soon opening up factories, fitting them out with looms and encouraging people, from within the trade or without, to receive training in silk weaving and work there. Many hand loom cotton weavers from Lancashire, where the trade was in decline owing to the advent of the steam loom, flocked to the town to take up these new jobs. One was David Rowbotham. He was born *"on a common near Castle Shane, Ireland"* in 1783, one year after his father and an elder brother, both weavers, were imprisoned for attempting to emigrate to America and thereby take their trade to the renegade ex-colonies. Much later, Rowbotham spent some time on the Sussex coast before making his way north to Lancashire and working at the cotton hand loom. When the steam loom took his trade away he then brought his weaver wife Elizabeth and their two infant children to Macclesfield, arriving in 1816.

The manufacturers also managed to 'poach' the silk weavers' own apprentices along with lots of other boys, girls and women who had no experience whatsoever. It was the beginning of a factory system of weaving in Macclesfield. Henceforth there would be two types of weaver in the town; 'inside weavers,' employed in the manufacturers' weaving factories, and 'outside weavers' who either worked for them directly in their own homes or were employed indirectly in undertakers' loom-shops.

The prices paid for the weavers' work were much reduced. For weaving 'Bandanna' handkerchiefs, a staple item in the Macclesfield trade, the list price in 1813 ranged from 4s. 8d. to 5s. 6d. per yard wide 'cut' of seven yards in length, depending on whether they were plain or fancy; and a good workman could complete four cuts in a week. After 1815 the price paid for Bandannas was rarely more than the 3s. 6d. per cut paid by manufacturers such as John Ryle; and it could be as low as 1s. 9d. from others. A journeyman's deductions for loom rent, coals, candles and quill winding, before and after 1815, was about three shillings.

At the time that the strike began, early in November 1815, John Prout was aged 21. He had then completed his apprenticeship and had been working as a journeyman weaver for about a year, mostly weaving fancy Bandannas. When the weavers met to vote for the strike John put up his hand to stick out for the old price of 5s. 6d. per cut, then he 'turned out' with the main body. In a few weeks he, like most others, went back to work at 3s. 6d. per cut. But before he resumed his trade there was a document to sign, one which all weavers were presented with by manufacturers before they were allowed a warp to weave. This, like the one that John Ryle's workers were given, stated:

"I do solemnly declare, that I do not belong to any committee or associated body of weavers, and that no committee or associated body has any power or control over me, whatsoever..."[5]

A committee of weavers would eventually arise once more from the defeat of 1815, and John Prout and David Rowbotham would be leading lights in their affairs. But they would never again be as strong a force in determining prices for silk weaving. Neither would Macclesfield's silk weavers enjoy such a long period of stability and the good living standards they had before Waterloo.

References

1. Letter by the Mayor to the Duke of Portland. quoted in Malmgreen, Gail, *Economy and Culture in an Industrialising Town: Macclesfield, Cheshire, 1750-1839*. PhD thesis 1981.

2. John Corry *History of Macclesfield*. 1817.

3. Commission of Inquiry into Handloom Silk Weavers, 1838 (see Macclesfield Courier 6/10/1838).

4. Macclesfield Courier (M.C.) 25/11/1815.

5. Second Report of Select Committee on Ribbon Weavers of Coventry and Leek and the Silk Weavers of Macclesfield 1818, page 64, evidence of John Ryle.

RUFFIAN ASSEMBLIES.

A Radical meeting, c. 1817.   *(BM)*

Chapter 2. Radical Macclesfield

After November 1815, when Macclesfield's silk manufacturers gained the upper hand over the prices paid for woven silk, the conditions of those who wove it became more and more onerous. Not only were the prices paid for each type of woven article reduced, but where before the price for weaving a whole 'cane' containing 21 cuts, or 147 yards, was fixed in advance, some manufacturers altered it week by week according to the state of the trade. With incomes much reduced, many weavers left their homes for smaller houses, often for those with only four windows on which no window tax had to be paid. Others were forced to apply to the parish for relief - so many of them that the parish overseers had to borrow over £1,000 to support them. In 1817 the desperate weavers petitioned Macclesfield manufacturers:

"We hereby beg permission to call your attention to the truly lamentable situation into which the trade has been reduced and degraded, since the unprecedented reduction in our wages, and also the alarming increase of pauperism that daily presents itself...."[1]

In spite of its contrite tones, it had no effect on the majority of manufacturers.

Although some manufacturers tried to be fair in giving a price for weaving, there was always the problem of others, less scrupulous, undercutting them. One who aimed at fairness was Thomas Parker of Habgood and Parker. Having once himself been a silk weaver and a member of the weavers' committee in 1815, he was much more inclined to view them with sympathy:

"I can only say that, when a poor weaver has come to me for a warp, and with his hat in his hand, has said, "Can you give me a warp," his looks tell me that he has been pinched: his very face and countenance exhibit the strongest picture of misery and wretchedness. I have often given a man a warp because he wanted it, and I knew he must have it, although I could not afford to give him more than a certain price, viz. the same price that I give to the rest of the men; but if I had been so inhuman as some of the rest of the manufacturers, I would have said, "There is a warp, but I shall only give you 2s. for it," and if I had so said he would have taken it in order to get a little bread for his family."[2]

Whether the manufacturers made any significant gains from their actions is unknown. Parker claimed not, as they were *"underselling each other in the city."* Others said that by employing untrained labour in their weaving factories the trade fell into disrepute. However, one manufacturer stated that the effect was to open up the trade to more designs, and in two years there were more new designs being produced than in the previous ten.

In 1818, Macclesfield silk weavers joined with those of Leek and Coventry in petitioning Parliament for the Spitalfields Act to be extended so that wages paid to silk weavers were equalised throughout Britain. Macclesfield's manufacturers then counter-petitioned. A Committee of the House of Commons was set up in order to examine witnesses, both weavers and manufacturers. They recommended that the Act be extended for a trial period, but this was rejected by the Commons. It was later claimed that at least one weaver who testified before the Committee was unable to get work from manufacturers afterwards.

A strike in early September 1818 seems to have been attended with some intimidation, fomented by a well-known Radical agitator, John Bagguley, a servant from Manchester. A letter from the Rev. C.W. Ethelston of Macclesfield to Lord Sidmouth, the Home Secretary, read:

"I shall be able to prove that Baguley was in my neighbourhood on Friday last evening inciting the weavers to conspiracy against their masters. At his instigation vitriol was thrown into the warps of the weavers who were not in the combination for an increase of pay."[3]

Macclesfield, in the period 1816-1820, was to witness much Radical activity, most of it directed towards political change.

With the ending of the Napoleonic Wars a period of comparative prosperity for Macclesfield's silk weavers disappeared, but the majority of workers in Britain's manufacturing industries had not fared so well while they lasted. The changing fortunes of war had caused violent fluctuations in the demand for labour. Once the war was over and British industry re-engaged in peacetime production, commodities which had previously fetched high prices due to scarcity suddenly dropped in value. Falling prices were no incentive to investors or industrialists and the resultant contraction in production led to wholesale wage-cutting and unemployment on a far worse scale.

While the cost of food in general was lower, this did not soften the blow of reduced wages or of eking out an existence on parish relief, for the prices of essential items were maintained at high levels, sometimes higher than during wartime. Wheat, averaging 64s. 6d. per quarter locally during 1815, was thereafter maintained at a minimum price of 80 shillings a quarter through the Corn Laws, which restricted imports of foreign wheat until home prices had reached a level that protected British farmers. Although most of Macclesfield's food prices dropped by 30 % after the war, bread, the staple diet of the poor, was 30 % higher.

Taxation raised the cost of other essentials. Income tax, brought in as a wartime measure and affecting only the wealthy, was abolished in 1816 despite the vast national debt that the war had generated. Instead, the Government balanced its budget through taxing everyday items such as tea [taxed at 100 %], sugar, tobacco, beer, soap, candles and paper. The burden of this taxation fell most heavily on the poor, upon whom little Government money was ever spent - and who had no vote by which to show their disapproval.

To make the situation more desperate, the weather in 1816 was among the worst ever recorded. Spring was severely cold and on June 7th there were snowfalls on the high ground in Cheshire and Derbyshire. Heavy rain throughout August ruined harvests throughout Britain. The price of wheat at Christmas reached 170s. per quarter and the cost of a sack of flour had more than doubled since June. Samuel Higginbotham, a Macclesfield solicitor, was to say of this time, *"the privations which the people had to endure....caused a degree of mortality frightful to contemplate."*[4]

The result was widespread civil unrest and demands for Parliamentary reforms including universal manhood suffrage, so that taxation without representation was ended. These aims were not an entirely new feature on the British scene, not even in Macclesfield. Since the 1790's the town had its share of Radicals, some of them Jacobin sympathisers. Religious dissenters particularly came under suspicion. Tory *"Church and King"* mobs of self-appointed vigilantes vented their rage at the Calvinists' Townley Street Chapel, disrupting their meetings with violence and deriding the worshippers as *"Jacobins"*. In return, one Radical characterised such men, *"Billy Pitt's* [William Pitt, Prime Minister 1784-1804] *dancing dogs."*

After 1816 Radicalism drew increasing numbers of supporters within the town. On the 2nd January 1817 about 1,000 people gathered at Town Field to hear Radical activists from Manchester and Stockport, *"tried VETERANS in the cause,"* address them. The meeting had been called by twenty local weavers and mechanics, and a journeyman silk weaver took the chair. At this time Manchester reformers were busily touring northern manufacturing districts to drum up support for the Hampden Club of Westminster, founded by Major John Cartwright and Sir Francis Burdett with the aim of petitioning for Parliamentary reform. But when these petitions were delivered by Lord Cochrane at the State opening of Parliament on the 28th January, they were utterly rejected, having been preceded a so-called attempt on the life of the Prince Regent - his carriage window being broken by angry crowds. As a result, the Government clamped down on all reforming societies, suspended Habeus Corpus and banned all meetings of over 50 people.

Some Manchester reformers, led by John Bagguley and Samuel Drummond, then decided to petition the Prince Regent directly. This was permissible, they argued, by an Act of Charles II allowing for ten out of every twenty petitioners to do so. Their idea was of a great march to London, each man carrying his petition wrapped in brown paper and tied around his right arm with a white bow. They were also to carry a blanket each for sleeping on the ground or in churches along the route: hence was coined their name, 'The Blanketeers.' Although the organisers were completely open about their plan, the authorities regarded the whole idea with the utmost suspicion - even that it would incite a revolution. As hundreds set out from St. Peter's Fields on the 10th March, 29 men including the organisers were arrested and the marchers were harassed by dragoons, yeomanry and special constables all the way to Stockport, where another 167 were taken prisoner and a bystander killed. Four or five hundred continued on into Macclesfield.

The arrival of these 'revolutionaries' in the town was recorded by *the Courier*:

"The tattered habiliments and forlorn aspect of the many deluded, with the desperate looks and language of the few villains who deceived them, might well remind one of the march of the Marsellaise; and some there were that had augured a similar event of their expedition. But their feebleness and discomfiture were now too evident to every eye, to admit the prevalence of any other feeling than of compassion; nor will we attribute the kindness manifested by our fellow townsmen to any other than a good and generous motive."[5]

The marchers were generally well received, encouraged, fed and lodged overnight; though some were said to have slept in St. Michael's churchyard and five were arrested and placed in prison. Special constables checked lodging houses and cavalry patrolled the streets overnight. In the morning the remaining marchers continued their way south, through Leek and on to Ashbourne, where yeomanry expecting a body of 30,000 men turned about two hundred back and took another 25 into custody. Only one man reached London to present his petition to Lord Sidmouth. So ended what *the Courier* claimed was an *"insurrection of twenty thousand men......a wild and incensed multitude"* from which they were thankful for the town's *"deliverance"* in *"the hour of danger."*

The Seditious Meetings Act of 1817 was in force until July 1818 and Macclesfield was apparently quiet until a further year had passed. In the meantime radical protest persisted elsewhere, sometimes with men from the town present in the role of delegates. Macclesfield delegates attended a meeting held at Hunslet Moor, Yorkshire, in June 1819, when reformers protesting about high taxation resolved to abstain from using any taxed article, beer, spirits, tobacco and tea included, until they had Parliamentary representation.

Then in July 1819 the Mayor and magistrates of Macclesfield felt obliged to warn local inhabitants that a proposed reform meeting to take place near Christ Church might constitute a breach of the peace. *The Courier* also warned readers about attending this *"threatened meeting of firebrands"* while including a lengthy list of *"Church and King"* adherents who had signed public declarations of loyalty during a meeting at the Town Hall - most of whom were to act as special constables on the day. A letter published within from *"An Englishwoman"* decried the female reform societies.

The reform meeting took place on July 31st and was attended by about 1,000 people - 300 of whom were said to be special constables. Two carts were lashed together to form a platform for the speakers. Among these with local notoriety were Robert Swindells, a cobbler who in 1817 had served time in Chester Castle for selling seditious pamphlets, and Joseph Swann, a 35 year old journeyman hatter who also sold pamphlets in his spare time. John Richards, a 23 year old one-time schoolteacher from Rainow, latterly a journeyman silk spinner, also spoke to the crowd, as did a tailor from Sutton named Joseph Sutton and John Stubbs, aged 32 and a cotton spinner. The vast numbers of women and children in the audience, outnumbering men, were also addressed by a woman from Stockport Female Union Society, who urged then to form a similar women's union in the town. After the meeting, seven of the speakers were arrested.

Two weeks later, an event in Manchester was to have serious repercussions in Macclesfield, as in many manufacturing towns in the north-west. On Sunday 15th August Henry 'Orator' Hunt, a national figure in the agitation for universal suffrage, arrived in the town by coach on route to Manchester. After a short meeting with some local

Henry 'Orator' Hunt holding his white cap of liberty

supporters he continued his journey. Hunt was to address a mass meeting at St. Peter's Fields on the following day. It was this gathering - of 50,000 working people, clad in their best clothes, waving banners and branches of laurel and wearing white caps of liberty - that ended in horror. Without provocation, magistrates arrested Hunt and read the Riot Act, then the unarmed men, women and children were cut down by the sabres of the mounted Yeomanry and Hussars. Eleven people were killed and a further 400 injured in the massacre, which has ever since been known under the infamous name 'Peterloo.'

Tuesday 17th August was a day of high tension in Macclesfield. Trouble was expected once news of the events at St. Peters Fields reached and aroused the town's working people to exact retribution upon those who opposed reform. It began at dusk, when about 700 men and boys gathered in the Market Place, shouting abuse and threats in the direction of the Guildhall and throwing stones through the windows of *the Courier* office. Mayor Samuel Pearson, along with magistrates, constables and four armed musketeers, then mounted the Guildhall steps and by lamplight read the Riot Act. The volley of stones that followed had them beating a hasty retreat to the Macclesfield Arms Hotel, after which the crowd completed the destruction of *the Courier* office windows and forced the door open. Next on their list was the home of Thomas Grimsditch, a local lawyer who, as a

STEEL LOZENGES

will stop their pain,

And set the Constitution

right again.

My L.—ds and G—tl—n,

The foreign powers

Write me word frequently

that they are ours,

Most truly and sincerely,

in compliance

Two cartoons, above and opposite, that appeared following the Peterloo massacre in 1819. *(BM)*

Cornet in the Cheshire Yeomanry, had gone to St. Peters Fields on the fateful day, though arriving after the massacre. Once his windows and their frames and shutters were completely destroyed the mob raged down Mill Street, breaking more doors and windows at the Theatre Royal, the Savings Bank, the Mayor's House, the Town Clerk's house and the News Room on Park Green.

It was as they turned their vengeance on the home of ex-Mayor Thomas Tunnicliffe that the tide turned. Tunnicliffe and another man had armed themselves with swords and were mounted on horses, and when they rushed the mob their action allowed the Mayor and

A FREE BORN ENGLISHMAN! THE ADMIRATION of the WORLD !!! AND THE ENVY of SURROUNDING NATIONS!!!!

about thirty or more special constables to begin rounding up the ringleaders. After a battle lasting about an hour, with brickbats and stones littered all over Park Green in the aftermath, the streets were finally cleared of rioters. Soon afterwards the sound of a bugle call announced the arrival of the Cheshire cavalry and at this the Mayor read the Riot Act once more in the Market place. Only two criminal charges resulted from the riot, one man being a silk weaver named Ralph Wright. But the destruction was severe, with forty homes needing repairs which cost over £1,000. For several days afterwards the town was patrolled by constables and the cavalry.

The reform meeting near Christ Church in July resulted in charges of Seditious Conspiracy against the Radical speakers. They were said to have vilified Parliament and aimed *"to excite a spirit of discontent and disturb the public peace."* A *"True Bill"* was found against seven men by the Grand Jury at Chester Quarter Sessions in October 1819 and six were tried at the next

The Old Guildhall, Macclesfield. *(MMT)*

Quarter Sessions in January 1820. In spite of defending themselves *"with no small share of ability,"* four, Swindells, Stubbs, Richards and 66 year old Stockport shoemaker, Joseph Burtenshaw, received sentences of two years at Chester Castle and were bound afterwards to keep the peace for a year on sureties totalling £100 each. Joseph Sutton obtained the clemency of the court on account of his large and totally dependent family.

The hatter, Joseph Swann, received a total of four and a half years imprisonment, for he was additionally charged with blasphemous libel, having sold pamphlets which implored people to reject the Bible and read the works of Tom Paine instead [1737-1809, father figure of British Radicalism, supporter of both American and French Revolutions and author of *The Rights of Man*, 1792]. Swann had been warned at the earlier quarter sessions not to continue selling pamphlets, but a man working for prosecution lawyer Thomas Grimsditch had later managed to buy one from Swann's wife. Both man and wife were then hauled before magistrates, where owing to her advance state of pregnancy and with four children at home Mrs Swann was released. Joseph Swann was sent to Knutsford House of Correction to be fettered with felons while awaiting trial at Chester. When Sentence was passed on him there at the January Quarter Sessions, *"Swann, with a vast deal of apparent sang froid, held up his RADICAL emblem - a white hat bound with crepe - and exclaimed "Han ye done? is that all! Why I thowt ye'd got a bit of hemp for me, and hung me!"* [6]

William Cobbett, 1763-1835.

Swann's wife then had to support the family on 9s. per week from the parish. In 1817, when Swindells was serving a term of imprisonment for selling seditious pamphlets, his wife and baby had died from neglect while another child was taken to the workhouse. To ensure no repetition of this sorry affair, Mrs Swann was financially assisted by national Radical figures Richard Carlile, publisher of Thomas Paine's works and the journal *Republican*, and William Cobbett, whose weekly *Political Register* had a nationwide following.

During Swann's incarceration, the Radicals' most hated adversary, Lord Castlereagh, committed suicide. Cobbett then penned a mocking obituary, *"CASTLEREAGH HAS CUT HIS OWN THROAT AND IS DEAD! Let that sound reach you in the depth of your dungeon......and carry consolation to your suffering soul."* It was addressed to Swann.

After 1820 the impetus for radical change was dissipated locally as improvements in living standards gathered pace. But Richards, Stubbs, Sutton and Swann were to continue agitating for many years to come.

References
1. Second Report of Select Committee on Ribbon Weavers of Coventry and Leek and the Silk Weavers of Macclesfield, 1818, evidence of Thomas Kelly.
2. Ibid. page 108, evidence of Thomas Parker.
3. Letter from the Rev. C.W. Ethelston to Viscount Sidmouth, Macclesfield, 7th Sept. 1818. HO 42/180, quoted in Aspinall A. *The Early English Trades Unions.*
4. M.C. 19/5/1849.
5. M.C. 15/3/1817.
6. M.C. 13/1/1820.

Macclesfield from Windmill Hill c. 1820.   (MMT)

Chapter 3. Boom to Slump

As the third decade of the nineteenth century got under way, the lives of all associated with Macclesfield's silk industry began to improve dramatically. In May 1822 *the Courier* reported:

"the silk manufacture of this town is now rapidly expanding and the capital embarked upon it is very considerable."[1]

During the previous year, the House of Lords had recommended reducing import duties on raw and thrown silk while retaining a prohibition on imported silk goods. From 1824 the duties were to be lowered from 5s. 6d. to a mere 3d. per pound on raw silk and from 9s. 11d. to 7s. 6d. per pound for thrown silk. Anticipating a surge in demand for Macclesfield's products, new silk mills were soon under construction and hundreds of houses for workers were being built. The demand for bricks was so great that cartloads of bricks caught fire in the streets from being taken too hot from the kiln at the brickyard on Macclesfield Common and the bricksetters themselves were in a position to obtain as much as 4s. per day for their labour, *"such is the demand for workman at the present time."* Land values rocketed: an estate near the town which was earmarked for housing increased in price from £10,000 to £30,000 over a short period.

Macclesfield's population expanded rapidly as hordes of people flocked in to take part in this bonanza. A population of about 7 or 8,000 in 1790 had risen to 24,000 by 1822 and was to reach around 32,000 within three more years. Many came from the depressed cotton-weaving districts of Lancashire and a sizeable portion from Ireland. In January 1823 *the Courier* proudly reported:

"an enormous increase has taken place in the trade and extent of this ancient town. Two considerable villages have risen within the year 1822, upon the estates of John Ryle and Thomas Smyth Esqrs.: while six extensive Silk factories have been finished and four more are in a state of rapid progress towards completion. Our numerous and daily increasing population, are in the enjoyment of that steady and ample employment, which secures to them the possession of all comforts, and many of the luxuries of life; and, we have been gratified by the admiration expressed by strangers, at the sight of those crowds of healthy young men and beautiful women, who pour from our gigantic factories in the intervals of labour...."[2]

The writer continued in glowing terms to mention the *"peace, good order and mutual benevolence"* among all classes in Macclesfield.

Yet it was not all *"peace, good order and mutual benevolence,"* for in

April 1824 a bitter dispute arose between silk manufacturers and millmen. Aiming to take full advantage of the booming trade, the employers wanted to increase their employees' hours from 11 to 12 per day, plus the usual two compulsory 'overhours.' The millmen turned out immediately and later gathered in the Market Place, where serious riots had to be quelled by the yeomanry and militia men. Only then did manufacturers offer an extra hour's money, but the millmen still refused because the extra hour would interfere with late shopping on Saturdays, their pay day. Manufacturers then promised an earlier finish on Saturdays if the extra hours were made up during the week, but this too was rejected. Claiming the longer hours would be more beneficial to the workers than themselves, the manufacturers next issued a notice insisting on the extra hour. Then they sat back to await the return of their workforce, which they felt assured *"may yet be enforced by privation and suffering."*

While they waited the millmen were busily circulating handbills in the town, stating that their opposition was on account of the very young children employed in the mills who would be adversely affected by the extra hour:

"It is a well known fact that children very young are employed in the above branch: and can we as men submit to a proposition as highly indecorous as to increase the hours of labour, knowing that it would not only affect the present ages, but ages yet unborn?"[3]

With this argument they gained much sympathy for their case; and when a subscription was raised among townsfolk their employers were beaten. The manufacturers were also much criticised by the London daily newspaper *the Morning Chronicle*, which deplored their attempts to increase the hours of both men and children, and condemned them for *"openly combining in defiance of the law."* The newspaper was actively hostile to the Combination Acts but stated: *"These Laws exist and we find that the Masters of Macclesfield have distinctly violated them.."*

The Combination Acts were in fact repealed only a few months later; but the law was still heavily biased against employees in matters of industrial relations. During the millmen's strike a thirteen year old boy, *"in humble circumstances"* had turned out with fellow workers. He and some other boys were then brought before a magistrate charged with leaving work unfinished under the 1767 Master and Servant Act. The magistrate was himself a silk manufacturer and during the hearing the boy's mother, a Mrs Hunt, realising this, spoke out, *"You are not fit to judge my son......Sir you have no right to commit these boys, you are in the same trade."*[4]

Despite her efforts the boy was sentenced to the maximum penalty, three months gaol at Knutsford, which he served throughout on the treadmill. But Mrs Hunt was not beaten, for on her son's behalf she brought an indictment for wrongful imprisonment against the magistrate, which was heard at Chester Assizes in April 1825. The verdict went to the plaintiff and she was awarded £20 in damages.

The year 1825 also saw the silk boom reach its peak. In February *the Courier* carried an advert addressed to *"Overseers, Guardians of the Poor and Families desirous of settling in Macclesfield."* It stated:

To Overseers, Guardians of the Poor, and Families desirous of settling in Macclesfield.

WANTED IMMEDIATELY,

FROM FOUR to FIVE THOUSAND PERSONS from Seven to Twenty Years of age, to be employed in the Throwing and Manufacture of Silk. The great increase of the Trade having caused a scarcity of hands, it is suggested that this is a most favourable opportunity for Persons with large families, and to Overseers wishing to put out children as Apprentices, to insure a comfortable livelihood for them.

Application to be made (if by Letter Post Paid) to the PRINTER of this Paper.

(CRO)

The Courier did voice doubts that their instant arrival might pose lodging problems, but went on to mention that not less than a thousand houses were about to be built and that several plots of land were marked out for four to five new silk factories. Many of these new houses featured loom-shops on the top floor and looms in the town now numbered 5,325 - about 4,000 more than in 1815. Factories had increased from 32 in 1814 to 58 by 1823, and by 1826 were to number 70. Since the early 1800s, most new factories were steam powered and built beside roads from which coal could be delivered rather than adjacent to a water source. This frenetic scene of construction was described by one manufacturer in February 1825:

"The Master erected factories: the operatives entered into building associations with the surplus of their earnings, and hundreds of cottages sprung up in every direction: the rush was on to take them, and before the plaster was dry on the walls they were occupied by families who found immediate and lucrative employment."[6]

With such a demand from employers for people to work in their mills, the price of labour rose. In mid February 1825 there was a short turn out by silk workers who, *"aware of the very prosperous state of the trade, demanded a considerable advance of wages."* The manufacturers complied within 24 hours and their workers returned to the mills. Prosperity seemed to have made manufacturers most agreeable, for *the Courier* recorded; *"the best understanding now exists between them* [silk workers] *and their employers."* Within weeks the town's silk weavers made renewed calls for a list of prices and a general increase of about 10% on their current wages. Unfortunately for them, the silk trade boom was all but over. All they could manage was to resist the lowering of prices for 'Persians' in November that year.

John Prout had married eighteen year old Elizabeth Etchells at Gawsworth Church on the 16th January 1816. By 1825 the couple had produced five children and were living at Crompton Road in a house with a loom shop on the top floor. They may have been purchasing it through one of several building societies set up by silk workers in the 1820's, possibly the Macclesfield Friendly Building Society, which had property in Crompton Road. As an undertaker, Prout employed several journeymen at his looms, weaving several types of light, figured and fancy silk goods - articles with equally fancy names, such as 'gros de Naples,' 'Persians,' or 'sarsnets'. Their wages were about 19s. 7d. per week less loom rent of about 2s. 6d. He also employed some child quill winders, paying them one shilling per week. Speaking of these years he later said:

"there was a degree of comfort attached to the situation of a weaver in Macclesfield, their wages were never to any great amount, but yet it appeared to afford them the competency that might be considered sufficient to produce the comforts of life....I could support my family with the decency that becomes an honest and industrious man."[7]

All this; the satisfaction of producing beautiful silk goods and of earning an adequate living, was soon to end.

While the increase in trade encouraged Macclesfield's town council to embark upon a grandiose neo-classical Town Hall, replacing the ancient Guild Hall, and manufacturers and others were calling for a Silk Exchange to be built, and were rushing to subscribe £25 per share to the £4-5,000 already raised, a recent Act of Parliament was beginning to take effect in the town. This Act, brought into being by ardent free trade disciple and President of the Board of Trade, William Huskisson MP, in 1824, would reduce the import duties on

Garret houses in Crompton Road.

thrown silk from the previous 7s. 6d. to 5s. and allow foreign manufactured silks to be imported into Britain. Some of the town's merchants proposed to form a company to import Italian silk almost immediately, but the general feeling was one of gloom at the prospect of competition from foreign imports. By April 1825, when a site in the centre of Mill Street was being cleared ready to begin construction of the Silk Exchange, the silk trade, both in Macclesfield and London, where much of its capital was raised, soon began to stagnate.

South Elevation of the Town Hall, Macclesfield.

Above: Drawing showing the south elevation of the new Town Hall, 1825.   *(MMT)*

Below: Jacquard loom. *(SM)*

Fears were expressed by manufacturers that capital would be withdrawn from the town in order to purchase finished goods from the east or Europe. They could neither compete on price or on quality with foreign silks; and some countries were far better equipped for manufacture. The Jacquard loom, invented in 1808, had only recently percolated into Britain. Less than 500 had been brought in at enormous expense to manufacturers and just two individuals possessed the *"elaborate machine of great value"* which perforated the cards from which their mechanisms operated. The first few of these new looms had arrived in Macclesfield during 1824. By contrast, there were said to be 20,000 Jacquard looms in the French town of Lyons alone; nearly all of them owned by the operatives themselves.

Gloom at future prospects was soon transposed into a silk trade slump. The new duties, which should have been effective from November 1825, were postponed until July 1826, but had already depressed the value of Macclesfield silk by up to 50%. By December 1825 some manufacturers had become bankrupted - one leaving debts of £70,000 - while others put their workers on a shortened week or laid them off entirely. Worst affected at first were silk throwsters. From 18,000 hands employed in silk throwing alone, upwards of 5,000 were unemployed. Thousands of children previously employed in the mills were said to be playing in the streets, where *"Satan finds some evil still for idle hands to do"* and where they would soon loose all the *"good impressions made upon their infant minds at our noble and numerous Sunday Schools."* Sixty to eighty families who had been brought in when the demand for their labour was high, left town altogether. Others found alternative work:

"The Army - In consequence of the lack of employment, this town has become a rare recruiting station. Numbers of able fellows are now seen parading the streets with the visual emblems of military enlistment on their hats, instead of being employed in the manufacture and production of the same."[8]

Meetings were soon being held by people from every branch of silk manufacturing. Manufacturers and throwsters met at the Macclesfield Arms on the 6th October to express their alarm at the relaxing of silk duties, and when its effects began to bite, the workers themselves gathered together. On the 30th November, silk weavers and dyers meeting at the Roe Buck Inn appointed a committee of sixteen men to prepare a memorial to the Board of Trade, urging them to repeal the Act and restore the duty to its former amount. Among the sixteen were John Prout and also William Parker, a 29 year old undertaker with

VALUABLE SILK MACHINERY, RAW SILK, AND SILK GOODS, WARE-HOUSE FIXTURES, &c.

TO BE SOLD BY AUCTION,

BY MR. JOHNSON,

At the Depot Mills, Macclesfield, in the County of Chester, (by order of the Assignees of Mr. JAMES ROWBOTHAM, a Bankrupt,) on TUESDAY, the 14th, and WEDNESDAY, the 15th Days of MARCH Instant; VALUABLE SILK and SILK GOODS, consisting of a quantity of Dappiona raw silk, in long slips; Reggio raw silk; Valentia raw silk; Brutia raw silk; ten cuts of soft warp bandanas, 35 inches; eighteen dozen of 7-quarters damask shawls; three dozen of 6-; quarters ditto ditto; Reggio and Valentia gum sewings, Brutia sewings, 3 cord; a quantity of Italian, Organ, and Tram, thrown; eight sets of 1800 reeds and harness entered; a large quantity of fine Italian Organ, of various colours, wound on the bobbins; Italian Tram, of various colours, wound on the bobbins; Waste Silk; Linen, wound and unwound; Button Molds; and Hand Reels.

All the valuable *NEW MACHINERY*, lately used by the said Bankrupt, consisting of nine excellent throwing mills, 207 dozen spindles, with 1¼ sets of reels to each mill; thirteen spinning mills, 242 dozen spindles; gearing for 22 mills; twenty-four mill horses; twenty-five engines, 1359 swifts; nine doubling engines, 324 bobbins; two soft silk engines, 160 bobbins; warping mill; forty-five gross of engine bobbins; forty-two gross of tram ditto; forty-seven gross of shaft ditto; fifteen gross of sewing trams; warp and shute bobbins; ninety skips; range of shelves, with slides; counter, &c.; excellent counter, seven yards long, mahogany top, with twenty-one drawers; ditto ditto, 6½ yards long, mahogany top, with seven large silk bins; large mahogany writing desk, or pulpit.

Sale to begin each Morning at Ten o'Clock.

The Auctioneer begs to call the attention of the Public, to the above Stock of Machinery, which is entirely new,

Advert in the Macclesfield Courier, 11th March 1826. *(CRO)*

a house and loom shop in Arbourhay Street, Hurdsfield. At a further meeting, held at the National School in Duke Street on 12th December, the committee's memorial was approved and duly sent off to Parliament in the hands of the County's M.P.s. Duke Street National School was also the venue for a late December meeting of foremen, stewards, warehousemen and millmen, who likewise sent a petition to the Board of Trade. A reply from William Huskisson came just after Christmas: he sent his regrets that the silk trade was so depressed, mentioned that the prevention of silk smuggling was the reason for the Act and added that there was *"no justification for departing from the decision."*

January 1826 saw a further Macclesfield Arms meeting of manufacturers and throwsters: this time they also intended to petition and lobby Parliament. A week later, at a meeting chaired by the Mayor, the same men were contributing to the relief fund set up for the town's unemployed silk workers - the sums subscribed ranging from the £30 given by John Ryle down to 10s. This charity provided the destitute with *"a compound made from pearl barley, a small quantity of rice, treacle and black pepper"* and up to 20,000 quarts were given away weekly. It also provided bread and potatoes, *"the latter of which was boiled down into some sort of jelly and in that state, with a sprinkling of salt, was devoured."* John Wright, a 35 year old silk steward who lived in Roe Street, was one who was appointed by the charity to distribute this food. He later said of this time:

"I have often seen men eating their food with their tears; and while they have been eating their scanty morsels, tear after tear, like a plentiful shower, have dropped from their eyes."[9]

Figures given early in February put the unemployed as numbering almost 12,000 while the 5,000 or more still in work were on half-time. Thirteen of the town's largest manufacturers and throwsters had been reduced to bankruptcy - one closure costing 1,500 hands their jobs.

A general meeting of operatives held in the National School in early February, for *"the repeal of that obnoxious Act,"* saw 1,300 people crammed inside while hundreds more, who could not be accommodated, stood outside. The Chairman, William Parker, first thanked the charitable fund upon which many families were totally dependent for sustenance. At a proposal that if their latest petition was unsuccessful they should then petition again for the repeal of the Corn Laws, loud cheering broke out, although Parker warned them not to attack the powerful agricultural interest in Parliament.

Duke Street National School. *(MMT)*

The thirteen man committee that ran these proceedings was composed mainly of undertakers like William Parker. One of many weavers of Irish origin, Parker had arrived in Macclesfield as a child around the year 1800. Since then, probably in the lean years of 1816-20, he had, like other townsmen, travelled widely in search of work - to London, Dublin and Manchester - before returning and settling down to married life. Another committee member was David Rowbotham, the Irish born ex-cotton weaver who had come to Macclesfield in 1816. By 1823 he was an undertaker with home and loom shop above it at Prestbury Lane End, where his wife also wove and their five young children would in time become weavers. Secretary to the meeting was yet another undertaker, Thomas Cope, a relatively local man, having been born in Buglawton, near Congleton about 1790. Cope had spent the years 1808 to 1817 with the Royal Regiment of Artillery, serving three years in Quebec before returning to his trade in Macclesfield. By 1825 he had a house and loom shop at Fountain Street, where his weaver wife Mary had just produced a baby girl, the first of six children, all of whom were destined to follow their parents' trade.

The effect of the several petitions already received was to arouse some interest among MPs. Late in February 1826 a Mr. Ellice MP put down a motion in the house of Commons for a committee to be set up to examine the Silk Laws.

On the Saturday, after this was scheduled for debate, a crowd of thousands of weavers awaited the arrival of the London Mail coach and news of the result in the Market Place. They dispersed peaceably after hearing that the debate had been postponed for a week. But after "post-time" on Sunday, rumours were soon spread that the debate had taken place and the Commons was against the setting up of any such committee. The next day, Monday 27th February, saw a gradual build up of people in the Market Place reach 5-6,000 in number by seven o' clock. Anger built up, stones were thrown through shop windows and gas lamps were smashed. Finally some shops were broken into and bread was stolen; then two of the town's aldermen were tripped up and robbed among the crowds. Special constables were then sworn in, among whom were several members of a weavers' committee. These, with the aid of the militia, had restored order by nine.

On the following morning, this *"Weavers' Committee"* signed an advert in *the Courier* disassociating themselves from the *"riotous proceedings of last night, at a time when our more wealthy neighbours have used every exertion to alleviate our distress."* Of the fourteen signatories, some, including William Parker and Thomas Cope, had run the meeting of all silk operatives in the National School. Others included John Prout, in the role of committee secretary, and his younger brother William, who lived at Arbourhay Street, Hurdsfield, as did William Parker and another committee member. Their committee would soon bring about a resurgence of the silk weavers' role in trade matters.

Two days after the riots, the Commons debate actually took place. During it, Huskisson said of Macclesfield:

"In 1825 such an excitement, such speculations were set on foot as no person could believe possible ....speculation was never carried to such excess as in that town."[10]

He mentioned by way of example the infamous advert of 19th February for 4-5,000 persons "wanted immediately:" *"Can any man wonder...... after such inhuman efforts to induce so many destitute children to flock to the manufactories .....after such an influx of population .....at most of these newcomers being out of work."*[11]

Yet as Huskisson must have known, it was not only newcomers who were unemployed. Conditions in the town worsened as 1826 wore on. The fund for the relief of the poor reached £3,000 in April, thanks largely to a subscription of £1,000 from His Majesty King George IV, but all this counted for little against a shortfall in weekly wages of £7,000. By August, when the

DISTRESS IN MACCLESFIELD.

24th April, 1826.

THE Committee have the grateful task of communicating to the public, that HIS MAJESTY has been pleased to CONTRIBUTE ONE THOUSAND POUNDS, in aid of the Subscriptions raised for the Relief of the Poor of this Town—an act of munificence which can but enhance the affection always entertained by them towards his Majesty's person and office.

This princely gift will enable the Committee to vary the nature of the food distributed to the poor, and thus make some addition to their comfort.

They regret to add, that the number of unemployed poor continues to increase, and that MORE THAN ONE HALF OF THE POPULATION of the Town *have no means of subsistence,* except those provided by this Charity. The distress may be best appreciated by the fact, that although the Subscription appears so considerable, being upwards of £3000, the amount of wages now paid weekly in the town, is upwards of £7000 less than it was six months ago. They are therefore under the necessity of repeating their appeals to the humanity of the public.

	£	s.	D.
I. Watts Russell, Esq. M. P., Ilam Hall	20	0	0
Sir Rich. Brooke, Bart. sub.	2	0	0
Ditto ditto donation	3	0	0
The Rev. Sir Philip Grey Egerton, Bart.	15	0	0
The Rev. Richard Egerton Warburton	2	0	0
Messrs. Bover and Nicholson, Warrington, by T. Boden, Esq.	2	0	0
T. B., Manchester, by the Mayor	10	0	0
Col. Parker, second subscription	10	0	0
S. P. Humphreys, Esq. of Bramhall	5	0	0
Macclesfield Gas Light Company, forty tons of Coke, value	33	6	8

Notice in the Macclesfield Courier, 29th April 1826. *(CRO)*

unemployed figures had risen to 14,000, it was stated that 2,719 families comprising 11,965 persons were in receipt of relief from the fund, and these were all people whose average earnings from parochial relief did not exceed 10d. per person per week. The parish would provide men with paid work in breaking stones for the highway, but this, as one man with a wife and three children complained, paid only a shilling a day. In one case a family of nine were living on 7s. per week from the parish. The Assistant Overseer said in defence that they had great difficulty in collecting poor rates and in some instances tempers had flared up - men *"gone to all extremes"* had broken the windows of the workhouse.

Sometimes tempers flared at the least provocation or for unjustified reasons. Yeomanry returning from Manchester duties that May were greeted with scorn by large crowds of the unemployed, who later assembled in the Market Place. They then marched to a factory in Crompton Road where about 130 steam powered cotton looms were situated. The mob attacked the factory, breaking windows, then gained access and smashed one of the looms. The militia and special constables restored order and *"a strong detachment of infantry"* was later sent into the town.

By July 1826 the town was looking decidedly down-at-heel; *"unoccupied factories and dilapidated houses presented themselves in every street."* The once much-vaunted idea of building a Silk Exchange never proceeded beyond the planning stage. At Christmas the numbers of families on poor relief in Macclesfield alone, excluding Sutton and Hurdsfield, rose from a previous high of 57 to 332.

References
1. M.C. 30/5/1822.
2. M.C. 4/1/1823.
3. Report of the Select Committee to Inquire into the Law Respecting Artisans, Machinery, Combinations of workmen, etc. 1824, page 600, evidence of Francis Reddish.
4. M.C. 23/4/1825.
5. M.C. 19/2/1825.
6. M.C. 21/1/1826.
7. Select Committee Report into the State of the Silk Trade, 1831-32, page 810, evidence of John Prout.
8. M.C. 10/12/1825.
9. Select Committee Report into the State of the Silk Trade 1831-32, page 823 evidence of John Wright.
10. M.C. 4/3/1826.
11. William Huskisson Speeches, London 1831 Vol. II, page 249; quoted in Malmgreen, Gail, *Economy and Culture in an Industrialising Town: Macclesfield, Cheshire, 1750-1839.*

Rules, &c.

FOR

SILK WEAVERS.

MACCLESFIELD, FEB. 20, 1826.

Brother Tradesmen,

If there were none but honest men in the world;—if men always acted upon principles of justice and truth, and did unto others as they would others should do unto them, there would be no necessity for men to unite for their common protection and support: but since this is not the case, and because there are Manufacturers, who, if it were not for the liberal examples of others, and being in some measure compelled by their servants, would never give what might be termed a fair price for their work.—In this case it becomes neces- sary that we should unite, in order to keep these men up to the legal prices of the town.— But this is not all, we have our Trade to guard in a political point of view, and if we are not unanimous amongst ourselves, we shall be un- prepared for any attainment whatever: more-

Rule book for the silk weavers' trade union, February 1826.

Chapter 4. Petitions and Pamphlets

In January 1826, a Macclesfield manufacturer complained to *the Courier:*

"The repeal of the <$iCombination Laws> had let in the accursed union system, and rendered general strikes or "turn outs" of the hands legal."[1]

Freedom to unionise had a quick response from the recently formed silk weavers' committee. Its Secretary, John Prout, was soon at work writing *Rules & Orders for Silk Weavers*, a short pamphlet published on the 20th February. In this a brief introduction states the basic premise:

"If there were none but honest men in the world; if men always acted upon principles of justice and truth, and did unto others as they would others should do unto them, there would be no necessity for men to unite for their common protection and support..."[2]

The call was for weavers to form a union. Each loom-shop, depending on how large, was to appoint a committee of four or five hands together with a chairman, a secretary and a treasurer, who would make weekly or monthly collections. From each shop would also be delegated two sober and trustworthy persons to sit on a Central Committee which would preside over the trade within the town. Both undertakers and journeymen would form the membership and the seven year apprenticeship system was to be strictly adhered to. In spite of all this, the union as such was a somewhat loose-knit arrangement.

Its energies were first directed towards Parliament rather than local manufacturers. The main item on the agenda at a meeting in March, when Chairman Thomas Cope addressed his audience as *"Brother Tradesmen"* rather than the customary *"Gentlemen,"* was to petition for the repeal of the Corn Laws. John Yearley, a weaver originally from Spitalfields but latterly of Nixons Yard, off Barn Street, then made a vigorous attack on the Laws, after which a committee of six men, including Cope, Yearley and David Rowbotham, were deputised to draw up their anti-Corn Law resolutions.

Nothing further seems to have come of this until the 11th October, when John Prout stood before the union's members, gathered together at the National School. Ascending the *"Tribune"* where the master of the school usually presided over his pupils, he addressed his fellow workmen:

"Brother Tradesmen, we are met here to exercise one of the highest privileges of Englishmen, the right of petitioning; and our object is to obtain the total abolition of the Corn Laws..... Let us then conduct ourselves throughout the proceedings in a becoming manner."[3]

He then moved that Thomas Cope took the chair and under him the meeting passed resolutions that condemned free trade, the Corn Laws, high taxation and the large standing army being used as *"an instrument of oppression."* The weavers were also urged to end their "passive obedience." Cope proposed, sardonically, that as founder of the new principle of free trade, William Huskisson should present their petition. Later, John Prout stepped up on to the "Tribune" once again:

"It would be right to establish a Free Trade, provided all classes of manufacture and produce were placed on an equality, but we feel the grinding effects of what is now called Free Trade in this distressed town. It is notorious that the Silk Trade always flourished, when under the fostering care of the Government.....The protection has been withdrawn from our trade without any reciprocal good whatever: we are exposed to want, and in a short time we shall have to apply to the hard-hearted Overseer, in order to complete our misery. I therefore second the resolution as it stands."[4]

Their petition, when it was published that December, offended many people, both in Macclesfield and beyond. *The Courier* was of the opinion that it was:

"the most levelling attack that the veryest Radical, aye, even the demagogue Hunt himself, ever attempted at any of the seditious meetings."[5]

Later, a letter from the Rev. Bowles of Bramhall enclosing £7. 5s. for the relief of distressed weavers, stated that it would have been more had not the tone of their petition made his parishioners none too warmly disposed towards them. The offending paragraphs not only referred to the weavers being un-represented in Parliament but denounced the Corn Laws in this sarcastic vein:

"Your petitioners cannot contemplate the scene of distress without enquiring to what ends is all this unheard of misery inflicted - are these enormous sums of money thus wrung from a starving people for purposes equally urgent as to their wants, or that cannot be dispensed with? No, the greater part of them are wanted for no greater purpose than to gratify the insatiable avarice, to pamper the most lascivious appetite, or to indulge the most luxurious ambition and to keep in pay an immense militia and naval force in a time of profound peace, who are equally useless to the country, an insult to the people, and a disgrace to the Government which retains them for purposes which we need not name."[6]

John Prout, Secretary to the weavers' Central Committee, had penned the petition; and it seems that they later had reason to regret naming their correspondents in *the Courier.*

The new union was able to exert some influence over local trade, though not all weavers welcomed the Central Committee's power. One undertaker, forced by them to comply with the two apprentices rule and dismiss two extra, 'illegal', apprentices, complained that a *"set of jackanapes"* had *"set themselves up as dictators."* In October 1826, when one manufacturer was found to be paying much less than others for the same silk articles, he too was forced to comply with the union's ruling. Yet conciliation rather than confrontation was the union's preferred method, for in December 1826 they published a short pamphlet, *An Address to the Manufacturers*, which aimed to end *"all the differences which have unhappily too long existed among them."* *The Courier* noted:

"It seems upon the whole, to be well written, void of any bad feeling, and is certainly worthy of perusal."[7]

However, the pamphlet seems not to have had the required response: for by January 1827, during a strike by Critchley and Brinsley's weavers, the Committee published a handbill addressing other tradesmen in the town, aiming for their support. This, *the Courier* recorded, *"exhibits much of bad feeling."*

Most disputes were settled through arbitration however, which was possible under a new Act of Parliament. Each side was allowed to appoint referees who would decide the issue among themselves. The first such case occurred in December 1826, when manufacturers Powell & Sons refused to give out 'shoot' [silk for the weft] to several weavers in their employ who had put out a handbill claiming the firm was paying less than others. When these aggrieved weavers applied to the Mayor's court, he told them to go to a County magistrate as their employer's premises were in Sutton and not in the Borough of Macclesfield. They asked, *"Is Mr. Ryle one?"* The Mayor said he was. One weaver then replied, *"Aye; aye; but Mr Browne* [The Rev. John Rowlls Browne, Vicar of Prestbury] *is our point* [choice]." Browne, who was a known sympathiser with weavers, put their case to arbitration.

During arbitration, the six referees found difficulty in meeting together so William Adam, a 25 year old Scot appointed by the weavers, acted on his own. He awarded them £11. 18s. 6d. in damages from Powell and included 15s. for his own expenses. A few weeks later he again acted in an arbitration case, but could not agree terms with the manufacturer's representative. It was finally settled by a magistrate, who much reduced the award proposed by Adam, claiming it was *"exorbitant."* Within days *the Courier* printed a scurrilous piece:

"Levelling systems - "Liberty and Equality" - ****, the silk weaver, who has been for some time acting as an arbitrator, was at one time of his life (we do not know whether he is so now) a strong advocator for the 'levelling system'."8

As 1827 got under way there was a small improvement in the silk trade: some factories re-opened, a few throwsters were reported as wanting hands and because of this shortage there was an advance in millmens' wages. Meanwhile, the silk weavers decided to petition Parliament for legislation to regulate wages. In this they were acting in unison with other towns and responding to *"An Appeal to the Nation from the Committee of the General Association"* formed in February 1826, and which they may have affiliated to at the time that their own Rules & Orders were published. But at a meeting that April, William Adam, the arbitrator, spoke out against any such petition, saying that the Government would not listen - they never had in the past. His proposal was to petition the King himself, asking him to dismiss his government; an idea for which he was roundly hissed. John Prout was next on the rostrum:

"Mr Chairman, there are two sorts of people in the world - one distinguished by the abilities they possess - and the others in possession of none, but who wish to make themselves noted as oddities! (laughter) Such a one is the last speaker." (applause and laughter)"9

From mild derision Prout changed to a more serious note, justifying the tone of their previous petition against the Corn Laws in a lengthy speech. Although it was denounced as *"violent and inflammatory"* it was *"their good sense and better judgement"* which had approved the language used, he said. Now they wanted the same protection that landowners had through the Corn Laws; legislation to fix wages and prevent them being underpriced by competitors. Finally, in denouncing the current theory that over-population caused poverty, he gave vent to his Christian beliefs:

"GOD when he created man had said "increase, multiply and replenish the earth," and the infinite wisdom of the Deity never ordered an end without providing the means for its accomplishment. (long and continued applause)." 10

Having relinquished the post of Central Committee Secretary, Prout continued to draw up all their petitions. He also campaigned on the Committee's behalf via a serialised letter to *the Courier* that July and August. This was penned under the name *"Scipio"*; the pseudonym almost certainly a protective measure after the hostile reception awarded the anti-Corn Law petition. Part one of the letter opened in typical John Prout style - *"It has been the practice of mankind in all ages and nations..."* - and went on to justify their proposed *"Silk Weavers Regulation Bill"*. The second part added fine details of what they were aiming to achieve by it: prices for weaving were to be fixed by majority decisions at meetings between manufacturers and weavers, and could be altered only when the *"exigency of the trade may require."* The third and final part of his serialised letter - again including the inevitable reference to *"mankind"* - discussed any likely objections to the weavers' Wages Regulation Bill and admonished the Government for failing to provide justifiable reasons for rejecting their previous petitions. It concluded:

"Why should it be thought a crime to belong to a committee, as if there was something obnoxious, or dangerous in the very name itself? If it be admitted that the labourer has a right to do the best he can for himself, why should he not be allowed to exercise that right, in whatever legal way he likes, without incurring the displeasure of his employer?"[11]

In the meantime however, there was no such Wages Regulation Bill and prices fluctuated according to the whim of manufacturers. Lower rates of pay were announced at Thomas Hall's in October 1827 and his 200 workers promptly turned out. Hall then prosecuted 24 of them under a recently passed Master and Servant Act and ten were duly sent off by magistrate John Ryle to Knutsford House of Correction. The weavers' Central Committee, led by Thomas Cope, William Adam and Nicholas Lynch, a 26 year old Irish newcomer to Macclesfield, published handbills to be put out all over town and organised collections for the strikers. At the time, a new local newspaper, *the Herald*, financed by William Brocklehurst, brother of silk manufacturers John and Thomas Brocklehurst, was hostile to the strikers whereas *the Courier* showed sympathy. A call went out to boycott *"shopkeepers, publicans, hairdressers or other persons who still take in the Herald."* The strike lasted until well into January 1828, when Hall promised to stick to the list prices. However, he refused to re-engage the leaders of the strike, who were then supported from union funds.

When their first petition for the regulation of wages failed, the Central Committee met in March 1828 to petition once more. This new petition, the Chairman explained, was to be drawn up by their *"Corresponding Committee."* Questioned as to who these people were, he replied that it was best they remained un-named, for they *"had a delicate duty to perform"* in the way of law business. This had arisen from the strike at Thomas Hall's. Prior to it, one of his weavers, a man named Hardy, had been provided with two warps, one for himself and one for his son. But the son fell ill and the work was not completed as the strike commenced. As a consequence, Hardy was sentenced with the nine others to one month's imprisonment at Knutsford for breaking his contract under the new 1824 Act. He returned home only in time to bury his son, who had died in the meantime. Striking weavers from Hall's had held a meeting on the Town Field as soon as Hardy was released, on 14th December 1827, where they protested against the magistrate and collected 3d. per loom from all Macclesfield weavers to carry on a suit at law. Spitalfields weavers were equally appalled at the way in which this recent Act had been interpreted and were helping with the fund.

An action for false imprisonment was brought against the magistrate, John Ryle, at Chester Summer Assizes, but was declared a *"nonsuit"* because Hardy was one day late in bringing the action; the time limit having terminated six months after he left prison. The judge awarded him one farthing's damages - this apparently to prevent a second action - but the decision was subject to the Court of King's Bench in London. While awaiting this, *the Courier* published a damaging piece about the three principal witnesses against Ryle, claiming they were *"agitators"* who had obtained money for expenses at the trial and then absconded to Liverpool *"leaving their families at the mercy of the Overseers."* But despite such interference, the *"nonsuit"* was set aside by the Court of King's Bench in November 1828, as the six months time limit had been complied with. Their verdict went to Hardy. The principle of the case was said in Court to be of great importance to all working in the silk trade

Yet the old 1767 Master and Servant Act, requiring a weaver to complete a warp once started, was still effective. A woman weaver, Mary Hill, was brought before the Mayor at the Town Hall Court in November 1828 charged under that law. She claimed the work was such that she could not obtain a livelihood and that she had not started it anyway. Nevertheless, she was offered the choice of completing it or committal to the House of Correction - and she chose the former.

In that month the silk weavers met at the Market Hall to send a memorial to the Board of Trade regarding their distress since the importation of foreign silks was allowed. Their wages were said to be 50% lower than in 1825; the 19s. 6d. then was reduced to 10s. 4d., less the usual expenses. Thomas Cope, now President of their union and in the chair, gave a powerful address:

"Now, since the Huskisson system had come upon them, like some wild and desolating inundation, or some destructive and overwhelming volcanic eruption, firm after firm and house after house had been overwhelmed by its desolating influence - consternation, terror and alarm had seized every breast - thousands had been deprived of the means of obtaining their livelihood - the workhouses were filled with paupers and the streets with beggars - and masters and servants, parents and children, all in one common mass had been hurled from a state of comparative ease and happiness to that of misery and degradation."[12]

Despite such moving oratory; despite their union; despite their petitions and their pamphlets; the situation of silk weavers in Macclesfield was getting steadily worse. They were not alone, for the general distress in the Town was once more approaching that of the terrible year of 1826. Soup kitchens doled out nourishment for the needy, at 1d. per quart, and at Christmas there were 199 families on poor relief in Macclesfield alone. As 1828 moved on to 1829 there was a renewed distribution of the rice, pearl barley, black treacle and pepper compound to those in dire need, though the money to pay for such charitable deeds was fast running out.

On the 21st February 1829, *the Courier* proudly announced:

"A pamphlet has just been issued from the press entitled "A Practical View of the Silk Trade" with which we are very much pleased. It is written by John Prout, a weaver residing in this town, and has for its object a complete exposure of the results of the measures of 1824."

THE SILK TRADE.

Just published, price 3s. 6d.

A PRACTICAL VIEW of the SILK TRADE, embracing a faithful Account of the result of the measures enacted in 1824 for the encouragement of that Manufacture.

By JOHN PROUT.

Macclesfield : Printed and sold by J.Swinnerton ; sold also by Yates, Congleton.; Claye, Stockport; Sowler Manchester; and Nall, Leek.

The pamphlet, in sixty pages quarto and priced at 3s. 6d., was published by Swinnerton's, the now amalgamated *Courier* and *Herald* publishers. Its preface included the usual John Prout opening sentence in which 'man' in the abstract again figured:

"It is a principle in man, when not destitute of reflection, if he should be in a suffering condition, to investigate the cause..."[13]

Prout's investigations had led him to study the trade both at home and abroad, and quote from the Select Committee Report on Artisans of 1824, together with two volumes, *Analytical Exposition* and *Analysis of Commerce*. He then compared conditions in 1823 to those in 1829 with devastating thoroughness and concluded with a total figure for loss of revenue from silk duties to the Government of £459,567.

A Practical View of the Silk Trade was written by Prout in direct response to another pamphlet, *A View of the Silk Trade*, by Richard Badnall of Leek, who had attempted to show that the 1824 measures were beneficial to the trade. Before putting his argument to the contrary, Prout first used humour to demolish Badnall's credibility. Of Badnall's leather tanning process to cure hides in days rather than months, set up in Leek, Ashbourne and Derby, Prout stated, *"it is now defunct and forgotten, unless it be remembered to be laughed at amongst other emanations from Laputa."* Of Badnall's process for silk dyeing, which ruined thread and left it utterly useless, *"long remembered by those who were so unfortunate as to entrust silk to the visionary's care."*

Also to be mocked were; Badnall's patent winding machine, which ruined his partner and whose children were in Leek workhouse; his throwing silk for sewing scheme - *"abandoned with great loss"*; the discovery of a mine on his estate from which Roman cement could be manufactured - *"foolish speculation";* and his authorship of a book called *Legends of St. Kilda* - tales as remote from reality as his *View of the Silk Trade*. Finally, an estimate of Badnall's for establishing a throwing mill was shown to have omitted certain essential expenses; such as the wages of key workers in the process, oil for machinery and the entire cost of lighting the factory. But in spite of Prout's derisive wit, his erudite argument and his comprehensive facts and figures; or that his pamphlet was somewhat naively addressed to the Duke of Wellington in the hope that the man *"pre-eminently the defender of England, will also prove himself the protector of its suffering artisans"*, it had little or no effect on the fortunes of Macclesfield's weavers.

Their next move was to try once more to have the silk measures overturned. At a meeting chaired by Thomas Cope in the Market Hall that February, a new petition was urged by David Rowbotham and also John Richards, one of the local Radicals imprisoned for sedition in 1820. Later that week, millmen gathered at the same venue to draw up a similar petition heard their chairman, silk steward William Boothby, report that of well over 10,000 mill hands in employment during 1825, only half now had jobs and wages were

50% lower. The town's manufacturers, numbering 56 in 1823, were reduced to 36 by bankruptcies.

Two months later, the weavers, millmen and other silk workers joined forces. A public gathering of all silk workers was held at the Sunday School and attended by 2,500 people. Asked first by chairman William Boothby to remember that the place was devoted to religious purposes, an *"inflammatory"* speech from the floor, detailing William Cobbett's plan for Radical reforms, lasted an hour long. Otherwise there was occasional humour. Robert Crook quoted the MP for Dover, who had stated that five articles used most by the working classes had increased in sales, proving that they were now better off. The first of these articles was tallow; *"a pity he* [the MP] *could not be fed on it for a month (laughter)."* In reality, Crook said, people were using the candles to work longer hours, *"instead of proving the happiness of the people, it proved only increased slavery - (loud applause)"*[14]

The meeting resolved to petition Parliament yet again; this time seeking an indemnity for the losses they all had suffered owing to the Silk Act, as previously had the town's manufacturers and throwsters. Neither petition was successful.

From the formation of their union in 1826 through to 1829 Macclesfield's silk weavers had petitioned Parliament repeatedly: for the repeal of the Silk Act and the Corn Laws, for the regulation of wages, and then, when it was finally realised that Parliament were intransigent on these issues, for an indemnity for the losses they had suffered. Not one of these petitions had the slightest effect. By 1829 their condition was every bit as bad as in 1826. Having been able to earn wages approaching a £1 per week in 1824-5, their average over the succeeding years was about 7s.

As a result of this failure, the Central Committee had changed in composition by 1829. Instead of being mostly undertakers it included many inside weavers. These were mostly young men, who, without the responsibilities of an undertaker, could afford to be more militant. Also, unlike undertakers in their relatively isolated loom shops, they worked in close confinement with many other like minds in large weaving sheds, where information was quickly disseminated and acted upon. Under their influence the main thrust of the weavers' Central Committee changed. They no longer looked towards the Government to alleviate their distress, but rather to local conditions over which they might exert some control. The list of prices once more became the central issue.

A list of prices for weaving was still operating in the town, albeit at low rates compared with before 1825. However, when in May 1829 it was discovered that John & Thomas Brocklehurst's of Hurdsfield were paying up to 30% below the list, other manufacturers stated their intentions to follow suit. The weavers struck immediately. That evening a thousand men and boys congregated in the Market Place and then marched down to Hurdsfield, demolishing gas lamps and breaking windows along the route. Once at Brocklehurst's they smashed almost all of the factory windows and were gone before the militia arrived. At the following day's meeting the weavers voted to continue the strike until Brocklehurst's paid by the list. Peaceful protest was now emphasised and 3,000 marched without incident through the town.

Brocklehurst's own weavers joined the strike next day and swelled numbers at a further meeting to upwards of 4,000. They called for the Mayor to intervene, then marched through the town once again. This time a carnival atmosphere prevailed, for they were headed by a band playing music, men dressed as mourners, others carrying black flags and other emblems, and one with a pole surmounted by a small loaf decked out in black crepe. Sympathetic shopkeepers gave out loaves and other provisions to the strikers. Weavers' committee man Nicholas Lynch later said, *"the masters gave their sovereigns and the shopkeepers their bread to aid the men against that tyrant Brocklehurst."* Another, similar procession was held the day after, during which some men pushed a loom decked in black crepe on a handcart. On it was the inscription; *"silk machinery to be sold by auction, by W. Huskisson."* At the loom was a weaver; with a red herring suspended just beyond reach of his mouth.

Brocklehurst's justified their lower rates as paid only when weaving for stock; this to keep their weavers fully employed. Their continued refusal to pay list prices ensured that the main strike ended after a week, although Brocklehurst's own weavers stayed out awhile longer before submitting. Afterwards, in spite of determined attempts by the weavers' Central Committee to keep manufacturers paying by the list, the situation deteriorated. Some weavers withdrew their delegates from the Committee and accepted lower prices. Some manufacturers began to send their silk into Lancashire, where it could be woven more cheaply by unemployed cotton weavers. A few Macclesfield weavers even went into Lancashire aiming to seek such work for themselves, walking the twenty miles or more to Manchester, plodding homewards with a heavy warp in a bag on their backs, and weaving it at prices 25% lower than elsewhere in town. Soon, the weavers were divided into separate interest groups. Those employed directly by manufacturers, especially in their weaving sheds, were first to get work in time of shortage. Because of this, undertakers and journeymen working outside were often forced to accept the price a manufacturer would offer, even if it was well below that of the list.

The latter half of that year was one of further decline. The earnings of working people were reduced to *"a bare and miserable subsistence"*. Week by week, 20,000 quarts of soup or gruel were distributed among them. Families on poor relief that Christmas numbered 320 in Macclesfield, almost attaining the record figure of 1826, when 332 families had sought assistance. A *"Townsman"*, writing to t*he Courier* that December related how hundreds of poor people had been visited one evening, when it was discovered that not one in ten had as much as a blanket:

"It is evident, that the poor, generally speaking, must sleep in their wretched day clothing, and huddle together, often upon the bare floor, to preserve warmth."[15]

Blankets, like other bedding and clothing, had been long since taken to the pawn shop. In the years between 1826 and 1831, John Prout and his growing family fared badly:

"I have suffered in common with my fellow workmates; I feel it at the same time that poverty does not necessarily infer degradation, because we may be poor from causes over which we have no control ....my own condition has considerably deteriorated. I have been exempted from the payment of poor rates and parochial assessments on account of the poverty of my situation."[16]

Where previously he had worked with pride on light and valuable, highly figured fabrics, he was now weaving only coarse plain goods, when employed, and then for much less money. Worse perhaps

An elaborate early 19th century Macclesfield silk pattern by a Brocklehursts' weaver.

were the problems of raising children in such times. By 1831, John and Elizabeth Prout had six children ranging in ages from the eldest Mary, at thirteen, to baby Harriet, born that year. He mentions that children were obliged to go barefoot and not able to attend Church or Sunday School because of the want of clothing; and writes of children "*who present a spectacle of misery in their countenances*". This was from personal experience, as a further statement illustrates:

"when I have seen my children surrounding the table, and heard their cries for food, embittered with the reflection that I had none to give them, I have frequently wished that a protracted life of misery might be closed by premature disease."[17]

Yet children could be an advantage to a weaver and large families were commonplace. John Prout's children, like many others in these mean, lean years, were often able to contribute small sums to the family budget; for whenever possible they were put to work in throwing mills.

References

1. M.C. 21/1/1826.
2. Rules and Orders to be Observed by the Silk Weavers of Macclesfield, Feb. 20th 1826.
3. M.C. 14/10/1826.
4. ibid.
5. M.C. 10/2/1827.
6. M.C. 9/12/1826.
7. M.C. 2/12/1826.
8. M.C. 2/12/1826.
9. M.C. 14/11/1827.
10. ibid.
11. M.C. 18/8/1827.
12. M.C. 8/11/1828.
13. Prout John, *A Practical View of the Silk Trade*, 1829.
14. M.C. 25/4/1829.
15. M.C. 29/12/1829.
16. Select Committee Report into the State of the Silk Trade, 1831-32, p. 810, evidence of John Prout.
17. ibid.

Chapter 5. The Child Mill Workers

Child mill workers c. 1820.

A child's day in Macclesfield's silk mills started at six o' clock in the morning. At precisely that hour the mill doors were slammed shut and any latecomers were fined heavily. For that reason it was not uncommon to see children leaving home at any time between four and six o' clock and running through the streets fastening their clothes, as many a poor home did not possess a timepiece of any description. The factory clock, high above the imposing entrance of many mills, offered no guarantee of accuracy, for it was sometimes set fast. Inside these mills, other clocks might lag behind. By this method many manufacturers gained a minute or two from each employee, day by day and week after week, man woman or child.

The 76 hour working week begun in the year 1800 was still the norm throughout the 1820s and lasted well into the 1830s for both adults and children. Starting at six o' clock they would then work until eight, when a twenty minute breakfast was allowed. Lunch was taken from two till three and was followed at five by a twenty minute teatime break. The day ended at eight o' clock. Only

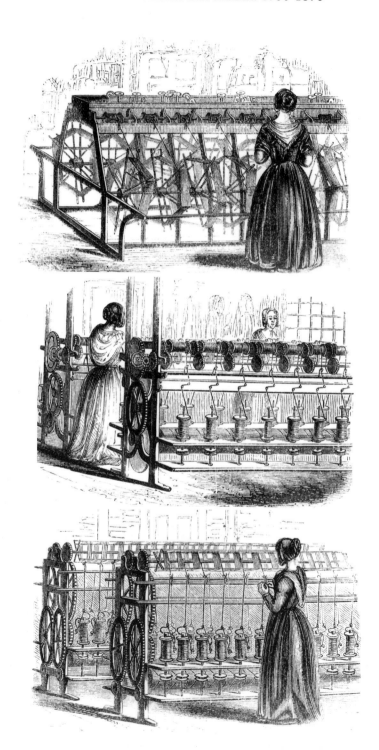

the very youngest beginners were allowed any remission and they worked two hours a day less, until they were sufficiently experienced.

The mills in themselves were not 'dark' or 'Satanic' and compared favourably with cotton mills. There was no cotton dust or 'flue' to pollute the air; the machinery was lighter in construction and less noisome; and the heat was much lower than inside a cotton mill - at most about 75°Fahrenheit. Mill walls were regularly limewashed and the work itself was generally clean; so much so that the women and girls who worked there, about 70% of all millworkers, were able to dress neatly and their appearance was often favourably commented on by strangers to the town. Less wholesome was the use of candle lighting for six months of the year owing to the length of the day, as this caused smoke and soot. The mills were also very crowded with workers but only had limited sanitary facilities; it was said that the stench from the privies often permeated the whole mill.

Children were taken on from the age of five upwards. If they were apprentices their term was for three years, which they were legally bound to serve. Their masters could sack them at will. Discipline was not particularly harsh; it was commonly claimed that children were never beaten. The silk stewards under whose charge they worked carried rods or leather straps, and as they paced up and down the rooms they would constantly strike the wall or part of the machinery near to the child, just to give them a warning. In some cases it would be to keep the child awake.

Children were employed at almost every process in silk throwing. When the raw silk arrived at the mill it was in rough parcels of hanks called 'books' which girl 'sorters' would divide up into various qualities and remove any waste. The next process, purifying the silk by soaking it in hot water, was a man's job. After that, the silk was taken to the Winding Room, where the hanks were wound on to winding frames and then on to bobbins under the direction of women 'danters.' The danters were assisted by 'engine piecers,' usually the younger girls, who as the silk was wound pieced any broken ends together - and it broke constantly! From the Winding Room the bobbins went next to the Cleaning Room, where the silk was drawn between two smooth blades to remove dirt and irregularities before being re-wound on frames managed by boys or girls who also pieced any broken ends. Next, in the Spinning Room, two or more ends were 'doubled,' twisted together and 'thrown' by women

Opposite page: Women workers in a silk throwing mill.
                   Top to bottom: Winding, Spinning, Doubling.   *(MMT)*

'doublers.' These rooms were the hottest and noisiest in the mills, for the spinning frame spindles revolved at 3,000 revolutions per minute and were packed tightly together so that each piecer, usually boys, could manage as many as forty spindles each. Once wound into hanks for either 'organzine' [warp] or 'shoot' [weft] it was sent off to the premises of a silk dyer to be dyed. Back in the throwing mill the dyed hanks were re-wound on to reels and bobbins, each winder working 22 ends. Women and girls were always employed in this process as men's fingers were considered too clumsy. The final stage was for the organzine to be put into the hands of skilled women 'beam warpers,' who on their warping mills would prepare warps for weavers, while the shoot [or 'shute'] was wound on to a 'draw frame' awaiting use in a weavers' shuttle.

The work in itself was not arduous, but in almost all cases the children had to stand the whole day long and their opportunities for movement were limited. In the case of small children they had often to stand upon stools in order to reach their work. The very nature of piecing, requiring concentration and sharp sight, was the cause of 'piecers squint,' particularly among the little girls who assisted the danters. Worst of all was the danger to life and limb posed by unfenced machinery.

Any child first entering such an establishment would have found it a traumatic experience. An eight year old, Adam Rushton, a farm labourer's son from Hurdsfield, took employment at Green's factory in Commercial Road in 1829. There, as he later wrote, *"The close, impure air seemed to be stifling me... the clangour of machinery deafened me."* He was put to work piecing, having been shown how by a girl. Starting with six 'swifts' [winding frames] he graduated in stages to twenty and more. As a beginner his hours were from six in the morning to six in the evening with one hour and 40 minutes in total for meals. After a few months he did the full 6 a.m. to 8 p.m. day. His pay was 6d. per week for the first month; 1s. per week for the next two months and finally 1s. 6d. per week as a regular wage. After eight months the mill shut down with 100 hands thrown out of work.

Rushton's next job was at J & T Brocklehurst's factory in Hurdsfield Road:

"Taking me to the end of a side of swifts, the Steward, Mr J.B. said, "start here, and let us see what thou canst do." For a time my fingers trembled so much I could hardly do anything at all. "Humph," exclaimed he to the Danter; "he is not up to much." "Let him alone a bit; he is frightened," said the Danter. When he came back I had eight or ten swifts going round. "Get him a dozen," said the Steward."[1]

On the following day Rushton was given twenty swifts and in a few weeks he was piecing at 25 swifts. The silk was inferior Bengal, difficult to manage even by older hands, and the strain upon the eight year old was very exhausting.

At the end of a year, during which he felt his health was failing, his 1s.6d. per week wage was raised to 2s.6d., *"which sum was a great boon to my mother in the management of the home."* He was by then piecing in the cleaning room and was fortunate to have a window close by overlooking woodland, which boosted his spirits. When he became thirteen he was promoted to the spinning mill and his wage increased to 6s. per week, 1s. of which his mother allowed him to keep. Later he worked in the warehouse, earning 7s. and keeping 2s.

The long term effects of this labour had a debilitating effect on children. Adam Rushton's long hours of piecing left him spiritually and physically exhausted:

"this crushing slavery had to be endured. Hence my appetite failed, never to be fully regained; the ruddy colour left my face never to return; and chronic weakness took possession of my limbs, and retarded growth."[2]

The silk steward, John Wright of Roe Street, whose own employment in mills began at the age of five, noticed similar symptoms among children aged seven and upwards in his charge at Brinsley and Shatwell's throwing mill:

"The tediousness and the everlasting sameness.. ....preys much on the spirits and makes the hands spiritless....Excessive labour often leads to a total loss of appetite, a kind of languor steals over the whole frame, enters into the very core, - saps the foundation of the best constitution and lays our strengths prostrate in the dust."[3]

In some cases these symptoms may have been terminal: Rushton claimed, *"untold numbers went in this way to untimely graves."*

When millmen had gone on strike in 1824 to resist the lengthening of the working day, they had claimed it was on behalf of the children: *"We told them that they had made cripples enough already in Macclesfield,"* they said. John Wright also spoke of children who had been crippled by the long hours of standing. Some were frequently carried to the mills, being unable to walk because of the *"excessive labour and confinement"*. In this he spoke from personal experience: his two sisters had needed carrying back and forth until eventually they were so crippled they were unable to attend at all. In about 1820, when Wright worked at Barker and Pearson's, one of the largest mills in Macclesfield, scarcely half of the men employed there would have passed fit for service in His Majesty's forces; for even those who were straight in limb were often stunted in growth.

However, it is very likely that the effects of diseases such as rickets and a poor diet would have contributed greatly to such physical deformity and lack of stature. Adam Rushton's factory breakfast and tea sometimes consisted of small doughcakes baked with gooseberries inside. These were so small they could not satisfy a growing lad's appetite. At home the staple food was oatmeal with milk and though they ate bread and butter, this was carefully rationed. On Sunday's *"a grand treat at dinner"* was provided by way of a small portion of beef with potatoes and apple or gooseberry dumpling to follow. Rushton's *"retarded growth"* can perhaps be largely attributed to this diet.

That children were physically punished when working was always denied: Wright and other observers were in full agreement that children were never beaten. Yet one severe case was brought before the Mayor at the Borough Court in November 1828. A silk steward was charged with a violent assault on an engine piecer who worked under him, a girl aged about ten. In *"chastising"* the girl for not attending to her work he had struck her head, rendering her almost deaf, and had then kicked her on the hip, badly bruising her. The steward attempted to blame a boy for the kick but it was proved in court that he could not kick high enough. A fine of 10s. and costs were the steward's punishment. He would have been earning about 14s. per week. Other, less serious, offences of this nature would have not reached a court - or *the Courier.*

In fact, it is quite likely that in some mills at least, regular beatings did take place. Throwing mill owner and magistrate Samuel Thorp, a Quaker by religious conviction, had often said *"If the children cannot do without a beating, he had better be without them."* It was at Thorp's mill, at "Clock Alley," Hurdsfield, in November 1833, that eleven year old engine piecer, Sarah Stubbs, died after taking a beating from a silk steward:

"Her "ends were down," and he cried out to her, "Sally get those ends up there" ...He had a strap in his hand ...He then came up the "Alley," in which the deceased was working, and hit her three times over the head and once over the arm. Her head was bare. They were hard blows."[4]

The strap measured 16 inches long and was 1 inch wide at its thickest end. The girl cried a little and later complained of pains in her head, then she was sick after teatime. Thorp was away from the mill at four o' clock, when the incident occurred, and the girl could not be taken home immediately because his workers were all locked in. She left the mill at seven p.m. and died two days later. The House Surgeon from Macclesfield's Dispensary, Dr. Fleet, said death was due to concussion and inflammation of the brain following the beating.

Thorp's Mill, Hurdsfield.

The steward, an elderly man, had often struck other girls in a similar fashion. He was sent for trial on a charge of manslaughter. *The Courier* defended this *"unfortunate man":* he had been quiet, orderly and industrious for forty years. With character references from Thorp and some aldermen of the town, he was found guilty with a recommendation of mercy at Chester Assizes - and gaoled for two months.

Yet the death of a child in one or other of Macclesfield's silk mills was no rare event. Though the work itself was considered light, the frames, spindles or bobbins at which they worked were driven by complex systems of shafts, gearwheels, pulleys and belts - all of it unfenced until the mid 1840's. Inattentiveness could be at least dangerous or at worst fatal. Injuries, however serious, rarely reached the pages of *the Courier* and were probably not considered to be "news." Fatalities did, but were treated as not uncommon occurrences:

"Last week another of those unfortunate circumstances too frequently attendant on silk machinery, occurred at a factory near the Common in this town. A young boy ....whose clothes had got entangled in the machinery, met his death by strangulation."[5]

During the boom years in the silk trade there were three such deaths in a space of less than eighteen months:

"A little girl about seven years of age was caught by her clothes, and drawn between an upright shaft in the engine room and a wall; and before she could be extricated from her perilous situation, life was extinct in consequence of the violent crush."[6]

"Ralph Boothby, about five years of age, was unfortunately caught by one of the shafts or wheels belonging to the machinery, when he was immediately killed upon the spot."[7]

"..William Downs, about eight years of age ....the shaft caught the strings of his pinnafore [sic] which coiled round, and the pressure became so great as to cause the dislocation of his neck, and he died immediately."[8]

Two more children were to die in almost identical occurrences during 1827 and 1828. These fatal accidents caused little comment in *the Courier* largely be due to the fact that the death of a child through any number of other accidents - run down in the street, burnt to death at the home fireside, scalded to death in kitchens or drowned in ponds and pits - were almost weekly happenings.

That parents risked the health, welfare and happiness, even the lives of their children in such establishments, is to the modern mind almost unthinkable. But these were the children of poor working people who had, in most cases, no other course of action. Although it was often cynically said in Macclesfield that there were persons who lived entirely off the labour of their children, the majority would have much preferred an alternative. School was never an option: although many workers would have liked to send their children to a day school, poverty obliged them to put them to work in mills at an early age. A full week of tedious, demoralising and strength sapping piecing, plus a very elementary instruction in the three 'R's' at one or other of the town's Sunday schools, was the best that many a Macclesfield child could hope for.

References
1. Rushton Adam, *My Life as Farmer's boy, Factory Lad, Teacher and Preacher,* 1909. page 32.
2. ibid.
3. Second Report of Children in Working in Factories, 1833.
4. M.C. 23/11/1833.
5. M.C. 29/7/1815.
6. M.C. 10/5/1823.
7. M.C. 20/12/1823.
8. M.C. 23/10/1824.

Chapter 6. Parliamentary Reform and Strike, 1832

Although the list of prices was always of concern to Macclesfield's weavers, other much less insular issues came to the town during the early 1830s. These were nationwide movements for change, each of which would gain adherents from among weavers, inside or outside, young and old, as with other silk workers. Growing pressure to reform the Houses of Parliament and widen the franchise to include a better representation of the people was one. First to arrive though was The Association for the Protection of Labour, a national association intent upon fixing the rates of pay in every trade.

This was the ambitious brainchild of John Doherty, secretary to the cotton spinners union in Manchester. Defeat in a protracted strike in 1829 had led him to the belief that a much larger organisation would prove more effective. At first, he envisaged a nationwide union for cotton spinners, but no sooner had it been launched than he was entering into a far larger project, one to embrace all trades. In March 1830 he first published the *United Trades Co-operative Journal*, which was to be the mouthpiece of this new organisation. The National Association for the Protection of Labour followed in July. Before the inauguration, delegates from Doherty travelled the country seeking support.

Two of these delegates came to Macclesfield early in June 1830. Prior to their arrival, notices had been posted advertising the meeting and its aims on the walls of an empty factory in Brook Street. On the evening of the 7th, the largest room of the factory was filled completely with cotton and silk trade operatives, as many as 2-3,000 of them. One of two local speakers was John Richards, the silk spinner imprisoned for sedition in 1820. The other was Reuben Bullock, a 55 year old silk weaver of Roe Street and a contributor to the *United Trades Co-operative Journal*. It was he who urged the formation of a Macclesfield branch of the new National Association in a lengthy speech. The resolution was carried and the town became the first to be recruited outside of Lancashire.

According to *the Courier*, the National Association had upwards of 80,000 members nationally and was in receipt of £500 per week by October that year. Such was the *"danger"* of this new union, the Duke of Wellington had been informed that *"Operatives are, at the will of the Committee, obliged to strike for wages, however satisfied with their present employ."*[1]

However, it was in support of very unsatisfied fellow workers elsewhere, whose low rates of pay posed a threat to themselves, that Macclesfield weavers responded. At a meeting in the empty factory that December, delegates from Ashton-under-Lyne told how a manufacturer there had set up in silk weaving and was paying 9d. per cut below Macclesfield's rate for Bandanna's and up to 3s. less for other items. The delegates argued that Macclesfield's manufacturers would be forced to compete and asked for financial assistance for a planned strike. The weavers agreed, and having already paid the sum of £1 to the National Association, passed over a further £10.

The strike at Ashton to obtain Macclesfield prices commenced on 3rd December 1830. Later, *the Courier* published news that the strike was over. This was hotly denied in Doherty's new journal *Voice of the People* [his previous unstamped journal having been suppressed by the authorities] in January, which was of the opinion that this was a deliberate lie intended to undermine the support of Macclesfield's weavers. They had by this date contributed over £21 to the Association and the fighting fund for the Ashton strikers. But on the 19th February the *Voice of the People* reported that Mr. Hynes, secretary to the Ashton strikers, had disappeared along with over £100 from their fund. The Ashton strike collapsed almost immediately and the weavers returned to work on their master's terms; many being refused employment in reprisal. The monthly district meetings of the Macclesfield branch, held at the Bundle of Sticks [a symbol of union] beerhouse in Watercotes, continued from April until December, but no more contributions of money were made to the National Association. After an abortive attempt to mount a general strike of cotton workers in Lancashire that December, Doherty's National Association had ceased to exist by March 1832.

In the meantime, Macclesfield was simmering with agitation for the Reform of Parliament. At a meeting requested by the town's capital burgesses, held at the Town Hall in late February 1831, the protagonists for either household or universal suffrage clashed. Proposing *"a fair share of representation"* - meaning only household suffrage - was Thomas Grimsditch, the Brunswick Street lawyer who had prosecuted local Radicals in 1820. Several of the many weavers present then spoke against him, including William Forrest, a 35 year old undertaker from Park Square, Reuben Bullock, David Rowbotham and John Richards - one of those 1820 Radicals. Forrest's amendment to Grimsditch's proposal was worded in such an extreme form that it caused uproar. But when Bullock stood up, raised his spectacles and read a more moderately worded resolution favouring universal manhood suffrage and vote by ballot, the Town

Hall resounded with tremendous cheering. He was seconded by Richards and supported by the vast majority of all present. Grimsditch and the chairman hedged about this and wanted to stick to the original proposal when petitioning Parliament. Rowbotham too was inclined towards their view, but Forrest, again on his feet, railed against any compromise. At this, uproar ensued once more and the meeting ended inconclusively.

Macclesfield Town Hall, the 1825 front.

A second meeting was called two weeks later at the request of *"upwards of 80 respectable inhabitants."* They wanted to petition Parliament on the basis of the reforms already proposed in the House of Commons - these advocating household suffrage for urban rent-payers of over £10 per year. More than 2,000 people attended this *"harmonious and agreeable meeting"*. which was first addressed by several local dignitaries. Richards and Forrest then spoke in support of the resolutions. Forrest, undaunted by the loud cheering and laughter that greeted him - saying he had *"a face as hard as a weather beaten pilot"* - was now in favour of such a petition for the sake of unity: *"He would as soon as dance to the gallows than throw any obstacle in the way of it."*

Even so, he and others remained staunch supporters of universal suffrage and were to continue agitating for this until long after the Reform Act became law. Forrest, Bullock, Richards, and also the Rev. J.W. Morris, the Unitarian Minister of Dean Row chapel, were speakers at an April meeting of the National Association district branch at the Bundle of Sticks; where a unanimous resolution was passed to form a 'Political Union' and correspond with others based elsewhere, the most notable being at Birmingham. The amphitheatre adjoining the Bundle of Sticks was the venue for the Political Union's next gathering, on 6th June, when Richards and Joseph Sutton - a co-defendant from the 1820 sedition trials - addressed the crowd. The resolutions passed were in favour of universal male suffrage, annual parliaments and vote by ballot.

Another co-defendant of 1820 was campaigning in Stockport. Joseph Swann had resumed his hatting trade there after his four and a half years imprisonment but in November 1831 was charged for hawking unstamped Radical newspapers. At the magistrates court he proved to have lost none of his bravado and interrupted the magistrate frequently. He was sentenced to three month's hard labour at Knutsford for his insolence, but managed to get in the last word: *"I've nothing to thank you for; and whenever I come out, I'll hawk them again. And mind you (looking at the magistrate) the first that I hawk shall be to your house."*[2]

In December 1831 a meeting of around 400 people at Park Green saw the emergence of two young men, both of whom would be revered in Macclesfield and even more widely renowned for their oratory. John West, born in Dublin, had arrived in the town with his widowed mother when still a boy. He proposed the first resolution - for universal suffrage, annual parliaments and vote by ballot. He was only nineteen years old, but with his dark eyes, wavy hair, a ready smile and *"Olympian"* laughter he carried the crowd along with him when another, less charismatic speaker, quoted several philosophers and sections of the Bill of Rights of such length that he was eventually hissed from the stage. Even younger than West was a lad, seemingly about sixteen, who urged the crowd that *"union and co-operation"* were the best means to secure their rights. *The Courier* scathingly recorded that this *"raw, inexperienced youth"* spouted nonsense; but in time young Timothy Falvey would, like West, make his mark locally and nationally. All speakers were utterly scornful of the Government's proposed reforms; one man saying:

"It matters not to him whether he was governed by a boroughmonger, or a whoremonger, or a cheesemonger, if the system of monopoly and corruption was still to be upheld."[3]

Supporters of Doherty's National Association and the Political Union met later that month at the Bundle of Sticks, where with 2-300 people present to hear them, speakers - as *the Courier* saw it - *"abused the best institutions of this country."* Union matters and political agitation were about to be fused together in a heated battle over the vote.

In this John West soon came to the fore. He had made himself known to a wider audience of Macclesfield's inhabitants at a Reform meeting held at the Town Hall early in 1832. All was confusion until West mounted the platform. There he *"electrified the meeting with his powerful oratory and carried the majority with him...he so impressed our Alderley neighbours* [the Stanley family of Alderley Park] *that they would have become useful patrons of West if his proclivities had been more pliable."*[4]

Later that year, West used his speechmaking skills to support the well-known Radical, William Cobbett, in his successful bid to become MP for Oldham. For this he received a warm tribute from Cobbett. The defeated Tory, impressed by West's abilities, offered to have him trained as a barrister. West declined in order to continue agitating on behalf of his fellow workers.

The first shot in a protracted skirmish against silk manufacturers J & T Brocklehurst, both political and economic, was fired by John West in a letter to the *Poor Man's Guardian* newspaper in March 1832. Headed *"Unjust and Tyrannical Employers"*, West attacked John Brocklehurst, who had "offered himself" as one of two prospective MPs for a new Macclesfield constituency, as being *"of no benefit to the country at large."* A printed document followed which Brocklehurst was said to give to his weavers:

"You must take this material and weave it on the following terms:-
No particular price is now fixed; such a one will be given you as Mr. T. Brocklehurst's looker-over considers the work worthy of, being governed by the state and quality of the work. If the warp or work be spirited, or sized, or dressed, or short more ends than ordered, or be detained longer than they think proper, one half the wages to be deducted, and as much more as the damage may amount to. Marks at the end of pieces to be woven in or five shillings will be deducted. For ruffled or soiled bobbins sixpence will be deducted, and for bobbins one shilling each. (cost him about one half-penny each) All short weights to be paid for by the weaver." [5]

West concluded that this was a *"specimen of the numberless instances of tyranny practised by him over his workmen."*

Brocklehurst's weavers, led by William Parker, quickly responded on their employer's behalf and refuted West's claim as *"an abominable misrepre-*

JOHN BROCKLEHURST
1788-1870
M.P. for Macclesfield for 16 years—1812-1868.

John Brocklehurst, *(MMT)*

sentation." The Political Union had no right to interfere between them and their master and they highly approved of his conduct. Brocklehurst himself was quick to point out that he had not *"offered himself"* as a prospective MP for Macclesfield, but had been solicited to do so by two hundred respectable householders. Neither had he given such a document to his 500 weavers. Yet it obviously did exist, for he then stated that it was only used in instances *"in the country"* and then as a caution, never acted upon.

Sending weaving into *"the country"* was an insoluble problem for Macclesfield's weavers. When the Central Committee heard in March that a Government Select Committee was to be set up to enquire into the *"State of the Silk Trade",* they deputised Thomas Cope and David Rowbotham to go into Lancashire and investigate matters. The two weavers found about 9,000 silk hand-looms operating there, many worked by ex-cotton operatives; as Rowbotham himself once was, having come to Macclesfield in 1816 from Lancashire when the hand-loom cotton trade declined. Unemployment was still rife in 1832 and willing hands were eager to work underprice.

With this evidence, Rowbotham, Cope, John Prout and two other weavers, together with John Wright the silk steward and another mill operative, were deputised to go to London and stand before the Select Committee of the House of Commons. This had been set up as a result of pressure by John Brocklehurst; and twenty members were to sit examining witnesses almost daily from March to July. The Macclesfield men were called on the 19th July 1832, when all seven told of the decline of the town's silk trade and their fortunes. Rowbotham claimed to have been worth £150 in 1825, but was reduced to about £10: *"my money is all gone, my property is rendered of little value,"* he said. Prout had prepared a table of prices paid for a variety of silk goods, covering the years 1815 to 1832, and this illustrated how wages had fallen overall by about 60%. Bandannas, which before 1815 earned up to 5s 6d. per cut, now paid only 2s. 3d.   He explained that his average wage was 6s. 6d. per week net after deductions, but without taking account of 'casualties' when work was spoiled. His conclusion about the situation in Macclesfield was thus:

"poverty has produced demoralisation, and demoralisation disaffection to his Majesty's person and Government: in short, we are obliged to have soldiers to keep the peace whereas the constables formerly did it."[6]

The Select Committee's *"voluminous"* evidence was presented to the House without them having formed any conclusions.   Nothing of any worth came from it.

It was the municipal economics of the situation that mostly concerned the newly enfranchised householders of Macclesfield.   At a meeting convened by the Mayor and requested by rate payers and other inhabitants in September 1832, it was reported that several manufacturers were sending work out of town when there were still many unemployed weavers within - and who had to be supported from the poor rates.   Gross expenditure in Macclesfield alone, excluding Sutton and Hurdsfield, had risen from a previous high of £8,670 in 1830 to over £9,500 in 1832; and would have reached £12,000 if they had not reduced the poor allowance from 1s. 6d. to 1s. or 10d. and made any able person break stone.   They were concerned to prevent further rate increases.

The weavers had already made concessions.   A strike that July had resulted in an increase in prices which many manufacturers were reluctant to pay.   When several then began to send work to places outside the town, the weavers had requested a committee of shopkeepers to mediate and had abided by their conclusions.   As a result they were generally weaving for the lower price paid before the July strike.   Yet some manufacturers were still sending their work elsewhere.

By October discontent among the weavers erupted in a demand for the price list to be raised, this time considerably more.   Once again the town's shopkeepers offered to mediate.   Instead, the manufacturers met representatives from each weaving shop, appointed by the Central Committee, but they were inflexible on paying more than the pre-July rates.   After several fruitless conclaves the weavers prepared for a strike.   So too were manufacturers, the County magistrates, and the Mayor and magistrates of the Borough, who issued notices that protection would be given to all who wished to remain at work.

TO THE

Inhabitants of Macclesfield, and its Vicinity·

Gentlemen, and Fellow Townsmen,

In consequence of the many misrepresentations which have been, and are now circulating through the Town, respecting the present unhappy but just contention between the Silk Weavers of Macclesfield, and Messrs. BROCKLEHURSTS; we feel ourselves imperiously called upon to publish to you, and the country at large, the real state of the case :—

Perhaps it may be thought somewhat strange to call this a contention between the Silk Weavers of Macclesfield and Messrs. Brocklehursts, seeing that not one half of the Weavers are employed by them; but when it is re-collected that it depends upon them, and them alone, whether the price of weaving is to be reduced, as we shall herein after shew, not much less than Fifteen per Cent, we think we are perfectly right in attributing to *them* the whole disturbance of the Town. That this is the case, we have only to refer to the language of those who propose to *reduce* the price of their weaving to the same level as that paid by the Gentlemen aluded to above; who say, " they have no other reason for reducing their weaving, but because they are beat out of the market by Messrs. Brocklehursts, in consequence of the low prices paid by those Gentlemen, for the manufacture of their goods."

If nature had been as lavish in bestowing upon Messrs. Brocklehursts a philanthropic disposition, as providence has in blessing them with the good things of this world, *they*, of all the men in Macclesfield, would have been the most calculated for benevolent actions, and extensive usefulness :—Happy would it have been for the Town if this had been the case!

If there be a Firm in the Town which is more calculated than another to give a liberal price for their work, Messrs. Brocklehursts is the Firm ;—possessing, as they do, a large capital, an extensive trade, and besides, being themselves Bankers, would, we think, justify the conclusion, that at least, they could afford to give as *much* for their work as other Manufacturers; but this does not appear to be the case.

It is said, " that there are but a few looms, in proportion to the whole number employed by Messrs. Brocklehursts, that are making goods at a less price than is paid by the rest of the Town ;" insinuating thereby, that all the other descriptions of goods manufactured by this Firm, are paid the same by them as by other Manufacturers; this is far from being correct :—At one description of work, called Brusells, there is nearly, if not all out, thirty per cent of difference in the price of weaving. Messrs. Brocklehursts are paying for a 36 inch. three single Brusell, 7s. 6d. per dozen, while other Masters are paying 11s. for the same kind of work.—For Black Bandanas, 36 inches, Messrs. B. are paying 6s. 6d. per dozen, while others are paying 7s. 6d.—For Bordered Bandanas, 34 inch. they are paying 6s. per doz. others 7s.—Black Fringes, Messrs. B. pays 6d. per dozen less for 36 inch.—34 inch. 1s. 32 inch. 9d. &c.—For Gros de Naples, Messrs. B. pays 6d. per yard, others are paying 7d.—For Persians, they pay 8d. others 8½ per yard.—It is said that Messrs. B. have nearly 200 looms of this kind of goods, that the most of these are 20 inches wide, the others 18 inches, and in order to have both done at the same price, he gives his weavers three broad ones for one narrow one. Without enumerating any more descriptions of works, we trust the above will be sufficient to prove, that what we have said above is true, namely, that if Messrs. B. are not brought up to pay the same price as other Masters, we must submit to a reduction of Fifteen per Cent.—And in order to shew that Messrs. B. are below other Manufacturers in the Throwing department, as well as the Weaving, we submit the following Statement, which has been furnished by the Millmen's Committee.

	Prices paid by Messrs. Brocklehursts.	By other Masters.
Mill-men, 8s. per week,	- - - - -	18s.
Soft-silk Piecers, 5s. per week,	- - - -	5s. 6d.
Tram Piecers, 5s. ditto,	- - -	6s.

It is to be remarked that the above is the average of the Wages.

Messrs. Brocklehursts have endeavoured to shelter themselves from public odium, by alledging as an excuse for their conduct, that they keep their men better employed than others, which they say more than counterbalances the losses which they sustain in the low price of their labour. Whatever degree of importance may be attached to this argument as it respects their own firm, there can be none at all, as it regards the influence which their low prices have upon the whole Trade of the Town ; for what does it matter to another Manufacturer, whether Messrs. B. keep their firm well or ill employed ; so long as they pay a less price for their work. While this is the case they will always be enabled to under-sell the other Masters in the Market. So that it appears that the low wages paid by Messrs. B. have as great a tendency to lower the price of Goods in the Market, when their firm is kept well employed, and more so, than when it is but partially employed. There is one thing more respecting Messrs. Brocklehursts conduct, of which we think it right to inform the Public, namely, that while other Masters are content with charging their Journeymen, who work inside the Factories, three shillings per week for loom standing, Messrs. B. charges their men six shillings.

We shall close our Address with a few words to our Brother Tradesmen ; to you we say, be firm and persevering,—commit no acts of violence, and may the *God of Justice* enable you to triumph over the oppressor.

The Committee.

A poster criticising the Brocklehursts, 1832.   *(MMT)*

The strike began in the 15th October. A crowd of weavers numbering 2-300, headed by a man banging a drum and another playing the fife in the customary fashion of calling a strike, marched through town knocking on loom shop doors, surrounding factories and persuading others to join them. Handbills with the disputed list of prices were distributed to those who swelled their midst's and manufacturers were given a paper with an ultimatum; as was one, William Jackson:

"Sir, agreeable to the determination of the meeting this morning the trade have resolved that if you do not comply with the list price for two thread sarsnets which is laid down at 4d. per yard, your weavers will have to strike work."[7]

Some who wove articles where prices were not in dispute were allowed to remain working. The strike committee issued them with their own 'Certificates of Protection', illegally headed by the King's Arms, which were to be displayed in their windows and illuminated by candle at night-time.

One manufacturer was singled out for most of the weavers' hatred - J & T Brocklehurst's of Hurdsfield. Before the strike they had 300 weavers manufacturing gros de Naples at 6d. per yard when other manufacturers paid 7d. per yard; and they steadfastly refused to pay the extra penny. Late in October a mob surrounded Thomas Brocklehurst's home, Fence House. They demanded meat and drink, destroyed some gardens and finally threw a large stone into a room where Mrs Brocklehurst and her young family were sheltering. After this, special constables were sworn in and military aid in the form of the 15th and 53rd Hussars arrived from Manchester.

Manufacturers then retaliated in the time-honoured fashion. The 1767 Act that enabled them to bring prosecutions against weavers "wilfully neglecting their work" for more than eight successive days, was ruthlessly applied. More than fifty weavers were brought before magistrates to serve as examples to others. Some pleaded that they feared for life and property if they remained at work, and most were discharged, having either agreed to return, had proof of having worked, or because their masters interceded on their behalf at the last minute. A few staunchly declined to return until the strike was over. These, thirteen men in all, were sentenced to one month's hard labour at Knutsford House of Correction. One of them was John Prout.

Whether Prout was in total agreement with the strike is doubtful. Few undertakers were on the Committee and some of those who had once been members were still working. Comments he later made suggest he would have preferred a more conciliatory means of settling the dispute. However, he did

Tho.ˢ Brocklehurst Eʃ.   Fanny B.   Sarah Goodwin   John Hall
                                       Goody! Nurse   the Butler.

Fence House, home of Thomas
Brocklehurst. *(MMT)*

Thomas Brocklehurst, 1791-1870.
(MMT)

Knutsford House of Correction. *(Mrs J. Leach)*

Frost's Mill Park Green owned by Corbishley and Barker in 1832. *(MMT)*

join the strike. Prout's employers, Corbishley and Barker of Park Green [at Frost's Mill], then prosecuted him and one other of their weavers, who was discharged after giving proof of having worked at his loom. In court, Prout offered no such evidence and pleaded guilty. One reason for this is suggested by Reuben Bullock, who was writing a pamphlet, *On Mending the Times*, as the strike progressed:

"...one I know, whose good sense could have evaded the law but I am told that he had such a good opinion of his employers, and believing them to be true Christians, that he had no idea of their pressing conviction, so he spoke the truth, but notwithstanding that, and his good character, nor his being a man of letters, and an author, - notwithstanding his superior talent, having been twice deputised to London to meet the House of Commons; - and notwithstanding his delicate constitution, with a wife and nine children, without the means of subsistence, he is now confined to Knutsford prison, where he may correct his ideas about true Christianity."[8]

There was considerable local sympathy for the strikers, even from *the Courier* who decried the low wages they received. Even greater sympathy came from further afield:

"This is a lamentable struggle: for no one can behold the pale cheeks and meagre forms of the poor operatives, without experiencing a heartfelt sympathy for their sufferings, and an ardent desire for the amelioration of their condition; but still the painful conviction forces itself upon the mind that trade has no bowels of compassion, and no sense but that of self interest."[9]

Desperation on the part of the weavers was soon to lead to violence. *The Courier* claimed that the weavers' strike committee *"consists principally of several Irishmen."* Most, as were John West, Nicholas Lynch, Patrick Jacobs and William Butterworth, worked as inside weavers. Two were undertakers who had previously sat on weavers' committees: Matthew Wilshaw, from Park Lane, on the Roe Buck Inn committee of November 1825, and Joseph Agnew, from Roe Street, a Central Committee member in 1826. John Cronan was said to be a silk twister but served on the Roe Buck committee and was a regular speaker at weavers' meetings. Every evening this group of men would address crowds of striking weavers thronging Waters Green from an upstairs window of the Nags Head public house. These gatherings were occasions on which lists of 'Knobsticks' - men ignoring the strike and still working their looms - were read out; and of whom West had said, *"We must look after them."* Unless a protection paper was displayed prominently the *'Destroying Angel'* would visit them, often at night, and stones would be thrown through their windows. The stones were sometimes wrapped in a paper signed *"An enemy to Knobsticks"* and were addressed *"Mr. West, the Editor of the Knobstick, at his office, the Nags Head."*

One undertaker, a near-neighbour of John Prout and Central Committee member during 1826-8, was Solomon Etchells:

"There was a procession of silk weavers last Friday through Crompton Road, accompanied by a drum and fife about half-past eleven o' clock in the morning. I was at work until they came near my house. I had been at work since the Monday before.

When they got opposite my house they began to shout, saying, "Turn out, Etchells Knobstick," and at that time a stone was thrown through my window. I had no protection paper in my house."[10]

William Prout, John's younger brother, also a committee member in 1826, did have one of these protection papers. As one of William Jackson's outside weavers he was allowed to work throughout the strike.

By the end of November cracks were appearing in the solidity of the strike. Brocklehurst's men felt aggrieved that they stood accused of being the first to have accepted lower prices

108 Steps, from Central Station.

The Nag's Head public house, Waters Green. *(MMT)*

before the strike. At a meeting held at the White Lion in Hurdsfield, they urged others not to trust "*the fallacious promises of the Central Committee*", resolving to return to work and by so doing set a "*beneficial example*" to others. Manufacturers made it plain that returning weavers would receive only "*such remuneration as circumstances will allow*" and those who returned to Brocklehurst's had also to suffer the hostility of crowds who stood outside the factory groaning and hissing at them. Yet with this break in the strike, the committee's power was thought to be "*on the wane.*"

The authorities were then busily collecting evidence of "*violent and intemperate*" speeches made by members of the strike committee from the Nags Head. William Butterworth, less guarded than his colleagues, at one time told the weavers gathered below the public house window, "*You know that some of*

An Appeal to the Public.

At a MEETING of the SILK WEAVERS in the employ of Messrs. J. and T. BROCKLEHURST, held at the Sign of the White Lion, Hurdsfield, November 21st, 1832,

JOSH. WILLIAMSON, in the Chair;

The Weavers of Messrs. J. and T. Brocklehurst have come to the determination of going on with their work, and deem it necessary to lay before the Public the facts of the case.—It was determined by the Meeting to take into consideration the many fallacious statements, and gross misrepresentations, industriously circulated relative to the character of our employers, and that we feel it an imperative duty on our part, having been in their service for a number of years, and being well acquainted with these matters, consider ourselves justified in attempting a refutation of those groundless and malicious accusations; which are mainly attributable to the unfortunate struggle between masters and workmen, and which struggle we presume would have long since terminated, but for the contest contemplated at the approaching Election.

It was Resolved,

That the Weavers in the employ of Messrs. J. and T. Brocklehurst, without any longer trusting to the fallacious promises held forth by the Central Committee, that eventually a victory would be obtained over the Manufacturers, do at once return to their work; and thus by showing a becoming confidence in the good will of their employers, as regards ourselves,—ensure to themselves a candid and just return of upright and friendly feelings on their part, and in doing so to set a beneficial example to their fellow Weavers of the Town; for it is now too evident that the struggle has been maintained on unsound principles; and if persevered in, can only terminate in an extension of weaving in distant places, and thus add to the already ruinous competition of Foreign Goods, that is crushing down the value of labour throughout the country.

That with respect to the unfortunate struggle between masters and their workmen, to which we have alluded before, we have to say we deplore it in common with all the sober and thinking part of our Fellow Townsmen, as being destructive of the true interests of all parties; and we have further to say that we should be happy to discover a more conciliating disposition on *both sides*, for we are persuaded, were this the case, there are men to be found in every shop who would come forward with their best exertions to conclude this unfortunate difference. Much has been said by men of corrupt minds respecting Messrs. Brocklehursts' being *the first to reduce the prices of weaving*, and that they should have said if other Masters came down to them, they would come lower still. This is a *palpable untruth*, as we could point out *by name*, different Masters who *reduced before them*, and others who NEVER GAVE THEIR PRICES AT ALL!—and we can assure our fellow townsmen and the public that our Masters, when compelled to reduce, (which they did in order to compete in the market with other manufacturers,) assured their Weavers, that it gave them the greatest possible pain to lower their wages; and they gave their word that they would reduce no lower this winter, and that they hoped in the coming Spring they should be able to advance their wages. The prices then offered were the prices they had been paying for some years.

We feel ourselves compelled, as men, also to notice the many FALSEHOODS that have been stated before hundreds of the people relative to our *Funeral Box*. The plain facts of the case are

these :—The Weavers met in order to raise a subscription to defray the expences of funerals ; they discussed the subject, drew up the rules, and then applied to their Masters to permit their Clerks to collect the subscriptions from the Weavers, and to pay the allowance of the box, in case of death, viz. four pounds on the decease of any Weaver or his Wife, and one pound for a child, and to keep the accounts relative to the Box. The Masters said it would be troublesome to the Clerks; but, notwithstanding, as the plan was likely to be advantageous to the Weavers, it should be done. This has been done for years, and *the accounts of receipts and disbursements put up in the Camp, or Weavers' Taking-in Room, for their information.* Now, with these facts before our eyes, can we help feeling indignant at the men who have repeatedly said thatfour pounds have been paid out of a subscription, and the rest pocketed by the warehousemen, and that five pounds had been given to three men sent on a mission to Stockport?

With regard to what is called *Late Money* many false representations have been circulated, but the *facts* are as follow :—The Weavers are required to be in with their work by Seven o'clock on Saturdays, and Nine o'clock on Mondays, and if later, they are liable to a forfeit of two-pence for each loom; but it ought to be remembered, that there are four days in the week that Weavers may take in work without any additional forfeit, which is certainly a great advantage in many respects, a privilege *not permitted at any other warehouse in the town;* and when we consider the number of Weavers employed by Messrs. Brocklehursts, it is impracticable for the warehousemen to get through their work without some restrictions on the Weavers, to compel them to bring in their work in the early part of the day.

We have already said, that but for the contest that is contemplated at the approaching Election, this unhappy struggle would long since have terminated. The Public, we think, will be satisfied of the truth of this statement, if they refer to two or three placards that have appeared on the walls of the town, particularly one signed "Joseph Smedley," dated the 1st of the present month. Whatever may be the cause, this gentleman being so very liberal in his invectives against our employers by his pen, and particularly by his tongue in different companies, indulging such acrimonious feelings—causing out with such rash and unbecoming expressions as we are unwilling to pollute our paper with—we say, whatever may be the cause it is best known to himself, but we very much doubt the truth of his assertion, when he tells us in one of his paragraphs, which we give in his own words—"having no private end to obtain, nor any party to serve, there are none whose frowns or applause I need care for, my object is to accomplish a national good, by preventing the Borough of Macclesfield from becoming a close one, which would have been the case, had not a gentleman of known independent principles, come forward to represent your interests in a Reformed Parliament." We think it is very evident that he has Mr. Grimsditch's party to serve, and from his conduct it is quite clear he is willing to serve it in a way not very commendable to himself, or to his party. But let us, for a moment, look at the worthy individual thus introduced to our notice, as a gentleman of *known independent principles.* Now, as to his

independent principles, we know very little about them, but we do know he was a very active gentleman in the honourable Cavalry, which acted so distinguishable a part in the memorable scenes of the 16th of August, at Manchester. It is true, the Macclesfield Troop did not reach the honourable scene of action; but he, and the rest of his companions in arms bravely drew their swords, and marched as far as Stockport on the occasion. We also know that this gentleman of *known independent principles* was very active in the prosecutions of Swan, Richards, Stubbs, and the other poor Reformers, who were incarcerated in Chester Castle, for adhering to those very principles which are now the fashion of the day. These, and other instances that might be adduced, are not, we think, very satisfactory proofs either of the liberality of his principles, or of the extensive scale of his reformed creed.

The next article we would notice is towards the latter end of his bill, where he takes his leave of Mr. Brocklehurst. His words are as follows :— " Of such an illiberal candidate I fearlessy declare that, if the new Parliament is constructed of such members, the sun will have set on the industrious classes of this kingdom." Now let us see wherein the illiberality of Mr. Brocklehurst consists : We have already seen his Address in which he states his political principles, and we appeal to the good sense of our candid fellow-townsmen, and ask them if there is not as much liberality displayed in his Address, as in those of the other candidates? Besides, some of us are not only Weavers, but Electors also, and have conversed with him on these subjects, and we have no doubt but, at the proper time and place, he himself will shew publicly, both to friends and foes, that though he does not drink-in all the wild and visionary ideas of some, yet he is prepared to go *farther in the cause of Reform than his opponents are willing to admit,* and as far as the real friends of the country can desire. For instance, he is an advocate for *Triennial Parliaments*—he deprecates *that part of the Reform Act, which requires that the Electors shall be clear with their rates and taxes* (a shameful clause), as if the laws already in force were not sufficient for that purpose, without exposing the Electors' private affairs, and depriving one-half of the Electors of England of their right of voting, as is the case at Birmingham, where, out of a population of one hundred and fifty thousand, only *four thousand* have the privilege of voting, and many other places are similarly situated ! He also told us that, in his opinion, the ten pound clause was very well in London, Dublin, Edinburgh, or such like places; yet for Macclesfield, and similar towns, the *sum ought to be considerably lower.* As to his abilities, as a commercial man, to protect the local interests of the town, we think there can be but one sentiment. His past services relative to the Silk Committee of the House of Commons are sufficient to set this question at rest for ever, and afford a pleasing guarantee for his future conduct. With these *facts* before them, we presume the public will see the inconsistency of Mr. Smedley, or any other man, charging Mr. Brocklehurst as being an illiberal candidate, or stating that his return to Parliament would blast the interests of the working classes.

With these remarks we close the subject, with the observation that the cause is poor indeed, that requires lying and calumny to support it ; whereas, truth will ever stand upon its own merits.

Signed, on behalf of the Meeting,

JOSEPH WILLIAMSON, Chairman.

Several hundreds of the Weavers in the employ of Messrs. Brocklehurst have already come forward to sign the above.

Poster put out by Brocklehursts' weavers in the 1832 strike. *(MMT)*

TO THE

PEOPLE

OF MACCLESFIELD.

Another hand-bill has made its appearance, with the title of "*An Appeal to the Public*." This hand-bill was written by Mr. Thos. Brocklehurst, and is signed by Joseph Williamson, as the Chairman of a Meeting of Messrs. Brocklehurst's weavers. Mr. Williamson is said to be one of a number of Weavers through whose agency Messrs. Brocklehurst continue to keep down the Prices of the bulk of their Weavers; no doubt he is well paid for it. But how was the Meeting held? What was the conduct of the party assembled? I will tell you. Admission was denied to numbers of the Weavers--some were dragged from the Room--and the whole business was conducted under the Watching and Warding of the County Constables and the Special Constables of the Township. Some 50 or 60 Weavers, (*including Putters-Out, Stewards, Book-keepers, &c.*) were present, and although they were packed and guarded as described, the numbers, on putting the Paper to the Vote, were nearly equal. The Chairman, however, chose to declare the Motion carried, and then ensued a scene of Drunkenness and confusion most discreditable.

The principal object of their hand-bill is to make you believe that Messrs. Brocklehurst "were not the *first* to Reduce the Prices." No doubt Messrs. Brocklehurst would be glad to throw the odium upon other Masters; but it is, in fact, a paltry attempt to deceive you: the thing speaks for itself. *They* were the cause of the Turn-out, by refusing to give the Prices paid by Mr. Pearson. Their refusal still to pay the same prices keeps the Weavers from work. It is well known that they have always paid *less Prices* than other Masters; *they* were the first to employ *Country Weavers*; and *they* carried it on for many years before any other Master. At length the other Masters did the same, and for a very long time upwards of *ONE HUNDRED THOUSAND POUNDS A YEAR!* has been paid away for Weaving *out of the Town!*

Look to that, ye Shopkeepers, Innkeepers, Tradesmen, and Property Men! What is the consequence? Universal Poverty reigns throughout the Town. The Working Man is Half Clothed, and but Half Fed. The Tradesman suffers by *Additional Rates*, and the general trade of the Town is in a state of depression bordering on ruin. But to return to Prices ---I was present before the County Magistrates when it came out that *Messrs. Brocklehurst were paying 6s. 9d. per dozen only for 36 inch Blacks, whilst Messrs. Potts and Wright and other Masters were paying 7s. 9d. per dozen*. This is *a Fact*, which cannot be denied; and one fact is worth a thousand surmises. I shall never forget the confusion of Mr. Thomas Brocklehurst when Mr. Potts raised his hands in astonishment. Other Items of Prices were found to be much the same. Mr. Brocklehurst has made Mr. Williamson and his party to say in their paper that they could point out by *Name* different Masters *who Reduced before them*; but he has made them state a *barefaced Falsehood*, as it can be proved that Messrs. Brocklehurst *Reduced before any other Master*.

Fellow Townsmen, I ask you,--Ought they not to have been the *Last* to Reduce? Is it right, that they, with superior advantages as Bankers, and in possession of Wealth, should have *Reduced at all!* No, my Friends; but I entreat you to enquire into the reason of continuing Country Weavers. Is it for cheapness? No. The Prices in Lancashire, taking into account the inferiority of the articles made, are as high as the Prices of Macclesfield. What then can be the object? Why, in plain English, it is to keep down the Prices of labour here, already so miserably reduced.

A Poor Weaver.

November 23, 1832.

J. WRIGHT, PRINTER, MILL STREET, MACCLESFIELD.

A further poster replying to the one on the previous page. *(MMT) us have some influence with the Destroying Angel!"* Nicholas Lynch quickly shut him up. The Special High Constables, who had gathered such evidence, arrived at the Nags Head with a large force of men one day in late October and arrested West, Lynch, Jacobs and Wilshaw, then took the remaining committee members into custody later. When arrested, West had papers upon him which gave instances of actions taken against "Knobsticks." One was a note that the *"Destroying Angel"* had visited a bread and cheese shop in Crompton Road and *"delivered a broadside."* Another was a letter from a poor widow in Cotton Street who had had her windows broken twice by mistake; the *"Knobstick"* lived two doors away from her house. West, Lynch, Butterworth and Jacobs were placed on bail totalling £100 each to stand trial at Chester Assizes, while the others were discharged.

With the committee arrested it was at first though the strike would end, but another was hastily formed and it continued as before. After a further week, the manufacturers decided to *"cede the point at issue"* and the weavers returned to their looms. The strike had lasted seven weeks, and victory was theirs - or so it seemed. Yet although their upwardly revised list of prices was generally accepted, Brocklehurst's refused to pay more for gros de Naples, preferring to abandon that trade entirely. In time, others followed suit. Many manufacturers continued to send work elsewhere.

TO THE

PUBLIC.

In consequence of Seven of the Weavers being Apprehended last night, we, the Body of Silk Weavers, do assure the Friends and Well-Wishers to the cause, that every Exertion of the Trade is now being made to procure the best Legal Assistance in their power, to obtain Justice for the above Men whom the enemies of the cause wish to Sacrifice to their own purpose.

November 27th, 1832.

Signed by Order of the Trade.

Poster announcing the arrest of strike leaders in 1832. *(MMT)*

As the strike came to a close the general election took place, the first under the newly reformed Parliament. Macclesfield itself was to elect two MPs where before it had only formed part of the county constituency. But of its 718 inhabitants, who as £10 householders were qualified to vote, only 80 were weavers. Nevertheless, on the occasion of the Reform Bill having become law that June - when riots occurred in some cities - workmen from Potts and Wright's Brook Street silk factory paraded through town with a band playing and banners waving in its honour. They then had *"an excellent dinner and plenty of good, strong ale at the expense of their spirited employers."* Later, three of Potts and Wright's weavers were to be among those sentenced to imprisonment during the strike.

The placards placed around town during the election on behalf of the Tory candidate, Thomas Grimsditch, infuriated some weavers. They recollected the fact that he was one of the Yeomanry sent to Peterloo, *"but did not reach the scene of the horrible action"*, and that he was also the prosecutor of Swann, Richards, Swindells, Stubbs and Sutton in 1820. However, as far as the weavers or any other 'non-electors' were concerned, not one of the candidates, Grimsditch, Brocklehurst or John Ryle, were worthy to be their M.P.s and at the hustings they showed their displeasure in no uncertain manner

The election took place in the second week of December. On the first day, crowds numbering upwards of 15,000 people gathered about the hustings centred in Waters Green; where they also leaned from upstairs windows overlooking the scene, stood on rooftops to gain a better view still, or were positioned on the high ground that surrounded it. John Ryle was first on the hustings and he was just reminding the multitudes that he was neither a Whig nor a Tory, when cries of *"Short Time Bill"* [for shorter hours for children - see Chapter 5] and *"Tax on knowledge"* [the 4d. stamp tax on newspapers and journals] upset his continuity. Then John West, still on bail over the strike, pushed through the crowds and said he would like to ask Ryle some questions. After some hesitation Ryle agreed; but at West's query whether he would support the Short Time Bill, his reply, at first inaudible and then on request repeated louder, was that he had not made his mind up. A similar equivocation followed West's question on whether Ryle would vote against the *"knowledge tax."* There was then total uproar among the crowd and Ryle stood down.

Following Ryle, the Liberal candidate John Brocklehurst mounted the hustings, ushered there by several special constables who had been sworn in to guard him because of the animosity felt towards him by weavers generally. As he appeared a huge roar went up from the crowd which doubled then trebled in furore. The special constables locked arms to hold back the pressure from all around but were overpowered. In the midst of all the struggle and confusion John West and Nicholas Lynch climbed up on the hustings. Lynch had a very powerful voice and managed to shout loud enough for some to hear him over the clamour. He begged everyone to be quiet and listen to what Brocklehurst had to say, but the crowd would not be hushed. They chanted over and again, *"Hear West! Hear West!"* Both West and Lynch asked Brocklehurst if they could speak, but as they were not electors some gentlemen objected. The two weavers then stepped down from the hustings. Brocklehurst made a brief and hasty address which was unheard except by two or three who stood next to him, then he abandoned the idea of speechmaking entirely.

Thomas Grimsditch got the same treatment; a deafening shout from the crowds and not one syllable of his speech heard above the mighty uproar. The only sign to onlookers that he was speaking was from the vigorous motion of his mouth and hands. When the voting began and a show of upraised arms

FELLOW
TOWNSMEN !

An Appeal has been made to you by Messrs. Brocklehursts' Weavers, assembled at the White Lion, Hurdsfield, with the notorious Joseph Williamson, alias Anthony Whirity, in the Chair, in order to vindicate the conduct of their employer, from what they call " gross misrepresentations and fallacious statements, which have been circulated by men of corrupt minds." They deny that Messrs. Brocklehurst were the first to Reduce Prices, and that they could point out by name other Masters who Reduced before them. I DARE THEM TO IT. Now, Gentlemen, I would wish to put the following Questions to his Weavers, namely : Was he not the first to reduce the Three-Thread Grey Bandannas Three-pence per cut, and not more than two Manufacturers followed his example ? Is it not a FACT that Mr. Pearson is paying *Eleven Shillings* for his Ducapes, whilst he is paying but *Nine Shillings and Three-pence* per dozen ? Again : Did not he Reduce his 2700 Two-Double Sarcenets to *Five-pence Halfpenny*, with from 128 to 139 picks to the inch, while Mr. Pearson was paying *Six-pence Halfpenny* per yard, for the same works, although the labour was considerably less, it being one inch narrower, and only 90 picks to the inch, from which price he has never altered.
    I wish you to bare in mind that this respectable Shop-Meeting consisted of *Burgess, Sutton, Ravenscroft,* and about Seventy miscreants in the employ of our Illiberal Candidate. A small majority of this Meeting came to a determination (*not daring to do otherwise,*) to go to work, placing confidence in their employer. Now, Gentlemen, relative to his former conduct being a guarantee for the future, I should like to know whether he did not remain in London as much for the benefit of his own health as with a view of rendering any assistance to the Inhabitants of Macclesfield, as the cheapness of LABOUR is a prominent feature in his general line of conduct, although a participator in the Threadneedle-street gang, of Paper notoriety, should enable him to pay the same price for labour as any Manufacturer of minor importance. Moreover, did he not declare when he summoned his dyers into his presence, that if any of them joined the Union for the Protection of Labour, they should no longer work for him ? Again, their Weavers say that Messrs. Brocklehurst would pay their present Prices during the Winter. That statement, like all their others, *is founded on Falsehood* ; for the question was put to them at the Meeting, and was answered by two Reverend Miscreants in their employ, who stated that nothing had been said by Messrs. Brocklehurst which might be construed into a promise on their part to continue the present Price of Labour.
    With regard to his Late Money, I ask you if any of the Misrepresentations, which they have been compelled by their employers to say, are circulated ? I ask you, do they not remain uncontradicted, with the exception of a fellow named BARLOW, *the Putter-Out at Bullock-Smithy ?* and which circumstance compels me to call your attention to a placard signed Smedley, in order to bring Brocklehurst and his hireling from Bullock-Smithy face to face ; the former declares that the Late Money is a perquisite that his Warehousemen receive ; the latter was willing to swear in the presence of a meeting of the Inhabitants of Stockport, on Thursday, the 15th instant, that the Warehousemen never received a Fathing of the Late Money ! I will leave the question to be settled by these two worthies ; but this I know, that the placard in question has been the sole cause of Reducing the Stoppages from Four-pence to Two-pence, which leaves a pretty round sum to be pocketted by JOHNNY GRAB-ALL. I must also call your attention to a letter sent to him when in London, desiring him to give an explanation of his Political Principles, asking him, if elected, would he support any Petition, if its object was to extend the suffrage, shorten the duration of Parliaments, and the ballot. This letter, though signed by upwards of twenty of the Electors, and wrote as early as June last, remains unanswered to this day. Now Gentlemen, a few words to the Electors, as we are on the eve of an Election. You must be aware that the Franchise with which you are entrusted, places you in a great measure under the influence of the Working Classes, who expect through you to be virtually represented. May I ask you, who are in a Retail way of trade, who is it that gives you employment ? The answer must be the Working Classes, and depend upon it those classes will narrowly watch the conduct of, I am glad to say, the small number who are inclined to support, at the approaching Election the *Threadneedle-street* Candidate ; and I am fully satisfied that the virtually represented will take their small earnings to those Shopkeepers who support the Candidate they consider the most worthy to represent their Interests in a Reformed Parliament.

AN OLD WEAVER.

Macclesfield, Nov. 22, 1832.

Three posters, left and opposite, from the general election of 1832 in Macclesfield. *(MMT)*

TO THE

Electors.

Mr. **BROCKLEHURST** is at length come out—He has published his explanation "by the *advice* and with the *concurrence* of a number of Manufacturers"—He says, it was "*incumbent* upon him" by such "advice" and with such "concurrence"—I say it was *incumbent* upon him and his duty as a Man, without any such "advice" or "concurrence" to do more.—He is called upon to explain why he was the first to *reduce wages*, and bring on the strike which has inflicted so much injury on the Inhabitants of Macclesfield.—He was the *first* to employ Weavers out of the Town!—He is the author of all the Evil that has arisen from it—**ONE HUNDRED THOUSAND POUNDS A YEAR** *paid away for Weaving out of the Town!!!*—Has he not carried it on for more than a Dozen years?—Will he cease the practice, and employ the People of the Town?—He says that "he was *equally* ready to accede to the List prices being given", but that a meeting of Manufacturers was held in London—that *they* declined, and that *their* dissent was "in accordance with the sentiments he then entertained."—Thus shewing that *he* never had been "ready" either *equally* or *unequally*, and thus stultifying his own prior statement.

This is evidently a sidewind attempt to throw the odium, in no very courteous manner, upon other Manufacturers, who one would suppose to be almost blind to their own interests and subservient to his, for so long as he is allowed to rule, we may look in vain for returning prosperity.—In another part of his Address he talks of retaining "this branch of Manufacture to the Weavers of the Town." Mr. **BROCKLEHURST** knows how this can be done—Let him give up the employment of Country Weavers—No body doubts that he has the means of giving a *living price* for labour as well as others who are willing to do it. But, Brother Electors, past experience holds out no hope. He has in the face of Free Trade, doubled if not trebled the extent of his concerns, till they have become a **MONOPOLY**, which threatens the destruction of all competition, and unhappily at the present day it has become the practice *to compete on the Labour of the Poor.*

Brother Electors—I, in common with numbers of other Electors, *cannot conscientiously* and in *justice* to my *Fellow-Townsmen*, who have a right to look for virtual representation through us, *and will not*, vote for Mr. **BROCKLEHURST**, although I am one of his

Improvident Promisers.

MACCLESFIELD,
NOVEMBER 24, 1832.

BOROUGH
ELECTION

Mr. **BROCKLEHURST** has let the *Cat out of the Bag.* The Turn-Out was *not* for an *Advance* of Prices, as stated in the Macclesfield Paper of last week but one, but to prevent a *Reduction.* It now appears that a Meeting of Masters took place in London, to *enforce* the *Reduction!* **SO MUCH FOR MR. EDITOR.** I was much struck with his bold assertion at the time. He would do well to adhere to Truth; and not mislead the Public by publishing False Statements to serve an Individual.

But what Masters attended the Meeting? Mr. Pearson and many others were *not* in London, and we may fairly conclude the Meeting was confined to Mr. Brocklehurst and his "*advice and concurrence men.*" Who are these Invisibles? Whoever they may be, they will shortly see that the Independent Electors of Macclesfield will not pollute the Franchise by serving their unhallowed purpose. No! Mr. Brocklehurst must *not* be returned to Parliament.

A Shopkeeper.

was required, Mayor and Returning Officer Dr. Fleet could not make himself heard above the tumult and had to hold up cards on which were the candidate's names, 'Ryle,' 'Brocklehurst' or 'Grimsditch' - at which the Tory gained only a feeble response. This was afterwards corroborated in the polling station at Duke Street National School. Grimsditch made his views known later to an impromptu meeting of non-electors, when he claimed to be against the Silk Act and the Corn Law and for the Short Time Bill. He also said he had not until that day realised that bribery and corruption existed in the election, but now had proof that one candidate had been *"treating"* voters.

The election took three days to complete and the disturbances continued throughout, with violence awarded particularly to anyone wearing Ryle's colours. Two ex-Mayors were also attacked and several rioters arrested. The final result was Ryle 443, Brocklehurst 402 and Grimsditch 186. The defeated Grimsditch magnanimously congratulated Ryle in his final speech but not Brocklehurst; of whom he had passed evidence of *"bribery and treating"* to the Returning Officer, Dr. Fleet. Grimsditch's memory failed him somewhat when he claimed to have been a supporter of extending Parliamentary representation to all the people of England, but cries of *"False - falsehood"* interrupted him and restored reality. He did however, in the light of his experience on the hustings, say he was a convert to the ballot box. After the final speeches, a procession was formed and the two new M.P.s were carried in chairs from the Town Hall through all the town's main streets, lined throughout with its inhabitants; some on walls or rooftops, all of them cheering and flag waving, and members of the *"softer sex"* fluttering handkerchiefs from upstairs windows. A long night of celebrations followed, after which one drunk was discovered next morning fast asleep and completely naked. When awakened he shouted, *"Grimsditch for ever - no bribery and corruption."* However, all of Macclesfield's elections, right up to and including the worst of all, in 1880, took place amid wholesale bribery and corruption.

At the next quarter sessions of Chester assizes, to take place in March 1833, strike leaders West. Lynch, Butterworth and Jacobs were to face charges of conspiring to prevent men following their occupation. Just before the trials there was a short turn out of weavers who met on two successive evenings at Rushton's Meadow to decide how best to help the defence of the men. At the second meeting, Burgess, the local constable, informed all present that as there was currently peace in the town, and he wished to keep it that way, he would mediate on the defendants' behalf providing that no breach of the peace occurred. This was agreed and when they met once more on the following evening, Burgess informed them that the matter was terminated because all charges had been dropped. The announcement was received with resounding cheers.

What John Prout thought of this result was not recorded. He would have completed his term of imprisonment in mid-December, almost certainly exhausted and unfit to continue his trade for awhile, even though the strike was over. Hard labour at Knutsford House of Correction meant work on the treadmill, introduced into prisons in 1820. Positioned in a long shed, the wheel itself was about five feet in diameter and long enough for about ten men at a time to be on it. Ascending it by a step, the men would hold a bar before them and tread the wheel around, usually at the recommended rate of 48 steps per minute and for periods of between three to five hours a day. It was said to cause ruptures and was particularly bad for those with varicose veins. The sweating induced in treading it could cause rheumatic and pulmonary diseases. John Prout's *"delicate constitution"* would have been tested severely.

References

1. M.C. 16/10/1830.
2. Thompson E.P. The Making of the English working Class, 1963, quoted page 804.
3. *Poor Man's Guardian* newspaper, 10/12/1831
4. M.C. 22/1/1887.
5. Poor Man's Guardian newspaper, 3/3/1832.
6. Select Committee Report into the State of the Silk Trade 1831-32, page 814, evidence of John Prout.
7. M.C. 1/12/1832.
8. Bullock Reuben, *On Mending the Times,* 1833.
9. Liverpool Mercury; reprinted in M.C. 10/11/1832
10. M.C. 1/12/1832.

Treadmill as used at Knutsford House of Correction.

ON

MENDING THE TIMES:

ADDRESSED

TO THE

AUTHOR'S FRIENDS AND ACQUAINTANCES,

ENGAGED IN

MANUFACTURES;

BRIEFLY SHEWING THE TRUE CAUSE OF

LOW WAGES;

WITH A NATURAL, EASY, AND EFFECTUAL MODE OF

Improving our System.

———

BY R. BULLOCK.

———

Act ye must by Laws or Rules,
To guard your health and ease,
Or still remain your Masters' tools,
To grind you as they please.

———

MACCLESFIELD:
PRINTED BY J. LANCASHIRE, BRUNSWICK STREET.
1833.
—
Price Four-pence.

The front cover of Reuben Bullock's pamphlet. *(MMT)*

Chapter 7. Ten Hours

"Act ye must by Laws or Rules
To guard your health and ease,
    Or still become your master's tools
To grind you as they please."[1]

When Reuben Bullock penned these opening lines of doggerel for his pamphlet *On Mending the Times*, he was about 58 years of age. Born at Sutton, he had spent much of his younger life at Bolton, but returned to Macclesfield around 1818, since when he had variously worked as a silk spinner, manufacturer and weaver, and had fathered two girls. His pamphlet, 16 pages long, quarto in size and priced 4d., was addressed to: *"the Author's Friends and Acquaintances engaged in manufacture: briefly showing the True Cause of Low Wages; with a natural, easy and effectual mode of improving our system..."*

This was for all trades to combine and reduce their hours of work: through united strike action if necessary. By these means they would increase the value of their labour and hence raise wages. If the masters demanded wage cuts because markets were overstocked, then operatives should insist on working for less time, until the market for their products was restored. On a local note, he stated that if the hand loom weavers were not to work by candle light in the winter months, it would reduce their production by a quarter: *"labour must be able to become valuable; and the only way to give it a high value is to make it scarce."*

Publication of the pamphlet coincided with the new, all-embracing union set up by Bullock's acquaintance John Doherty, the Manchester bookseller and publisher. For almost as soon as his National Association for the Protection of Labour died, Doherty was forming yet another to replace it, The Society for National Regeneration. This campaigned for an eight hour day for working people without loss of earnings, and if employers would not comply then a national strike would ensue in November 1833. Doherty was also the foremost campaigner in the north-west for restricting the hours worked by children. In June 1830 he conducted cases against cotton manufactures at Bollington and Macclesfield who had been overworking children under the existing Factory Acts. The magistrates, John Ryle and the Rev. Browne, dismissed all cases except one.

A national movement to restrict the hours of factory children had begun in earnest about 1815, led principally by Robert Owen, an early Socialist and enlightened mill owner at New Lanark in Scotland. He had been successful only in that an 1819 Act placed restrictions on hours worked by children in cotton mills. The movement gathered pace during the 1830s, led by Richard Oastler, a Tory land steward. It attracted, amongst others, John Fielden, joint MP for Oldham, with William Cobbett, and owner of the world's largest cotton spinning factory at Todmorden, and Anthony Ashley Cooper, known as Lord Ashley [later Earl of Shaftesbury], a Tory landowner and evangelical Christian. Many operatives were also setting up *"short time committees"*, partly in the hope that by restricting children's working hours, adults hours would also be reduced, but mostly on moral or religious grounds. Opposition to any such reforms came from the majority of manufacturers in all trades.

Robert Owen, 1771-1858.

Early in 1831 a Bill was introduced into the house of Commons by Radical MP John Hobhouse aimed at limiting persons under eighteen in silk, cotton or wool factories to no more than eleven and a half hours per day. A second clause would have prohibited the employment of any child under the age of nine. At a general meeting of the silk trade called at Macclesfield Town Hall in March, the proposed Bill was discussed by both manufacturers and operatives. Both approved the first part but objected to the second clause other than for cotton mills, where the work was seen as much more laborious and unhealthy. At the time, about

Lord Ashley, 1801-1885, from an Illustrated London News cartoon.

4,000 children were employed in the town's silk mills - five hundred or more of them under nine years old.

Other working people were for the Bill in its entirety. A small crowd consisting mostly of heads of families gathered at the Bundle of Sticks on 4th April to hear Thomas Worsley of Manchester, an associate of Doherty, report on the progress of Hobhouse's Bill. He had just left London, where he said, some gentlemen were saying that work in silk mills was so easy that children could sit all the time and would rather be there than at school. Cries of *"False, false,"* greeted these remarks. The Rev. Morris of Dean Row chapel then proposed a resolution to support Hobhouse's Bill and spoke of the injurious effects that standing for long hours had on children, *"through which so many are crippled for life."* Children's morals were injured too, he said, for they matured too early through work as in the adage *"soon ripe - soon rotten."* He also mentioned parents who lived in partial idleness on the earnings of their offspring.

However, Hobhouse's Bill was lost; and although it was replaced by another from sympathetic Tory MP Michael Sadler, this too failed at its second reading. Instead, a Select Committee was formed, one whose report accused manufacturers of brutality and was therefore rejected as being too partisan towards operatives. When Sadler lost his seat in the 1832 election, the short time committee's asked Lord Ashley to lead them in the House. Ashley then brought a Ten Hours Bill before the Commons, but yet another Commission of Enquiry was set up.

Macclesfield's manufacturers were largely against any changes to the working day. Thirteen of them, including Thomas Brocklehurst, Samuel Thorp and the Pearson brothers, signed a declaration to that effect for the benefit of the Commission:

"In conclusion we beg to state, that the hours and nature of working in silk mills have not been hurtful to the health of the people employed in them, nor their morals ......and there is no necessity for any legislative interference on the subject."[2]

Other men of local significance supported their claims. Manager of Pearson's throwing mill since 1825, Samuel Higginbotham, said the work was not harmful and produced several letters from local medical practitioners to back his words. One stated that *"the occupation of children in silk factories is more conducive to health than confinement in an ordinary school would be."* Another, from Dr. John Fleet, the House Surgeon of the town Dispensary, aiming to combat claims of children being crippled by such work, stated:

"The nature of the exercise in silk factories is calculated more than any other to prevent these deformities; the muscles of the upper arm and lower extremities are maintained in constant action, and the consequence is the children grow up in stature perfectly straight, and free from all species of deformity."[3]

Yet Higginbotham overstated his case on the employers' behalf; he said that the 1824 millmen's strike was to prevent manufacturers from *"reducing"* the hours of work to 12 per day!

At a delegate conference in Manchester to discuss the Commission, instructions were given to local short time committee's about what information to gather and present before it. One was *"to obtain a full and correct a list as possible of all the cripples and maimed in their neighbourhood."* On behalf of Macclesfield's local committee, John Wright, the Roe Street silk steward, gathered together a list of all those in the *"cleanest and prettiest streets in town"* - namely Townley Street, Watercotes, Bank Top, Mill Lane, Park Green and Pickford Street - and found a total of 63 cripples, all said to have been caused through excessive labour and confinement in silk factories. This information, along with much else, he put before the Commission.

Not all factory reformers favoured co-operating with the Commission; and John Doherty was one. In setting up the Society for National Regeneration early in 1833, supported by both Robert Owen and John Fielden, he favoured direct action. A branch of the Society was formed in Macclesfield that February after a visit by Doherty and Owen; and although the presence of Reuben Bullock is unrecorded, that inauguration coincided with the publication of *On Mending the Times*, in which views sympathetic to the Society's aims were expressed. However, Doherty's Society for National Regeneration foundered, as did every other attempt at a general union for all workers. The national strike planned for November 1833 was first postponed then dropped. A series of lock-outs of its members by factory owners concluded its operations entirely in 1834.

The 1833 Government Commission of Enquiry resulted in an Act of sorts. It was brought in by Lord Althorp, after much back-stairs intrigue with manufacturers, and was framed to take the heat out of public opinion without being too effective in practice. The Act provided that after 1st January 1834 no child under nine was to be employed in any mill - except in silk mills where no lower age was set. Neither was any child under thirteen to work more than nine hours per day or 48 per week in a mill by 1836 - except in silk mills where a ten hour day, 60 hour week was permitted. All young people aged between fourteen and eighteen were limited to twelve hours per day or a 69 hour week, but a clause making it compulsory for children working less than a 48 hour week to attend school did not affect Macclesfield silk manufacturers at all, because of their 60 hour week dispensation. A clause, which was to have some effect, stated that four full-time Government Inspectors would enforce the Act.

One of these inspectors visited the town in December 1833 to explain the workings of the new Act. He was informed by manufacturers that hundreds of children under thirteen years old were employed in all silk operations and with their working week reduced to 60 hours *"any interference with their labour would abate in equal proportions the production of the adults employed in the manufacture and consequently reduce their earnings in the same ratio."*[4]

After this threat they turned to schooling, anticipating later compulsion in this area by making a prior claim that of every 100 under thirteen year olds employed, about 95 already attended schools and were able to read and write.

As if to underline the inherent dangers to children working in the town's silk factories, just for the benefit of the new inspector, an accident took place on the 16th January - two weeks after his duties commenced. A young girl, Hannah Plant, had her dress entangled in machinery, which dashed her against a wall. Although her employer managed to throw the machinery immediately out of gear, she was badly bruised and her arm broken. But she was so weak that no operation could be done and within a week she died. It was stated at the inquest that only a small expense was needed to box in the machinery. The verdict was *"accidental death"* and her employer was made to pay a deodand [fine] amounting to one shilling.

Other working practices continued just as before. On the 29th March *the Courier* carried an advert headed *"Factory Act"*:

"It having been represented to the Inspector, that sundry Silk Manufacturers and Throwsters, in Macclesfield and the Vicinity, pay no attention to the Factory Act, now in force, and that they continue to work their younger hands as if no such Act had been passed.....NOTICE IS HEREBY GIVEN, That such Irregularities will infallibly subject the offenders to the penalties prescribed by the Act.....R. Rickards, Inspector."[5]

Sub-Inspector Charles Trimmer lived in Macclesfield, but his area encompassed all of Cheshire and Flintshire, plus parts of Staffordshire and Derbyshire. His salary was £350 per year out of which he paid his own travelling expenses - encouraging him to spend a lot of time in Macclesfield. One difficulty of his job was knowing the precise age of a child, for both parents and others sought to elude the constraints of the new Act. Parents might offer a baptism certificate as proof, but these were often falsified by backdating, or else it was sometimes claimed the child was much older when baptised. A

FACTORY ACT.

*Factory Inspector's Office, Manchester,
22nd March, 1834.*

IT having been represented to the Inspector, that
sundry Silk Manufacturers and Throwsters, in
Macclesfield and the Vicinity, pay no attention to
the Factory Act, now in force, and that they continue to work their younger hands as if no such
Act had passed, to the great prejudice and incon-
venience of those who strictly conform to its provisions ;

NOTICE IS HEREBY GIVEN,

That such irregularities will infallibly subject the
offenders to the penalties prescribed in the Act.

The Inspector, therefore, hopes that this timely
notice may have the effect of checking the proceedings thus complained of, and obviate the necessity, which he would much regret, of having
recourse to compulsive proceedings for this purpose.

The Inspector expects to be in Macclesfield in a
few days from this date, when he will be happy to
confer personally with the Master Manufacturers
and Throwsters on all matters connected with the
operation of the Act, and to give such explanations
thereon as may be required

R. RICKARDS, Inspector.

Notice concerning the Factory Act, 29th March 1834, Macclesfield Courier. *(CRO)* surgeons' certificate was another method used; these based on strength, appearance, height and teeth. One child who had such a certificate, stating its age to be thirteen, was only three feet nine inches in height. Five years after the 1834 Act, Trimmer found that of the many children under nine years old in Macclesfield's mills, some as young as five were still working more than a ten hour day. The youngest children were often hidden when the Inspector arrived, sometimes in the machinery or in water closets, and most were reluctant to give evidence against their masters. Proving overworking by manufacturers was always a problem for him, for the factory clocks and time books were often tampered with.

Nevertheless, Trimmer was able to bring charges against three manufacturers in April 1836, the first under the Act. The infringements were of failure to keep proper time books, working children under eighteen for more than twelve hours, and of working children without surgeons' certificates. Fines were imposed ranging from £1 to £3. George Kent Pearson was one of these manufacturers: he claimed that every manufacturer in the town was guilty of the same, including the Mayor [Samuel Thorp] and its Member of Parliament [John Brocklehurst], and concluded by saying *"It would be much better to pay a superintendent to keep the children at their work, than to keep them from their work."* [6] Macclesfield's magistrates were not too keen on Trimmer either: they said he was *"over zealous."*

John Brocklehurst MP [family motto Veritas me dirigit - Truth is my guide] was another who subscribed to the view that work in silk mills was no more difficult for a child than sitting in a school all day. In 1836 he supported a Commons Bill designed to allow twelve year olds to work a full day rather than the ten hours permitted under the 1834 Act, this on the grounds that it was unjust to interfere with their right to work. He was also to repeat the claim that 96% of Macclesfield's child workers could read and write; to which Trimmer countered that the *"census"* was unfairly taken. In 1840, one mill owner discovered that of his 113 hands aged under eighteen, only 52 could read and write.

Lord Ashley's interest in the welfare of child workers brought him and John Wood, a factory-reforming worsted mill owner of Bradford, to Macclesfield in October 1836. There, as related in a Manchester newspaper, they *"now and then stumbled over a few crippled and deformed persons from long hours of factory labour."* In town their guide must have been Reuben Bullock, whose two daughters were then employed as silk workers. Three years later, when Frances Trollope was considering writing a novel on child labour in cotton mills and of coming north to gather material, Ashley wrote to her:

"On your arrival at Macclesfield be so kind as to ask for Reuben Bullock, of Roe Street, and at Manchester for John Doherty, a small bookseller of Hyde's Cross in the town. They will show you the secrets of the place as they showed them to me...."[7]

Instead of journeying by road as had Lord Ashley, Frances Trollope and her son, Thomas Adolphus, were able to avail themselves of the new railway and set off from London for Manchester via Crewe on 20th February 1839, avoiding Macclesfield. Whether she did consult Reuben Bullock is unknown, but Thomas Adolphus *"proved useful"* to his mother in collecting facts in places where it would have been difficult for her to look. One of these places may have been Macclesfield, for he later wrote of:

"the little group of apostles to whom Lord Shaftesbury's letter introduced us and whose intimate conciliables his recommendations caused our admittance....all, or nearly all of them, men a little raised above the position of factory hands, to the righting of whose wrongs they devoted their lives."[8]

But in spite of Thomas Adophus's fact collecting, Frances Trollope's *The Life and Adventures of Michael Armstrong, the Factory Boy*, the first instalment of which was published within six days of her northward travels, drew most heavily on a little book printed earlier in Manchester by John Doherty. This was the biography of one Robert Blincoe, a London orphan and poor law apprentice whose experiences at Lowdham mill, near Nottingham, and Litton mill in Derbyshire were fraught with the utmost hardship and physical abuse. Mrs. Trollope's novel was not very popular among the novel-reading classes she usually catered for, yet in its twelve, one shilling parts it had a following, as she later wrote, *"I don't think any one cares much for 'Michael Armstrong' - except the Chartists. A new kind of patrons for me!"*[9]

As a Chartist himself, one who was chairman at a dinner in Macclesfield honouring national Chartists figures William Benbow and Feargus O'Connor in October 1838, Reuben Bullock would surely have approved.

Lord Ashley's aim to get all factory children's hours limited to ten per day was well supported in Macclesfield. The *"Friends of the Ten Hours Factory Bill"* held a meeting at Duke Street National School in February 1842; their advertising placards headed *"English Slavery."* In the chair was John Wright and also present was a deputation from Manchester that included John Doherty. The first resolution was moved by Reuben Bullock, who claimed that ten hours a day in a factory *"was as much as full grown men could stand with impunity*

Love conquered Fear

Illustration from *Michael Armstrong, The Factory Boy*, 1839.

and much too long for children of tender years." In seconding this resolution, Doherty justified the manner in which the meeting had been advertised and quoted from factory inspector Horner's [Leonard Horner, Inspector for Macclesfield 1834-8] pamphlet, where he had designated the employment of children in factories as *"slavery."* In fact, child slaves in the West Indies had been limited by law to only six hours per day since 1831.

Yet once again the factory reformers were thwarted. Ashley's Bill was rejected in the Commons and in 1844 the Government brought in one of their own. This classed women with children, limiting both to twelve hours per day. In silk mills, under eights were now excluded from work altogether; eight to eleven year olds were limited to seven hours; and eleven to thirteen year olds to ten hours per day [nine hours in other trades]. There was also to be compulsory half-time education for all eight to eleven year olds [9-13 years in other trades] for which parents had to pay a nominal fee. Equally of importance in Macclesfield was the compulsion attached to the fencing of machinery.

Since Sub-Inspector Trimmer's first forays into Macclesfield silk mills, and the death of young Hannah Plant within a fortnight, there had been at least four more instances of unfenced machinery causing death to children. A youth had died in July 1834, three days after being strangled when the neckerchief he wore got caught a round a revolving shaft in a mill at Waters Green. Then a ten year old boy had been drawn between a wheel and a wall and killed at the Depot Mills on Park Green in 1837. Another boy was killed in a mill at Waters Green in January 1838, when a lever that caught in his shoe carried him around a drum and into some spur gears, and the following month a nine year old boy was caught by his handkerchief and killed while playing near an engine shaft at Brocklehurst's mill. In each of these cases the inquest's verdict was *"accidental death"* and the maximum deodand had been £1. In June 1846, after the new Act requiring machinery to be fenced was in force, twelve year old William Barrett called to his dog from the window of the Bank Top mill where he worked: as a witness related:

"....directly after he heard a scream and went to where the scream came from; then saw the boy caught in the shaft by the comforter and shirt neck .....The boy muttered in reply to the question what he was doing - that he was knocking at Turk - the dog's name."[10]

The shaft turned at a speed of 42 revolutions per minute. It was situated beneath the window and not boxed in. The boy died later.

A death such as this from unfenced machinery could cost a firm between £10 and £30 in fines and compensation. Yet a similar case in 1855, when a fourteen year old girl survived being caught up in unfenced gearwheels, although requiring an arm amputated, was dismissed. She received compensation from her employer of just £1.0s.6d.. Lesser infringements of Factory Acts usually warranted a fine of £2. The money collected in fines went to help fund schooling for working children. In the first year following the 1844 Factory Act, grants paid from the fund totalled £60 but had fallen to £25 by 1850; a possible indication that the working environment was becoming safer.

Still dissatisfied, Lord Ashley introduced a new Ten Hours Bill in January 1846, but soon afterwards resigned when the Corn Laws were finally repealed. His place was taken by John Fielden. A resurgence of interest in Macclesfield began with a meeting at Parsonage Street Chapel that February, one week after Ashley's resignation. In the chair was Reuben Bullock, but making a long and emotional speech was John West, by then a well-known Chartist orator. In proposing a resolution to support the Ten Hours Bill he said:

"Macclesfield above all towns he knew showed the marks of the factory system in the number of cripples to be seen in its streets ...he knew of one family in which there were already four cripples."[11]

He also called for the total abolition of married women working in factories. The resolution to petition Parliament was seconded by John Wright. When presented in the house of Commons early that March by MP Thomas Grimsditch [elected at his third attempt, in 1837], it contained 10,000 signatures, among which were those of many of the town's clergy.

Once again, the Ten Hours Bill proposed by Ashley failed to find enough support in the House of Commons. Soon after however, the Tories were defeated and a more sympathetic Whig Government was returned. John Fielden introduced another Ten Hours Bill in January 1847. As before, this was accompanied by a meeting of Macclesfield supporters, again under the chairmanship of Reuben Bullock. It was to have been held in the Town Hall but so many people turned up that it was transferred to the National School in Duke Street. This time John Wright of Roe Street moved the first resolution, to reduce the hours of both children and females, and the Rev. Mr. John Wright of the Methodist New Connexion seconded him. John West, on a personal note, called for a law to prevent all married women from working. It was agreed once more to petition the Houses of Parliament.

Fielden's Bill passed through the House of Commons in May. It limited all women and children to ten hours per day and was to become law the following year. However, under an unaltered part of the 1844 Act, machinery could be run from 5.30 am to 8.30 pm, allowing employers to operate a *"relay system"* of different shifts. When this was contested, a decision favourable to employers was ruled by the Court of the Exchequer. Although the relay system was not operated in Macclesfield, operatives *"feeling an interest in securing the objects of the Ten Hours Act - now imperilled..."* held a meeting in March 1850. Numbered among the speakers were Reuben Bullock and five Reverend gentlemen from the town's churches and chapels, one being the Rev. John Wright of the New Connexion, while another regular was the Rev. W.R.B. Arthy of St. George's, who had attended all meetings since 1839. Yet from personal experience it was the other John Wright who spoke most ardently:

"The factory system had done its worst to him, and he resolved to do his best to improve the conditions of the factory hands."[12]

He thanked God that he had no children and said that factory workers still wanted a ten hour day, not twelve, even with reduced wages. After a nation-wide outcry by Short Time Committee's everywhere, the Government came to a compromise agreement with Ashley; a ten and a half hour day for women and children with outside limits of 6am to 6pm. But this was not enough; children could still be made to work shifts.

John Wright of Roe Street died in February 1851, aged 57, and after that date Reuben Bullock, by then 76 years old, no longer took a leading part in the Short Time movement. The mantle of support for the Short Time Bill passed to the local vicars. A meeting at the Town Hall in February 1853, aimed at petitioning Parliament to restore the Ten Hours Act and restrict shifts, had the Baptist Minister Rev. Mr. R. Stocks in the chair, while three others, the Rev. Arthy, the Rev. C.N. O'Pratt and the Rev. Abercrombie gave their support. Another cleric was the Rev. Joseph Rayner Stephens, a Wesleyan minister and one-time Chartist from Manchester, whose outspoken attacks on the treatment of child workers dated from the early 1830s. When he mentioned factory clocks with two faces, one outside going fast and one inside going slow, he was soon told from the crowd, *"There's plenty of that game in this town and I can prove it."* Another shouted, *"There's some of those clocks at Hurdsfield."* Principal speaker Samuel Fielden, of the Fielden Association at Todmorden, expressed surprise at the deformities of people in Macclesfield, for he had always believed the silk trade to be *"light work"* and that was why exemptions had been made in factory acts. The Rev. Stocks said he had resided in the town for 25 years and thought there was no town in England which had so many deformed people:

"Many of them had been worked at such a tender age, and for so many hours together, that they had become so deformed that they did not seem like human beings."[13]

The Rev. Arthy said his interest in the Ten Hours Bill stemmed from the fact that after working such long hours men often sought relief in intoxicating drink; if hours were shorter they might take advantage of the town's night schools to improve themselves.

Things were slowly improving for children though. The "normal day" other than "relays" was enforced after 1853, if not too harshly in Macclesfield. When in December 1858 Sub-Inspector Trimmer brought cases against five local manufacturers for working women and children beyond the 6p.m. deadline, local magistrate Dr. Swanwick imposed minimum fines of £1. In one case Swanwick said he though Trimmer was carrying the law to the extreme, as it was only half an hour over the time, but Trimmer retorted that the offence was on the increase. Later Acts of Parliament brought further improvement; in 1860 silk dying came under the Factory Acts, but it was a further seven years before unpowered workshops were covered.

Any exemptions that the silk trade still possessed were finally removed in 1875, when nine years old [10 from 1876] became the minimum age for employment as half-timers and thirteen for full time work. Macclesfield Chamber of Commerce objected, sending a deputation to the Home Secretary which also claimed to be representing the wishes of operatives. Yet at a crowded meeting of the Factory Acts Reform Association, mill workers had passed a resolution in favour of the Act. The deputation's plea to retain full time work from eleven years of age onwards was fully rejected. The Inspectors replied:

"as the work of the children appears equally continuous in this as in any other branches of labour, we cannot see any reason for the exemption of children over 11 from the rules as to half timers, which prevails in other manufactures."[14]

Half-timers required an exemption certificate proving that a certain educational standard had been attained before they could begin working. The beneficial effects of this system, begun in 1844, were slow in forthcoming; by 1862 only 452 out of 719 children applying for work in Macclesfield could read and write.[15] The problems it created within schools can be gauged from the situation at Duke Street National School, where of 27 pupils in Standard IV during 1880, 19 were half-timers. George Peachey, the Master - "Black George" to his pupils - recorded in the school log book; *"We seem to make little progress because of half-timers...it is all repetition."* By this time it had also been discovered that Macclesfield children were on average inferior in height, weight, chest measurement and chest expansion; endorsing the claims that local reformers had been making for the past forty-five years or more.[16]

Throughout this period the children themselves were largely passive, but there were times when they went on 'strike.' This seems to have occurred in August 1834 when numbers of apprentices left their employers, including Brocklehurst's, and risking prosecution for having broken the terms of their indentures - with terms of three months hard labour threatened - tried to get better wages elsewhere . There was another during 1850-51, when again it was not a unified 'strike' in the accepted sense, rather that for two or three months many children ran away from the mills where they were employed and went to others in search of better wages. Overall they gained an advance, either from new jobs or by being coaxed back to their old jobs at an increased wage.

By a curious coincidence, the original child that in real life was the inspiration for Frances Trollope's *Michael Armstrong, the Factory Boy*, Robert Blincoe, died aged 68 at his son-in-law's home at Sutton Mills, Macclesfield on the 12th December 1860.

References
1. Bullock Reuben, *On Mending the Times*, 1833.
2. Second Report of Commissioners on Child Labour 1833, page 23.
3. ibid. evidence of Samuel Higginbotham.
4. M.C. 30/11/1833.
5. M.C. 29/3/1834.
6. M.C. 23/4/1836.
7. Trollope T.A. *What I Remember*, Vol. II, 1883.
8. Ibid.
9. Trollope F.E. Frances Trollope; *Her Life and Literary work from George III to Victoria*, 2 Vols., 1895.
10. M.C. 14/6/1846.
11. M.C. 14/2/1846.
12. M.C. 9/3/1850.
13. M.C. 5/2/1853.
14. Report to Local Government Board, 1873.
15. Reports of Inspectors of Factories, 1862.
16. Report to Local Government Board, 1873.

Chapter 8. Owenites, Free Traders and Chartists

After their successful strike of 1832, the weavers settled into several years of uneasy calm, even though their wages were in no way comparable to the boom years before 1826. Issues other than direct improvements in their own trade occupied some. Reuben Bullock campaigned locally to have the town council's expenditure cut in order to benefit the poorer rate payer. In that same year, 1834, Bullock chaired a meeting at the Grapes Tavern, Sutton, at which he, David Rowbotham and John Prout spoke in support of a Parliamentary motion that would have lessened the burden of taxation. Weavers of Irish stock [as were about a third of all Macclesfield weavers], including Nicholas Lynch, John Cronan and Timothy Falvey, championed the repeal of the Anglo-Irish union - *"a union obtained by fraud and bribery"* - and the restoration of an Irish parliament. These and other nationwide movements for change each had their strong adherents in town during the 1830s and 1840s; and often the same figures supported more than just one cause.

As soon as the Reform Act of 1832 came into being, the general excitement which had gripped the town over universal or household suffrage died down. But though the £10 a year householders had won the vote and that particular battle, the old die-hard reformers of Macclesfield were not finished. John Stubbs, one of the Radicals imprisoned for sedition in 1820, chaired a meeting of like minds at the Union, a public house in Chestergate, in February 1837. This *"Radical Association"* was addressed by Mr Lloyd Jones, William Parker and Timothy Falvey. A committee was formed to carry out the objects of the Association, which advocated universal manhood suffrage, vote by ballot and annual parliaments. These demands, along with the elimination of property qualifications for MPs, payment for MPs and standard sized, single member constituencies, were to form part of the 'Six Points' of the 'People's Charter' first drawn up by the General Working Men's Association at London in May 1838 and later subscribed to by the Birmingham Political Union. The 'Chartists' would soon have a sizeable following in Macclesfield.

In the meantime Owenism [after the Socialist, Robert Owen] had gained some local followers, one of whom was Timothy Falvey. He was born in County Kerry, Ireland, in 1813, the son of a farmer whose financial ruin brought him and his family to Macclesfield in around 1820. Young Timothy and his two brothers were soon working as weavers - Timothy as an inside weaver at

Brocklehurst's. Since that first public speech on reform, as a youthful-looking eighteen year old in December 1831, he had become a local orator of some note. However, he was denied exercising his sonorous tones in championing Owenism before a crowded Theatre Royal at the bottom of Mill Street in August 1838, where 130 people filled the boxes and the one shilling stalls were crammed. At a lecture given by a Mr Easby against Owenism, Falvey was elected chairman and had to remain impartial. Mr Lloyd Jones, a respectable orator himself, took over, as Adam Rushton, the one-time child silk-piecer, now aged 17 and among the audience, noted: *"He had a fine presence and a good voice and imposing manner. His able defence of Owenism greatly troubled many Christian minds..."*[1]

The Owenites demanded that both the land and manufacturing industry be held in common ownership. Society was to be organised in colonies of two or three thousand people with equal rights, equal education, freedom of conscience, easy divorce and no punishment for offenders except counselling. When Easby stated this would undermine Christian principles, Lloyd Jones retorted:

"But what are the influences of your own Christian principles on the mass of the people? Look at the countless number of drunkards in your midst; at the armies of criminals, aye juvenile criminals; and at the tens of thousands of prostitutes swarming your city streets: and then say what your principles have done to save the masses of the people."[2]

Both speakers were hissed in turn but Easby got the most applause. Yet whereas Lloyd Jones figuratively *"took up the cudgels on behalf of Owenism"* - others seem to have done so literally:

"The controversy was not conducted in a courteous or gentlemanly manner and some damage was done to the theatre."[3]

Less than a month later, the Radical Association were denied their usual meeting place in Chestergate because the proprietor objected to them planning a visit by National Chartist leader Feargus O'Connor. Instead, they met by invitation of the Owenites at the *"Socialist's place"* on Bunkers Hill. Stubbs, once more in the chair, had just returned from unsuccessfully canvassing around town for signatures requesting the Mayor to hold a public meeting on further Parliamentary reform. He said: *"the shopocracy never intended to assist the working man and meant all reforms for their own benefit."*[4]

Having by then gained the vote in both national and local elections, Macclesfield's middle classes, as elsewhere, showed no interest in widening the franchise further. This 'betrayal' - as it was considered - precipitated many working people into the ranks of the Chartists. When the plans were made for O'Connor's visit, with William Parker and the Rev. Morris of Dean Row Chapel's support, Macclesfield's working women also demanded to play a part. At a meeting held at the Union Inn, the Dams, soon afterwards, they sent all the men outside and discussed what they should do. When the men were allowed back they were told - *"Resolved, that the women of Macclesfield join a procession on Monday and subscribe to a flag to be presented to Feargus O'Connor Esq.."*[5]

The arrival of O'Connor that Monday, 1st October 1838, was an occasion for Macclesfield's reformers to bask in the notoriety of Chartism's charismatic and nationally famous figure, the self-styled "Lion of Freedom." Irish born O'Connor was the leading light in 'physical force' Chartism, the founder of The Great Northern Union and editor of its newspaper, *the Northern Star*. He was accompanied into town from the Stockport road by a procession of hundreds of people, at the head of which fluttered three flags, bearing a rose, a shamrock and a thistle. Behind these was a large green banner from the women of the Union Inn, the Dams, showing in front the figure of a woman holding a staff and cap of liberty in one hand and a scroll in the other on which was inscribed, *"The People's Charter"*. On the reverse it proclaimed, *"The Patriotic Females of Macclesfield"*.

At Park Green a platform had been erected over several wagons arranged side by side and around it were crowds estimated at between 1-2000 by *the Courier* and 4,000 by others. But as it was the first Monday of Wakes week the town was also host to the annual processions of friendly societies and benefit clubs, and the bands which accompanied them. These, less well attended than usual because of the Chartist rally, occasionally passed through Park Green, their music causing considerable annoyance to the speakers.

Macclesfield's most venerable Radical, John Stubbs, was honoured as chairman for the meeting, and among other local speakers was ex-cotton spinner, but now Rainow schoolteacher, John Richards, a co-defendant from the trials of 1820. Another veteran of those early years accompanied O'Connor. William Benbow, a shoemaker, bookseller and coffee-house keeper from Manchester, had been a Hampden Club delegate in 1817 and was an advocate of 'physical force' both then and currently. He was also an enthusiastic disciple of Robert Owen. In 1831 he had published a pamphlet, *The Grand National Holiday and Congress of the Productive Classes*, which had a wide circulation.

More recently he urged working people to gain the six points of the Charter through a 'Grand National Holiday' - a general strike.

At the outset, Stubbs told the crowd they had the Mayor's permission for their meeting - the first such permission in the past twenty years. Stubbs had asked him that no special constables were sworn-in so they could police the meeting themselves, but the Mayor had replied; *"He had too good an opinion of the men of Macclesfield to offer anything of the kind."* But Stubbs hoped that peace would prevail and they would all go up in the Mayor's estimation. Local speakers, the Rev. Morris, John Richards and three weavers, William Parker, William Barnett and Samuel Simister, then had their say, with Barnett asking: "How was Macclesfield at present represented? One bank here [he pointed to Messrs. Ryle and Daintry's Bank across the green] ... sends a Tory to Parliament and the other [Brocklehurst's Bank in King Edward Street] sends a Whig." [6]

Then it was Feargus O'Connor's turn, the man whose every word the gathered multitude eagerly awaited to hear. In his powerful manner - having *"lungs of leather and a voice like a trumpet"* - he thanked the women who had made the green banner and did not stint in praising the Macclesfield reformers:

FEARGUS O'CONNOR.

"This is a glorious meeting. I call this a meeting of martyrs; for there are upon the platform several who twenty years ago were immured in dungeons for expressing the same sentiments which they now express here." [7]

Yet it was the Rev. Joseph Rayner Stephens, the Wesleyan minister from Manchester, whose words *"like sword cuts, or dagger thrusts, or pistol shots"* made the deepest impression on Adam Rushton - one amongst the mass of people. Stephens, another physical force advocate, favoured incendiarism as a weapon of defence. As one of the north-west's leading antagonists to the New Poor Law

Joseph Rayner Stephens

The Rev. Joseph Rayner Stephens

[see Chapter 12], he first made a virulent verbal attack on it. Rather than submit, shaven-headed, as workhouse inmates, they had the right, both scriptural and political, to pull every rich man's house down and burn every silk mill to the ground. As for the Charter and its opponents:

"They had a right to defend themselves; and if they should drive us to the necessity, we will do it, - (A voice - "We are ready and willing.") I am glad to hear it; I can tell you we are ready in Lancashire and Yorkshire." [8]

William Benbow, the next to speak, expanded this theme more guardedly:

"Now they were using moral force; but one of these days they would mix a little physical force...A little physical force of some of one kind would do good. Those who worked at the engines must cease; the stokers must supply no more fuel..."[9]

After this veiled reference to a 'Grand National Holiday' the main speakers of the meeting adjourned to the Union Inn, the Dams, where dinner for 60 people was prepared in O'Connor's honour. There, where Reuben Bullock took the chair and Timothy Falvey the vice-chair, the main toast was *"The Health of the Founder of the Great Northern Union, Feargus O'Connor Esq.."*

That Monday was the first of several days in which Assistant Commissioner S. Keyser of the Government's Hand-loom Weaver's Inquiry, then in progress, intended to interview weavers in town. He was disappointed that their meeting had to be cancelled so that the weavers could spend their day listening to the speeches of O'Connor and others, as he said:

"promising to redress all their grievances, rather than afford me the evidence as to the existence and cause of such grievances."[10]

But of those that Keyser aimed to interview, weavers Bullock, Simister, Barnett and Parker were there not just to listen, rather to speak as Chartists. Only David Rowbotham and John Prout attended as spectators. Prout, no Chartist himself, later observed:

"cries of universal suffrage, annual parliaments, and no property qualifications, have become the political creed of a large proportion of the trade, arising from the obvious reason that as they have nothing to lose, they might gain from a change."[11]

The Six Points
OF THE
PEOPLE'S
CHARTER.

1. A VOTE for every man twenty-one years of age, of sound mind, and not undergoing punishment for crime.

2. THE BALLOT.—To protect the elector in the exercise of his vote.

3. No PROPERTY QUALIFICATION for Members of Parliament —thus enabling the constituencies to return the man of their choice, be he rich or poor.

4. PAYMENT OF MEMBERS, thus enabling an honest trades-man, working man, or other person, to serve a constituency, when taken from his business to attend to the interests of the country.

5. EQUAL CONSTITUENCIES, securing the same amount of representation for the same number of electors, instead of allowing small constituencies to swamp the votes of large ones.

6. ANNUAL PARLIAMENTS, thus presenting the most effectual check to bribery and intimidation, since though a constituency might be bought once in seven years (even with the ballot), no purse could buy a constituency (under a system of universal suffrage) in each ensuing twelvemonth; and since members, when elected for a year only, would not be able to defy and betray their constituents as now.

Source: MMT

Such change was not to come. On the 12th July 1839 the Chartists' first petition, containing 1,280.000 signatures, was rejected by the House of Commons. On the 17th a Chartist National convention half-heartedly agreed to launch the proposed 'Grand National Holiday' originated by William Benbow, which instead of a 'Sacred Month' was now to last just three days. *The Courier* had previously indicated that trouble was expected locally:

"The Chartists - About six hundred special constables have been sworn in; in this town and will, we understand, be ordered to be in attendance at appointed places, in the different districts, if necessary..."[12]

Adam Rushton later told how Macclesfield Chartists mustered their forces and drilled them on the surrounding hills. John West was said to have armed himself with a home-made pike. The Chartists next met at Park Green on the 22nd July and this was followed by other meetings in early August, at the outset of the 'Grand National Holiday.' Leaders William Parker and John Stubbs failed to turn up at the August 12th venue - from fear of the consequences, it was said. In their absence William Barnett reluctantly took the chair while another speaker read a petition to Her Majesty the Queen urging her to dismiss her ministers. This was carried by vote and the meeting ended in a procession with men marching four abreast through town headed by a man beating a drum. At some point they were confronted by constables who confiscated their drum. A riot then commenced.

Although Stubbs had not attended that meeting, he was arrested along with William Barnett and seven others; the men being charged with conspiracy and using seditious language at the July meeting and of causing a riot on the 12th August. All except one man, John Weavers, pleaded guilty somewhat reluctantly, being *"unwilling to pronounce the word"*, at Chester Assizes in April 1840. They were released, bound on recognisances of £100 to behave themselves in future. John Weavers was additionally accused of being at the meeting on the 13th August, which had been attended by numbers of men from Liverpool and Stockport. This too had ended in a procession led by men with a drum and fife; but this time they had fiercely attacked the constables, throwing stones without provocation. While in prison awaiting trial, Weavers had been taught to read and write by William Benbow, who was also awaiting trial for his part in a seditious meeting at Stockport. In the dock Weavers read out his own defence statement, said to have been concocted by his mentor. It read as a fierce attack on the police and authorities. This could not have helped Weavers' case for he got six months hard labour and had to find sureties totalling £160 to keep the peace for two years. Benbow received a two years prison sentence.

With Macclesfield's principle Chartists bound to keep the peace on threat of forfeiting such large sums of money, the impetus went from the local movement for a year or two, although as it was strongly allied to both the short time and anti-New Poor Law agitation, its aims of gaining the six points were kept well aired. Nationally too, Chartism was in abeyance, with several of its leaders in gaol. The Rev. Joseph Rayner Stephens, arrested for uttering *"incendiary expressions"* at a meeting of Chartists on Kersal Moor, Lancs. in November 1838, had an eighteen months sentence awarded him at Chester in March 1839. In March 1840 O'Connor began a similar sentence in York gaol for *"seditious conspiracy"*.

Throughout this time, John West was busily making a name for himself elsewhere. Having established himself as an able spokesman in supporting the candidature of William Cobbett as MP for Oldham in 1832, he continued to oppose the "knowledge tax" on newspapers and the New Poor Law, and became a Chartist agitator and orator of note, speaking at meetings and conventions all over the north of England. His most notable impact in Macclesfield was a confrontation with Timothy Falvey over free trade at the Town Hall in 1841.

The Anti-Corn Law League, set up by Richard Cobden and John Bright in 1838, was a mostly middle class Radical-Liberal organisation that promoted Adam Smith's laissez-faire economics and sought to obtain its political ends by an alliance with Chartism. The League first sent a deputation to Macclesfield in December 1840, which included Cobden. At a small gathering in the Fence School they found fellow free traders in the Irish born Chartists William Barnett and Timothy Falvey. Falvey, Secretary to the Macclesfield Free Trade Association, spoke out *"against the wicked bread tax,"* defending his views against the protection interests argued by his employer, John Brocklehurst. Afterwards, Cobden warmly complimented Falvey on his speech and a long-lasting personal friendship was begun.

Richard Cobden, 1804-1865.

Further free trade meetings followed, but there were Chartists who were totally against the repeal of the Corn Laws, fearing it would reduce wages. At the 1841 meeting where opposites West and Falvey clashed was Adam Rushton. He noted:

"the fiery orator John West fiercely attacked the free traders. His language rushing like a cataract he denounced them as middle class traders seeking to increase their own wealth by keeping down the working classes."[13]

Then Macclesfield's other *"leviathan of the platform"* arose to speak:

"The fine looking Timothy Falvey, in sonorous, deliberate, clear and elegant language showed that Free Trade must benefit all classes and in many ways."[14]

This confrontation lasted five hours, but in the end it was West who *"vanquished his opponent in clear and overwhelming argument and so carried the meeting with him."* His speech was afterwards published in pamphlet form.

The pro-Corn Law *Courier* was unimpressed by Falvey's oratory, despite his *"gift of speech and economic opinions, enforced with fluency."* When, in February 1842, he was deputed to go to London on the League's behalf, the newspaper condemned him as a paid agitator who was clothed with *"the false pretences of the National will."* It was lamentable, it complained, that honest people should be *"deluded so easily by the speeches of such men."*

The Chartists' 'Grand National Holiday' strike of 1839 had been followed up with minor skirmishes in the North of England and a more serious insurrection in Wales. But the idea was revived by anti-Corn Law agitators in 1842, who hoped that such a strike would pressurise Tory landowners to demand the repeal of the Act. A strike at Stalybridge in early August, possibly engineered by anti-Corn Law millowners, created

Punch cartoon 1846 showing the benefits of free trade - cheap food, drink and tobacco.

such general discontent that it evolved into a widespread turnout of operatives throughout Manchester and Stockport. Gangs of strikers were soon roaming and begging all over the north-west countryside. The Charter became the central issue and in some places the situation ended in riots - the so-called 'Plug Plot' riots. Macclesfield was spared the worst of the violence but a vast crowd of strikers from Oldham, Ashton, Hyde and Stockport, swelled by colliers from Poynton, descended on the town on Friday the 12th. Many were armed with heavy bludgeons and at the Town Hall they demanded the release of three men thought wrongly to be held there. Their main aim thwarted, the mob then went around the town compelling factories to stop work. At Brocklehurst's, warehouseman Adam Rushton met their leaders at the factory door and took them to his masters in the counting house. A brief but civil discussion ensued between the two parties, then Brocklehurst's workpeople were released - as soon as the factory steam engine's boiler plugs had been removed and their fires put out.

Afterwards, mill operatives and weavers from all over town assembled on Park Green in their thousands and began to voice their grievances. They resolved to stay out on strike until the following Wednesday. A provision dealer in Mill Street, Michael Hall, then distributed bread and gave £20 worth of flour to the strike committee, which was handed over to the Stockport men. Before leaving, they threatened that men with homing pigeons would stay behind and if the mill workers went back to work the birds would be released, taking the news to Stockport within the half hour. Then they would return to Macclesfield and *"give it the devils"*. The strikers were said to number between 12-14,000; and there was not one soldier, mounted yeoman, policeman or special constable to be seen anywhere in town. Fortunately, no real violence or disturbances occurred.

The week that followed was enjoyed as an unaccustomed holiday by Adam Rushton, but for many others it was a time to convene or attend meetings, held every day at Park Green and addressed by ardent Chartists, such as Nicholas Lynch, Timothy Falvey and William Barnett. At the first it was announced that a proclamation from Her Majesty the Queen had been received earlier that day offering £50 and a free pardon to anyone whose testimony might convict a person inciting the riots. The crowd were warned by Lynch not to rise to the temptation and become spies or informers. On the following morning they first gathered again at Park Green then marched off to Prestbury, Bollington and Langley, where they made sure that everyone there was on strike too.

Meanwhile, the local Chartists'

A Manchester operative at the time of the 'Plug Plot' strike of 1842.

committee had sent delegates off to a Chartist conference at Manchester, held on Tuesday. Returning on Wednesday, the fifth day of the strike, the silk operatives gathered at Park Green heard them read *"An Address from the Executive Council of the National Chartist Association,"* which urged them not to return to work. This, *the Courier* claimed, was *"a declaration of rebellion and civil war."* The assembled workers were then asked whether the strike should be for obtaining *"a fair day's wage for a fair day's work"* or the Charter. The almost unanimous call was for the Charter and an *"Executive Charter Committee"* was formed. A few workers, more concerned with trade issues, then left to pursue their own aims [see Chapter 9]. The vast week-long strike had no effect nationally on altering the franchise, and, having taken place during a trade recession, no impact on wages either. Yet there were local benefits in the way of increased wages for some on their return to work.

Richard Cobden was back in Macclesfield in January 1845, when at an anti-Corn Law League meeting in Lord Street New Connexion chapel he was ably supported by Timothy Falvey. Since 1843 Falvey had been a full-time lecturer for the League, deputed to speak at meetings of village labourers in Dorset, Hants and Wiltshire, where any such agitation was ruthlessly opposed by landowners and had to take place under cover of darkness. There his personable style, *"plain yet eloquent"*, drew huge audiences and made him many friends, even among political opponents. It was Falvey's eloquence that persuaded the Marquis of Londonderry to throw the weight of his considerable voting power behind John Bright, during his successful bid to become M.P. for Durham in the 1843 election. But Macclesfield's weavers were not easily swayed and generally sided against free trade: a resolution condemning it was passed at one of their meetings that February. John Prout was among those opposed to the League. In spite of having drawn up the *"violent and inflammatory"* weaver's petition to have the Corn Laws repealed in 1826, he refused to sign the League's petition during the 1840s. He claimed:

"however wrong in their origin and formation, time and usage had given them another character, and that their annihilation would cause a greater evil than their present existence."[15]

The once hated Corn Laws were soon to be rescinded anyway. In 1846 the corn tax was much reduced and then finally abolished in February 1849. This was not so much because of the agitation by such as Cobden and Falvey; mostly it was to alleviate the consequences of a disastrous Europe-wide harvest in 1845 and the effects of the Irish famine.

Cobden was then one of two MPs that represented Stockport. In the 1847 election he was an absentee candidate, opposed by both a Tory and the Macclesfield Chartist, John West. West gained a winning margin over the Tory at the hustings but was defeated at the poll. Had he won outright he could not have served in the Commons, for he owned no property. Cobden, in Europe during the election, but returned as MP in both Stockport and the West Riding, chose to represent the latter, *"more distinguished seat"*. By that time he also viewed Chartists with disdain; his bitter personal animosity towards Feargus O'Connor, elected as MP for Nottingham in 1847, often vented during heated Commons' clashes.

Yet another union aimed at embracing all trades under one national body came to Macclesfield in May 1847. The National Association of United Trades for the Protection of Industry had originated in 1844, when a newly proposed Master and Servant Bill had been defeated in the Commons. This Bill would have empowered any employer to sue his workers for all breaches of contract, verbal or written; with an oath sworn by the employer or his over-looker alone being sufficient for the accused to suffer the penalty prescribed - two months hard labour. When the town's branch of this new organisation met at Parsonage Street chapel, with John West unanimously called to the chair, a Mr Peel lectured on its principles and aims; which were to enable the working classes to *"defend their interests against the attacks of the capitalists"*. The meeting pledged their support and arranged to elect delegates for a conference at Birmingham. But the following week less than 50 people turned up and a long discussion failed to agree on funding for the delegate - John West. No other meetings seem to have occurred.

By this date West had made his name as a Chartist orator, with a reputation that stretched *"from the Thames to the Tyne"*. His friend George Julian Harney, a national Chartist leader and *Northern Star* journalist, later wrote of West's audience *"numbering tens and hundreds of thousands familiar with the face and voice of John West, and from whom his eloquence and humour had oft drawn thunders of applause."*[16]

West and his wife Mary, both silk weavers, were often away from their Union Street [later Norton and then St.Vincent Street, Hurdsfield] home, travelling to meetings or conventions. It was during one such absence in 1845 that their second son, John Julian Harney West, named in part after the Chartist leader, was born at Sheffield. From this and remarks he later made it might be inferred that West shared Harney's Republicanism and idealisation of the

French Revolution. West's eldest son, Robert Emmet West, born in 1841, commemorated another of John West's heroes - the Irish patriot and martyr who was hanged in 1803. The West's own lives were not without some risk. After a speech in Belper during the mid 1840s, made in *"utter disregard of moderate opinions"*, West was followed to Leicester by law officers, arrested and committed for trial at Derby assizes. Charged with sedition, he refused legal aid and defended himself with great ability, for after a *"masterly and persuasive address"* to the jury he obtained instant acquittal. The judge afterwards complimented him on his defence, remarking that *"he left the court without a stain on his character, a credit to himself and an honour to his class"*. However, West was to suffer imprisonment for his beliefs sixteen times.

The general election of 1847 next saw the local Chartists in *the Courier's* pages. At Park Green that July, a meeting of *"non-electors.... all, we believe, Chartists"* was chaired by John Stubbs, who had been canvassing support for prospective Radical-Liberal MP John Williams. Welsh born Williams was the popular choice of Macclesfield's working people, even though most had no vote. Born at Ruthin in 1800 of poor parents and apprenticed to a local shopkeeper at age eleven, he had an appropriate background to represent them and his sympathies lay firmly with the underprivileged. *The Courier,* supporting Thomas Grimsditch and John Brocklehurst, the town's two MPs since 1837, proclaimed *"We will not recommend the election of a Chartist."* But not only was Williams in favour of the six points of the Charter, he was also for a reduction in taxation and the abolition of the New Poor Law as well - changes much desired by the poorer classes. Throughout his campaign he was supported by weavers Rowbotham, Stubbs and Simister; and also Timothy Falvey, who had declined an opportunity to stand for MP himself - as a free trade Liberal at Chichester. Williams, speaking from an upstairs window of the Angel Inn to crowds of supporters gathered in the Market Place, claimed that certain manufacturers had threatened to remove work from weavers who voted for him, though he exonerated rival Liberal John Brocklehurst from this accusation. Despite this he was successful in the election, defeating the Tory, Grimsditch. His fellow MP John Brocklehurst was much later accused of having his weavers walk in procession behind him to the hustings - after which he had stopped them half a day's pay for time lost.

The election of Williams was followed by several Chartist meetings at Park Green or the 'Chartist House' - a pub in Stanley Street - during April 1848; these just before and after the presentation of the third Chartist's national petition to the House of Commons. A few days beforehand, John West addressed a crowd of up to 3,000 people at Park Green; and he did not flinch from the possibility of conflict. He talked about miners, men who were often exposed to danger, being the *"advance guard"* on a march to London and spoke in support of the recent revolution in France [King Louis Philippe had been deposed in an uprising that February]:

"Kings could not do without people, but the people could do without Kings. Should England be behind in following the example which France had set?" [17]

The Courier recorded that because of the strong Chartist movement in town, *"every requisite precaution"* had been adopted for assuring peace, including the swearing-in of 2,000 special constables and the draughting in of a body of the Cheshire Yeomanry - later replaced by a company of the 6th Rifles.

They had good reason to expect trouble. The great petition, presented to Parliament on the 10th April, was rejected outright by the Commons as *"a gross abuse of the privilege"* and *"a derogation of the value of petitioning."* The House discounted all but 2 million of its 5,706,000 signatures, including those that were in the same handwriting - probably signed on behalf of those who could not write - and others, *"pug nose"* etc, that were pseudonyms. Yet of violence afterwards there was virtually none. Real fears of 'physical force' Chartists bursting into

A PHYSICAL FORCE CHARTIST ARMING FOR THE FIGHT.

Punch cartoon 1848 depicting a 'physical force' Chartist.

revolution, in Macclesfield, or even at the great Chartist rally on Kennington Common in south London, proved groundless.

Immediately after the rejection of the petition, Macclesfield's Chartists held three consecutive days of mass meetings, during which Samuel Bentote was elected as the town's delegate to a forthcoming National Convention in London - John West then representing Stockport. One week later, West told crowds at a further gathering that he was *"neither shot, hanged nor killed yet,"* but was about to be arrested; the charge being sedition. This followed a speech at Ashton-under-Lyne, where West's words had been *"highly seasoned to the pitch of a Lancashire artisan audience."* Nevertheless, he urged his fellow Chartists to continue agitating in spite of the "Gagging Bill" just enacted in Parliament. This they did, though with some caution at a May meeting at Park Green, arranged on Bentote's return from the National Convention:

"The speakers were more violent than usual in recommending the use of arms; but they all put such qualifications to their statements, that before concluding they had unsaid every word that they had said."[18]

Despite the talk of revolution, Macclesfield's Chartists were soon withering in numbers, as elsewhere. By late July *the Courier* could report: *"Chartism defunct - Chartism, in London at least.... is in its death struggle."* John West had a last word locally with his "Chartist Lecture" at the 'Chartist House' in Stanley Street that November. He was then out on bail to appear at Kirkdale assizes on charges of sedition - later to be found guilty and sentenced to twelve months in goal. But for the moment he was still free to hold and enthral an audience; and he advised them not to be *"led away by clap traps",* planned by the new Local Board of Health; He said:

"their Bath and Wash Houses and Model lodging houses, their Soup kitchens and their Lectures on Sanitary Reform are all a great humbug... Keep on agitating, notwithstanding the intimidation of the Government, till their object was obtained."[19]

Local MP John Williams also kept the main points of the Charter well to the fore in the minds of his constituents. In October 1849 he asked them:

"Just look at the House of Commons. What was it? Instead of being the mouthpiece of the Commons, it was the tool of the Aristocracy. (cheers) Away with property qualifications,. Why should not a fellow workman, a weaver for instance, be returned as a member? He would then be the mouthpiece of his order; and the order had no mouthpiece now." [20]

John West's late arrival at this assembly was greeted with wild cheering. He said he owed his very presence there to John Williams, for he had helped *"liberate him from a felon's dungeon"* - the gaol at Kirkdale in which he had

Macclesfield from The Hollins c. 1850.   *(MMT)*

been confined *"the victim of the perjuring and corruption of a Whig Government"* for twelve months. Williams had also made his time there more bearable, said West, for despite his political status, he had suffered the same hardships as any common criminal. He might have rotted in gaol for all that *"the other member"* [Brocklehurst] cared, he said bitterly. During his incarceration, his wife Mary gave birth to a daughter, also named Mary.

Few locals did *"keep on agitating"* as West had instructed them in his *"Chartist Lecture"*. The "Non-Electors" of Macclesfield that met at Park Green in March 1852 were not very numerous or boisterous. Nicholas Lynch, leading them, said the lack of enthusiasm was from thinking too deeply about what the speakers had said to give noisy demonstrations. But even John Williams was no longer the ebullient speaker of a few years before. His regular addresses to supporters from The Angel Inn's windows grew fewer and had lost their impact. *The Courier*, somewhat triumphantly, noted that he was often out of humour and the crowd had tired of his *"three-told tales"*. By that date the locals were also missing the foremost and longest served of Macclesfield's Radicals, John Stubbs, who died in November 1851. Chartism itself was a spent force by the mid-1850s, but demands for the vote by Macclesfield's working people was to be revived, and be rewarded with success in 1867.

References
1. Rushton Adam, *My Life as Farmer's Boy, Factory Lad, Teacher and Preacher,* 1909.
2. ibid.
3. M.C. 18/8/1838.
4. M.C. 22/9/1838.
5. M.C. 29/9/1838.
6. M.C. 6/10/1838
7. ibid.
8. ibid.
9. ibid.
10. Hand-loom Weavers: Reports from Assistant Commissioners, 1840 Vol. XXII, page 494.
11. M.C. 12/12/1840.
12. M.C. 6/5/1839.
13. Rushton Adam op. cit.
14. ibid.
15. M.C. 19/12/1840.
16. M.C. 19/11/1881.
17. M.C. 8/4/1848.
18. M.C. 27/5/1848.
19. M.C. 7/10/1848.
20. M.C. 31/7/1847.

'The threat of steam power', a mid 19th century cartoon.

Chapter 9. Tricks of the Trade

The years after 1832 saw no improvement in the weavers' trade, only an overall decline when compared to other tradesmen. By 1838, bricklayers and carpenters, who in the 1790s earned comparable wages to the weavers, had soared ahead with earnings of up to £1. 4s. per week, while weavers' wages had dropped to between 6s. 6d. and 9s. A millman's 8s. in the 1790s had likewise become 12s. 3d.; reversing the disparity with the more skilled hand-loom silk weaver. Whatever the list prices, manufacturers continued to avoid Macclesfield prices anyway, for the sending of silk out to be woven in Lancashire continued unabated. Even if they paid the full list prices, they had ways and means of garnering some back from the weavers' pockets and into their own coffers.

Since the early days of the 1790s undertakers had charged loom rents; and this comprised their entire profit from any journeyman working in their garret loom-shop. When, after 1815, manufacturers set up large weaving sheds, they also extracted loom rents from their weavers. But this was an additional sum to add to the profits they made on the woven silk. These loom rents had risen from the 3s. charged in 1817 to 4s. by 1835, and a Jacquard loom - almost entirely owned by manufacturers - could cost 5s. In September 1835, inside weavers at Thomas Wardle's factory left their looms, on which they were paying between 5s. and 6s., and went on strike. They returned only after some struggle to get Wardle's to accept the 4s. demanded by other manufacturers. At the Hand-loom Weavers' Inquiry of 1838, David Rowbotham told Assistant Commissioner S. Keyser that in the past two years when trade was slack, one manufacturer gave out work enough only for his weavers to pay their loom rent and have a shilling or two over. Samuel Simister gave an even worse instance: where weavers had been employed for six months without ever earning above the cost of loom rent and candles, such was the poor quality of the silk.

Poor quality silk from a manufacturer was at one time allowed for with an additional 2d. per yard over the list price, but by 1838 the situation was one of *"take it or leave it"*. Other extra allowances were once paid by manufacturers for the more complicated patterns which used several shuttles and for time lost changing a warp, but after 1826, when patterns were more complicated still and work changes more frequent, these were dropped entirely. However, deductions for so-called poor workmanship on the return of woven silk had increased dramatically since the 1800s when they were a rarity. During the 1820s a new process to improve texture and appearance, unique to Macclesfield, involved steaming the finished article to make it *"eyeable"* and to get the right *"feel."* Yet sometimes the dyes were poor and colours would run. For this a manufacturer might dock the weaver money or say *"the work does not feel sufficient; I shall stop you 2s."* Reuben Bullock told Keyser of a case where a manufacturer had stopped a third of the wages of six men who knew their work was good, but who dare not go to arbitration for fear of losing further work.

Probably the most onerous deduction of all was for lateness when outside weavers returned the woven silk back to the manufacturer. This could reach as much as 2s. depending on how much after the *"late hour"* - usually 9pm - they were. Sometimes the payment of late money ensured that a weaver would be able to obtain more work from that same manufacturer, encouraging him to be late. In times of slack trade, Samuel Simister claimed some manufacturers would only open their warehouses after the late hour, thus obtaining a weaver's work at a shilling or so less than their competitors.

The weavers that Keyser examined took care to be truthful and checked each other in this respect. William Barnett told how, in around 1827, he had been sacked from Brocklehurst's for resisting a reduction in the price for Persians, and was strongly critical of their current payments. He was taken to task over several inaccuracies in his statements; first by Rowbotham in front of the Assistant Commissioner and later by Thomas Cope and John Prout in letters to *the Courier*. Prout offered to meet with Keyser and Barnett to disprove the falsehoods. Having that January canvassed nineteen manufacturers, Prout claimed that Brocklehurst's were *"paying the highest standard in town."* Yet Barnett did make the point that almost all the other weavers who gave evidence were employees of Brocklehurst's. The risks of criticising an employer were all too apparent. William Parker was one who gave evidence, and his actions cost him his job. On being told this, Assistant Commissioner Keyser sent for Parker's employer, Charles Condron. Condron claimed that Parker was dismissed *"because he did not suit us."*

In spite of such risks, these weavers were well aware that little or nothing would be their reward from any Commissions of Inquiry and were mostly hostile witnesses. David Rowbotham told Keyser:

"Mankind judged of what would be by the past. They had seen the Government never had done anything yet in favour of the working classes and they did not think they intended to do anything now."[1]

They were right. Two years after the Hand-loom Inquiry the Government began considering a reduction on the duties of certain imported silks. The Weavers' Committee sent off a memorial against any reduction to the Board of Trade and in conjunction with weavers from Spitalfields and other places then petitioned the House of Commons through MP John Brocklehurst. As a result they got yet more interviews, this time with the Select Committee of the House of Commons on East India Produce, seated upon which was John Brocklehurst.

Once again, Thomas Cope and John Prout went through their well-rehearsed and oft-repeated reasons why the trade needed protection from any such competition and afterwards were thanked for their efforts, *"which will form a corner stone to build further upon - as they developed some sound principles."* Some of Prout's *"sound principles"* were derived from the fiscal policies of economist, Robert Montgomery Martin, a witness to an 1834 Select Committee. Reading from his evidence, Prout argued that Britain could not compete with foreigners because of the burden of high taxation on commodities, amounting to £11.7s.6d. out of every £22.10s. earned by a working man. He was also firmly against the export of machinery, where it

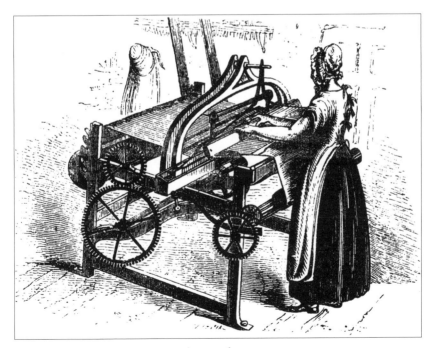

A power loom.

could be set up in competition against Britain, and when asked if this was not a profitable business to the country, replied; *"It may be to a few, but not to the aggregate of the community."* It was an attitude somewhat out of step with a society which in a decade or so would host the Great Exhibition, but Prout was quite vehement on this subject: *"I would rather that England be buried beneath the ocean, that that the steam engines and spinning jennies of Lancashire should rule the destinies of Britain."*[2]

He was reflecting what many workers in skilled hand processes, such as hand loom silk weaving, felt. Yet fears of power looms supplanting their skills were unfounded. Although some were used in weaving plain fabrics - Brocklehurst's had them from 1832 and another two manufacturers by 1838 - the hand loom would be pre-eminent in the fancy silk trade until much later.

For most of Macclesfield's weavers however, it was more immediate concerns about losing weaving work to Lancashire that occupied their minds. A meeting at Brocklehurst's Derby Street shed in August 1840 heard from Thomas Cope that price reductions were threatened by Macclesfield manufacturers, several of whom were getting their work woven more cheaply in Lancashire. Delegates had been sent to try to get Lancashire weavers to demand more money and most had agreed. However, the firm of Edmunds & Co. had been telling their Lancashire weavers that low prices were because of a glut in their warehouse; and as many were in debt to the company they were afraid to ask for more money. The Central Committee Secretary was John West, who wrote to the Courier outlining their case and naming the firm of Edmunds - a company owned by a London fishmonger - and its local agent M. Gibbon. It ended *".....if after Saturday the 22nd August, you do not agree to our demands, we must cease our labour for those masters who do not comply with our reasonable demands."*[3]

The dispute was soon concluded with a result acceptable to the weavers: Gibbon offered to pay more to Lancashire weavers, but would pay less than the list price for Persians in town. When this was announced before weavers assembled on Park Green, John West congratulated all on a favourable outcome; adding, in a reference to Chartism, *"It proved the advantage of moral over physical force."*

In spite of the evidence given by Cope and Prout to the Select Committee on East India Produce, and petitions sent from the weaver's to the Commons in 1840, the import duty on East Indian manufactured silks was reduced. The Central Committee petitioned against it once more in August 1841 and when winter came there was high unemployment and extreme poverty in town. In January 1842, 2,900 families were provided with coals, clothing and warm bedding, this in part from a subscription raised on the event of the christening of the Prince of Wales. By July the situation was not much improved, for silk weavers suffered severely from low wages and unemployment.

By and large, Macclesfield manufacturers abided by the list of prices, revised in February 1841. But when, during the 'Plug Plot riots' of August 1842, gangs of bludgeon-armed Chartist strikers from Stockport and other towns turned out local operatives from their garrets, workshops, sheds and mills, they stirred up a hornet's nest of discontent. The gathered mill workers and weavers who voiced their grievances at Park Green were only too eager remain on strike for a whole week, hoping they might return on better conditions.

The weavers, like other operatives who held separate meetings away from the political arena, aired several complaints. Most were about the same employer as two years before, the firm of Edmunds & Co. One, highlighted by 60 year old David Rowbotham that Friday, was of employing old men as inside weavers under the apprenticeship

Silk Manufacturers,

AND OTHER

INHABITANTS OF MACCLESFIELD.

GENTLEMEN,—We hoped that the disputes of the Silk Trade in this Town would, ere this, have been ended with honour to the Masters, and satisfaction to the Operatives ; but, we regret to state, we are grievously disappointed.

We are therefore reluctantly compelled to inform you, that although the sought-for advance on those miserable works, the Persians, has been generally given to the impoverished workmen, there are yet two gentlemen, Mr. Warland and Mr. D. Newton, who hold back, with cold hearts and selfish minds, refusing to do that justice which the other Manufacturers are ashamed to refuse.

In the interview the Committee had with Mr. NEWTON, he stated " that his weavers were perfectly satisfied with 2½d. per yard, and he did not see what right we had to interfere with them." We very much doubted the truth of this statement, and consequently sent a deputation to Hazel Grove and Bredbury, where, instead of finding the weavers satisfied, they stated " that they never had woven Persians at 2½d. during a winter ; and, if they could help it, they never would." And as a proof that they were sincere, they appointed a deputation to wait on Mr. Newton, along with a portion of the Committee ; and how, think you, Gentlemen, did this haughty personage receive these poor men that came so long a journey, to tell him that what he stated respecting them being satisfied was not correct ? Why, he slapped the door in their faces ; and, after the manner of the crook-backed tyrant, exclaimed, " I'm busy !"

The other gentleman always received the Committee courteously, and expressed his willingness to be even more liberal than we at present required. " A farthing per yard," he said, " was no object to him, that he would rather give a halfpenny." But his promise and the performance of them are two distinct things. He and Mr. Newton seem (like the Siamese twins) to be almost inseparable in their resolves ; and as we believe, from information received, that the farthing has been gained in the market, we ask, Gentlemen, what are we think of these honourable (?) men, who can thus quietly sport with the poverty of their workmen, and pocket the money which should be paid in wages to feed them and their half-famished families. We could admire their firmness and perseverance, if directed to a just and honest end ; but when we see them treading on the fallen, and greedily grasping from the needy, we blush for fallen humanity, and our hearts throb indignantly at the greatness of their injustice.

As long as there was a probability of bringing these Gentlemen to terms by other means, we refrained from adopting this extreme course ; but now that what we have already gained at so much trouble and expense is in imminent danger of being lost, through their inhuman obstinacy, we are compelled to let the world know who are the real oppressors of the poor Persian Weavers, and we tell these Gentlemen, that they are mistaken if they suppos: they can, as hitherto, rob the poor weavers of their rights, and not be amenable to the moral responsibility of public opinion.

Do they think they will be quietly allowed to hold their present unfair advantages ? No ! They may rest assured the Weavers will exert all the powers they legally possess to protect the other Masters in their upright and honourable conduct, and to prevent the ruin and degradation which our Trade is threatened with by the conduct of these two Gentlemen.

We trust their good sense and good feeling will cause them no longer to oppose the reasonable demands of the Trade, and not force us to still harsher measures, by appealing to their hands to cease to toil for them. They have yet an opportunity of terminating the dispute and bringing about a happy tranquility,—let us hope they will embrace it.

By order of the Committee,

JOHN CHADWICK, Chairman.
JOHN WEST, Secretary.

September 25, 1840.

A PUBLIC MEETING

OF THE

SILK WEAVERS,

WILL BE HELD ON PARK GREEN,

On Monday, the 28th of September,

ON BUSINESS OF GREAT IMPORTANCE.

EVERY WEAVER IS URGENTLY REQUESTED TO ATTEND.

Poster.   *(MMT)*

TO THE MANUFACTURERS,
OPERATIVE WEAVERS,
AND OTHER
Inhabitants of Macclesfield.

GENTLEMEN, AND FELLOW TOWNSMEN,—An advertisement has appeared in the *Macclesfield Courier* of this morning, *signed* by the Silk Weavers of Ormskirk, which, to use their own language, "contains serious mis-statements, unjust insinuations, and barefaced falsehoods." The Committee did not answer the letter of Mr. Gibbon of last week, because he has honourably consented to the wishes of the Trade since. As our only object was to obtain the additional farthing, both for the Country and Town's Weavers, we were contented to bear *some* blame, rather than excite any further ill-feeling, as our motto has always been peace ;—but, in justice to ourselves, now that the Ormskirk Weavers have *written* to deny that which they *positively affirmed* before a multitude of witnesses, we feel bound, for the sake of truth, to place the matters in dispute beyond all reasonable doubt.

The Ormskirk Weavers *now* say in their (?) Address, "that the Macclesfield Delegates stated to them, that, if they demanded (we say "asked ") the farthing per yard, they should have it," (they have got it without asking, thank the Delegates and their Master for it,) "as their looms were all full in Macclesfield." This latter part we emphatically deny ; we wish they were ; though we are certain that, "if every loom was made into two, it would not be possible to have all the work done in Macclesfield, which is given out here." Can this be true ? they triumphantly ask, when we state that hundreds are eating the bread of pauperism, in consequence of Mr. Gibbon having sent his work to this place ?" We say not "in consequence" but "WHEN" Mr. G. sent his work to you, hundreds were eating the bread of pauperism.

"They fearlessly assert they have borrowed money of Mr. Taylor." We wish we could *deny* it. That Donaldson, whose name is signed to the Address, owed Mr. Taylor £4, which Mr. T. lent him, and *the interest*, to re-pay his former Master, who returned Donaldson 2s. 6d., not, we presume, from the PRINCIPAL, but from the *penny per shilling*, which the Weavers in Ormskirk, aye, and North Meols, have to pay in "consideration" of the favour *so disinterestedly* bestowed ! Indeed, the "creeps" boasted of kindnesses received in this way ; and this is not taking away their independence forsooth ! Poor fellows ! proud should we be if they understood the *meaning* of the word.

They charge the Delegates " with wishing to instigate them so to offend Mr. Gibbon, as to cause him to take his work from them." To this we reply—the Delegates pressed them to use no violence in word or action, as the Macclesfield Weavers were determined to obtain their object by moral means, and the force of public opinion ; and as they (the Delegates) had learned that a very violent letter had been before sent by the Ormskirk Weavers, to Mr. Edmonds, who treated it with that contempt, which blackguardism always merits : and, as a proof that the Macclesfield Delegates did not so far commit themselves, the Policeman, who attended the meeting, retired before it was concluded, saying that *his* presence was totally unnecessary, as the Macclesfield Delegates asked nothing more than *moderate, just, and reasonable terms*. For the truth of this we appeal to the Weavers who attended the meeting—to the Resolutions passed—to the Addresses, which the Macclesfield Delegates wrote for them, and which were partially signed, and taken to Mr. Taylor, by Abraham Johnson and William Webster, who reported, that Mr. Taylor highly approved of them—and the Committee, whose names, strange to say, now appear in the Advertisement, affirmed them to be the most admirably adapted to obtain the farthing, without the *bare possibility of giving the least offence, and to which they were the first to affix their names !*

The Delegates next states that we assert, "Mr. G. was the first to teach them to weave ;" we unhesitatingly re-assert that "he sent his work to a *remote Village*, in Lancashire, *upwards of sixty miles* from Macclesfield," which must mean North Meols, as Ormskirk is but *fifty miles from this place*, and it is notorious that they are learning each other to fabricate Silk Cloth *even now* in that place. They first mis-understand us (we trust not wilfully) and then charge that falsehood on us, which they have so industriously and basely disgraceful.

They further state, "that one of the Delegates, in conversation with Donaldson, said 'that the reduction tended to reduce the Market and the Operatives' Wages, some only obtaining 7s., some 5s., and some nothing per cut.' And he, Donaldson, asked 'where ?' and the Delegate said, ' here at Edmonds and Co.'s' (this could not possibly refer to wages, even if it had been said ; as, to use an Irishism, where nothing can be got, nothing can be lost,) to which Donaldson replied, ' if the goods were made well, no abatements took place.' "

Now for the truth. The Delegates stated that they had learned at North Meols, in the universal consent of a large Public Meeting, that unprecedented abatements had been made ; Donaldson, (we call to witness Leigh, Cooper, &c.) instead of denying this fact, confirmed it ; but mark you, he gave a reason, to which the others assented, that the abatements were made, in consequence of the North Meols people being learned by Mr. T.; they, consequently, could not make the work perfect.

We have never affirmed that Mr. Taylor stopped wages for good work ; we hope he never will ; but that, as he had sent it to North Meols, he had to teach them to weave Persians. They, being cotton weavers, spoiled a portion of it, and *then* they were made to suffer for their ignorance of the trade.

We now, Gentlemen, and Fellow Townsmen, have stated the *truth* ; we have always spoken well of the Ormskirk Weavers, and cautiously avoided giving their names. Till now they have been in the secret depository of the note book ; but, as they have spoken one thing and written another, let them now be responsible for their utter abandonment of all honest principle, of all that confidence, which ought to characterise civilised man, and for that total disregard for truth, which the gratitude and integrity, they owe to the Committee, made doubly disgraceful.

They are either honest men or admirable deceivers or, *alias*, under *other influence.*

They affectionately parted with the Macclesfield Delegates, and repeatedly and voluntarily promised to write to the Macclesfield Committee to inform them of the very honourable and honest conduct of the Macclesfield Delegates, for which "they would ever feel gratitude and respect !" but "Oh ! how are the mighty fallen !" Burrows, especially, the Volunteer Delegate to North Meols from Ormskirk, we are confident would not have so basely signed his name he well knew to be untrue, unless under *coercion*, as his conscience must tell him, from the kind reception he gave to the Macclesfield Delegates, and the opportunity he had of seeing their conduct for two days, that their intentions were honest, and their motives above suspicion.

Then why so soon cease their exertions ? They said they would pay the price of a piece to assure the farthing from Mr. Edmonds. He has now that we have told him the truth solemnly and we say willingly promised. Why, after Donaldson saying, " if he was burned to death" he "should die the death of a martyr in the *good cause*," he had and others contradict in writing what they stated *viva voce* ? Because (the secret is out) they are "*taught*" according to the words in their own address, " to believe that their employment would be endangered by obtaining a farthing a yard in advance."

These simple facts founded in undeviating truth, are sufficient to answer their whole statements.

By Order of the Committee,

JOHN CHADWICK, Chairman.
JOHN WEST, Secretary.

AUGUST 29, 1840.

J. SWINNERTON, PRINTER, MACCLESFIELD.

Poster.   *(MMT)*

TO THE

Mayor, Magistrates, Manufacturers,

AND OTHER

INHABITANTS OF MACCLESFIELD.

GENTLEMEN,—Little did we think when, in the discharge of our public duty, we informed you last week that we had amicably settled our dispute with the Manufacturers, that we should so soon have to address you again ; but in doing so we have to announce, with feelings of pride and satisfaction, that the influential and respectable portion of the Manufacturers have honourably redeemed their promise, of agreeing to our just and reasonable propositions, and thereby prevent any confusion in the Town. But, Gentlemen, whilst we are compelled to speak in terms of respect and approbation of honourable Manufacturers, we ask you what are we to think of the conduct of individuals who by their perverse temerity still keep the Town and Trade in a state of painful suspense ! And who are they ? Men of *wealth* and *station ?* No ; but persons who have only the other day sprung from the ranks of the *Working Classes*, and who now, by a most unjust and unholy effort, wish to realise immediate and rapid fortunes at the expense of the whole community.

When the Persian Manufacturers informed us, Mr. Gibbon was the only person who stood in the way of settling this question, we brought it fairly before the public, and the same spirit of impartiality now compels us to mention the name of another *Gentleman*, who, with a sort of Quixotic Chivalry, appears determined to set the whole Town at defiance ; and this is no less a personage than a Mr. Heapy, who has gained for himself an unenvious notoriety by refusing to agree to the same terms as the other Manufacturers.

There were a few others who disputed the regulation, but who, whilst this Address was writing, sent in their adhesion to the Committee, and as it is our determination, if possible, " to throw oil on the troubled waters," we now refrain from mentioning their names. But, perhaps, you will ask (and justly so), why should Mr. Heapy be allowed to disturb the town ? Is he of so much consequence ? We answer, no. But it must be borne in mind, that Persians are a very peculiar branch of our trade ; and an apparently insignificant manufacturer may do much mischief, if allowed to proceed in his nefarious attempts ; and we can, in sober seriousness, inform Mr. Heapy, and also Mr. Potts, of the Soho Mills, that theirs is a fruitless contest, inasmuch as that they have the wealth, respectability, and intelligence of the town opposed to them.

Gentlemen, the Committee can state with confidence, that they are actuated by reason, and guided by discretion, in arranging the matters connected with the late dispute, and they have no doubt but that their efforts will meet with the approbation of the wise and good amongst all classes of their fellow-townsmen—for the prosperity of the town—the interest of the manufacturers—and the comforts of the operatives ultimately depend on the preservation of an equality in our prices. And we may mention one argument, independent of others, in proof of this, which is the conduct of the Manufacturers themselves, who invariably insist on preserving a regulation in the markets. Indeed, all classes in society have their protective regulations, and why should not the Macclesfield operative ?

In conclusion, the Committee, on behalf of the trade, return their sincere thanks to those gentlemen, who have by their honourable conduct, prevented a painful and protracted struggle, injurious alike to all parties engaged in it. And also to those kind friends who have sympathised with us in our exertions, and who, we trust, now that our position requires their assistance for the protection of Mr. Heapy's weavers and others, will not be found wanting, as proper persons will be authorised to wait upon them. We trust likewise, that Messrs. Heapy and Thomas Potts will see the propriety of agreeing to the same terms as their neighbours, and thereby bring the matter to a definite conclusion.

And now a word to the Weavers generally. The Committee have done their duty, and they trust that you will do yours by liberally supporting the men who are now resisting all the efforts which petty tyranny is making to reduce your wages.

By order of the Committee,

JOHN CHADWICK, Chairman.
JOHN WEST, Secretary.

Sept. 3d, 1840.

A PUBLIC MEETING

OF THE

SILK WEAVERS

WILL BE HELD

On Monday, September 7th,

ON PARSONAGE GREEN,

AT TWELVE O'CLOCK AT NOON.

J. SWINNERTON, PRINTER, MACCLESFIELD.

Poster. *(MMT)*

system and deducting a third or half their wages:

"It was disgraceful that old men, with grey beards like himself, should have to submit to such oppression."[4]

Chartist Nicholas Lynch would have talked politics, but restrained, replied to another speaker's claim that their union was too disorganised to be effective. In this he referred back to the strike of 1832 when a *"triumvirate as paid servants"* looked after them, referring by name to Matthew Wilshaw and William Butterworth, but not to West, with whom Lynch had long since fallen out. *"It was well that they should have such a body to protect their interests"*, he said. Lynch may have been prevented from working as a weaver after 1832, for he later owned a beershop in Watercotes. By the 1840's he was employed as an inside weaver at Brocklehurst's - perhaps why he no longer saw eye to eye with West.

Lynch soon took it upon himself to run the union. On Monday morning, at six o' clock, he called a meeting at Park Green, having advertised it by placards headed *"A Fair Day's Wage for a Fair Day's Work"* and inviting the women of Macclesfield to support their husbands, sons and brothers. They were asked by Lynch to co-operate with the men and not to prepare warps for Edmunds' agent Gibbon to send out into Lancashire until he paid the list prices. A *"married woman of decent appearance"*, a Mrs Challinor, responded, after first begging the excuse of the crowd for her imperfections as a speaker and that she was no scholar:

"She was a wife and mother, had been struggling, had been struggling all her life to keep her family in some degree of comfort, and now, when they could not get proper food, nor clothes, nor even clogs for their feet, it was high time they should give over working....It was a question of bread and cheese, and it would soon be one of bread, or no bread at all. She for one could not get bread and cheese, nor sugar in her tea. She would rather play and starve, than work and starve." (cheers)"[5]

She then proposed a resolution that women should not work for Edmunds until he paid by the list of prices in Macclesfield and elsewhere.

Next on the podium was Mrs Elizabeth Walker, *"of respectable appearance for her station"*, who addressed the crowd *"Sister Slaves of Macclesfield"*. After first characterising all manufacturers as *"oppressive monsters"*, she proceeded to elaborate on a typical working woman's life in the town: *"toil in the factories from their earliest infancy"* until they could toil no more, ending in the *"Bastille"*, where they would be *"fed on skilly and resin, and at last die like dogs, injured and unlamented"*. She was a small woman and

TO THE
SILK
WEAVERS
OF MACCLESFIELD,
AND OTHERS CONCERNED.

WHEREAS, a person in the name of LYNCH, engaging himself to Excite and otherwise Impose upon the WEAVERS and OPERATIVES employed in the SILK TRADE here, having maliciously brought forth Statements of a Personal and Defamatory Character against me, these are to inform those Parties interested, that such Statements are a FABRICATED COMPOUND OF FALSEHOODS, and the Instigators of such are respectfully given to notice, that in the event of proper Information being found, Proceedings at Law will be forthwith issued against them.

The Committee of Silk Weavers are respectfully informed, that in future no Communication whatever will be entered into with them relating to Works done in Lancashire, further than referring them to the Undertakers or Putters-out, *whose instructions are to act in accordance with the Regulations entered into by the Trade where such Works are Manufactured.*

M. GIBBON.

Macclesfield, August 16, 1842.

J. SWINNERTON, PRINTER, COURIER OFFICE, MACCLESFIELD.

Poster. *(MMT)*

when she explained she was like so many in town, *"stunted in their youth"* from working in mills, she was cheered heartily. Mrs Walker then seconded the resolution and it was passed unanimously. Lynch complimented the women speakers, adding that Edmunds had 23 warping mills preparing warps for Lancashire.

This meeting incensed Edmunds & Co.'s agent Gibbon, for he had placards posted on walls warning of Lynch *"engaging himself to excite and otherwise impose on the weavers"* and informing the Committee that he would no longer enter into any talks about weaving in Lancashire. At the weavers' next assembly, on the Wednesday, Lynch poked fun at Gibbon's placard, *"a grand effusion"* containing grammatical errors, and offered Gibbon free lessons

Wicked, but not Ashamed!

"I never wonder to see men wicked, but I often wonder to see them not ashamed."—SWIFT.

MARKET GARDENER AGAIN.

WHEREAS, a person "*in* the name" of GIBBON, has thought proper, in the profundity of his immaculate wisdom, to bring a charge against a person "*in* the name of LYNCH," for busying himself in imposing upon the credulity of the Weavers and Operatives of Macclesfield, by defaming the character forsooth of the said Mr. GIBBON; and he having "*given to* notice," (Oh, 'tis enough to make the shades of England's classic sons rise and protest against this "foul murder" of our mother tongue,) "*given to notice*," that, providing certain information can be obtained, "proceedings at Law will be forthwith issued." And he, Mr. GIBBON, respectfully informs any deputation of the Weavers, that for the future he shall refer them to his "putters-out," *otherwise* Carters, &c. who convey it to Lancashire and elsewhere. I would ask, if the exhibition of existing evils, and a discovery of the means to remove them, can be construed into delusion and defamation ! I say, No ! for, surrounded by unprecedented distress, it becomes an imperative duty to inquire into the cause, and we find that an inequality exists in our Prices, which, if not restrained, *will* in a very short time reduce upwards of 4,000 inhabitants of the Town of Macclesfield to irretrievable ruin. And amongst those whose cruel oppression and vicious conduct in withholding the Fair Wages of Labour stands foremost the Firm above alluded to, of which Mr. GIBBON is the Manager. For years past, in the Persian Trade, they have been the means of reducing the Weavers to the utmost limits of starvation ; but not only in this Branch of the Weaving Trade have they been notorious for their ill usage of the Weavers, but in some of the more valuable Branches of the Trade. By taking advantage of the poverty of the Country Weavers, they reduce the price of Weaving full 30 per Cent. below the price paid in Macclesfield. They employ upwards of 24 Warping Mills, whilst they only keep about ten Looms going in the Town. They have already been the means of stopping several hundred Looms here, by thus preying on the vitals of the Poor, and thereby underselling the more honest Manufacturer.

    Men of Macclesfield, consider this! when your infant offspring cry for Food, when their tears are embittered by the reflection that you have none to give, think of this Establishment, from whence, if not controlled, will arise the utter degradation of your families. Shall one London Capitalist be the means, by its servile slave, to distress the Weavers, increase the Poors' Rate, embarrass the Shopkeepers, withdraw 30 per cent. of wages out of circulation, and accomplish by his tyranny, what our greatest foreign enemy only threatened, when he said if "he could not conquer England, he would make it a place not desirable for any Englishman to live in !" The God of heaven, in his Providential government says, No ; suffering humanity says, No ! and the good sense of all responds to this declaration.

I remain, &c.

N. LYNCH.

MACCLESFIELD, AUGUST 16, 1842.

PEACE, LAW, AND ORDER.

J. SWINNERTON, PRINTER, COURIER OFFICE, MACCLESFIELD.

Poster.   *(MMT)*

in grammar from his young son Joseph. More seriously, he added that Edmunds were paying 1s. in Lancashire for goods worth 3s. in town and had invented a new name for Sarsnets, calling the same goods "Mulmocks" to avoid paying the list price. He was all in favour of forcing Edmunds & Co. out of Macclesfield and urged the weavers not to send their daughters to work for him: *"They had no right to work merely to satiate the cormorant appetite of a speculative fishmonger."*[6]

    Whether the silk weavers did get Edmunds to abide by the list is unclear. The weavers' Central Committee met with manufacturers on Friday, where *"a good spirit prevailed"*, except between weavers and those employers who sent work out of town. However, the *'Plug Plot'* strike was finally ended. It had benefited other silk workers, for millmen, stewards and others from silk factories had taken the opportunity to canvass employers and from their findings develop a unified wage structure for all. In future stewards' wages were to be 17s. per 11 hour day, six day week; millmen, 13s.; danters, doubler-peicers and reeler-pickers, 7s. 6d., and child mill-piecers doing 10 hours, 6s. 6d. The weavers did not fare so well: two weeks after the strike, they were naming another manufacturer paying lower than the *"fair"* manufacturers in town.

In March 1847, the whole list of prices question threw weavers into a state of utter confusion and divided them into two hostile camps. Parsonage Street Chapel was the venue where, under chairman John Stubbs, the gathering was informed that for the last five years Brocklehurst's, employers of 800 out of Macclesfield's 3-4,000 weavers, had been paying some of them under the list price for black Bandannas. These men had colluded with their employer in keeping this *"bottled up"* and accepted lower prices because Brocklehurst told them they had to compete with Lancashire, where he could get Bandannas woven at 3d. per yard less. The deceit had been discovered only recently by another manufacturer, who then demanded the same of his employees. John West, the long-term opponent of Brocklehurst's, was soon on his feet to condemn the town's MP, who so often said in Parliament of *"his desire to promote the interests of Macclesfield."* There should be no letting Brocklehurst's off paying by the list, he stated:

"a man who has been picking pockets for five years, might when he was detected, on the same principle, turn around and say "Oh I have been doing it now for five years and you must therefore let me off now (applause and clamour)"[7]

But others expressed fears that if Brocklehurst's were forced to pay by the list they would send all their black Bandannas to be woven outside town and 300 inside looms would stand idle at Hurdsfield.

A few days later, Stubbs chaired a further meeting which was asked to vote on a levy of 6d. per loom to finance support for Brocklehurst's black Bandanna weavers until they could find other employment. John Prout, who was most likely an undertaker for Brocklehurst's, spoke out against stopping these weavers from working and after going through a long list of previous attempts to keep up the price list, all unsuccessful, he mentioned that in so doing they had driven the weaving of gros de Naples and Persians entirely out the town and into Lancashire. He urged the weavers to withdraw their insistence on keeping to the list price for black Bandannas, but although seconded by

William Forrest, Prout's resolution came to nothing. West quashed all further argument and the 6d. per loom levy was carried unanimously. Brocklehurst's weavers were not happy with this arrangement at all. A letter to the Courier from George Brunt, Chairman of Brocklehurst's weavers' committee, stated:

"We are willing to work, but have been deprived of the opportunity of doing so for the last fortnight, in consequence of the untimely interference of a maliciously ill-disposed party..."[8]

Early in April, a public meeting was convened at the Town Hall to discuss the present condition of the silk trade and to adopt means of checking it from leaving the town. It was attended by silk weavers, shopkeepers and others. Stubbs was once more chairman and he straightaway expressed his opinion that the town had a right to expect Brocklehurst's to pay the list prices. Thomas Cope then spoke at inordinate length on trade affairs during his time as a weaver [since 1804], overrunning the time allotted to each speaker until uproar forced him to stop. The uproar was from John West's appearance in the hall, which was greeted with loud cheers. He then addressed the enthusiastic audience:

"No one could go further than him in declaring against the conduct of those manufacturers who after having their fortunes built up by their [the weavers] labour, took their work off to other places and left them to live in misery and want."[9]

He was pleased that shopkeepers were supporting them but warned:

"they would not allow them to determine the amount of wages they should receive....He would ask how the shopkeepers would like the weavers to be called in to decide the amount of profits which they should receive from their teas, their sugars, their bread and other stuff?" (cheers)"[10]

Nicholas Lynch next tried to make a speech, but he no longer commanded the respect he held as weavers' leader in 1842. He was now so completely out of favour that hisses, groans and taunts about his mid-1830's beer shop proprietorship finally silenced him. Yet although Lynch had been supplanted by the vastly popular West, not all weavers were entirely under his spell. When someone alluded to low prices paid by the manufacturer Charles Condron, West responded with a denial, saying that this was an opportunity for him to answer "certain calumnies" which were circulating around town. John Prout and others, he claimed, had been saying that he was being paid by Condron "for the purposes of throwing odium on Messrs. Brocklehurst's." His challenge for anyone to prove it was attempted by some, but Charles Condron was there to deny any such arrangement. After more stormy disagreements about the committee's composition of delegates, West moved a resolution that the meeting was:

"of the opinion that the present prices paid for silk weaving are miserably low and not sufficient for a workman to support his family in decency, and that any attempt to reduce them lower would be an act of cruelty, as well as injustice, and in no way calculated to advance the interests of the manufacturers, or benefit the town at large."[11]

The shopkeepers and townspeople present voted unanimously in favour.

With the 1847 elections following closely, John Brocklehurst was on the defensive. At a Townley Street School ward meeting he claimed to be paying wages of £1,800-£2,000 per week in Macclesfield and only £60 elsewhere: the fact that he sent any work out of town was in *"self defence"* in order to compete in certain types of goods. Brocklehurst's were still weaving the Bandannas which the strike that March had been over, but when challenged why he had 140 steam looms still working on them, John Brocklehurst retorted that only 16 steam looms were operating *"in order to give employment to some men who were suffering from want of it"* - and for this he was cheered. A further meeting held at Roe Street Chapel heard John Prout, a moderate voice in weavers' affairs and more a Liberal than a Radical, tell Brocklehurst:

"They were all desirous of having such a representative as Mr. Brocklehurst, but they would like him to do one thing, to bring all his work back into Macclesfield."[12]

But the debonair and charming Mr Brocklehurst, like other silk manufacturers and politicians then and now, would say one thing and do another.

References
1. M.C. 29/9/1838.
2. M.C. 19/12/1840.
3. M.C. 22/8/1840.
4. Macclesfield, Stockport & Congleton Chronicle, 13/8/1842.
5. Macclesfield, Stockport & Congleton Chronicle, 20/8/1842.
6. M.C. 20/8/1842.
7. M.C. 27/3/1847.
8. ibid.
9. M.C. 10/4/1847.
10. ibid.
11. ibid.
12. M.C. 31/7/1847.

The census return for John Prout's family in 1841.

Chapter 10. Home Comforts

In 1823, David Rowbotham had a house with a loom shop above it at Prestbury Lane End. As an undertaker he employed three journeymen and one live-in 'domestic' apprentice, while both he and his wife worked a full week at their looms. These six weavers would spend up to sixteen hours each day in what Assistant Commissioner Keyser later termed *"unvaried toilsome . labour";* working the loom treadles and snatching the baton which sped the shuttle back and forth across the alternating divide between the warp threads.   With Rowbotham earning 28s. per week, the highest wage, their gross earnings came to £7.14s.6d.   After paying their journeymen, the families' net earnings, including money from loom rents but excluding the cost of quill winding, rent, taxes, coals and candles, then came to £3.9s.6d. This sum, divided between Rowbotham, his wife Elizabeth, their five children and the apprentice, amounted to 8s 8d. per head.

By 1832 the two eldest of Rowbotham's children, a son and daughter aged 20 and 18, then worked with him and his wife as weavers. At this time he only employed two journeymen plus quill winders and there was no apprentice, the old system having been almost entirely done away with. Their daughter was the highest earner of the six weavers in the loom shop, at 12s. 5d. per week, and the gross wages of all who wove there was £3.1s.7d. The family's net earnings had dropped to £1.4s.10d. - only 3s. 6d. per head for his family of seven. Even then, Rowbotham could still claim:

"we are one of the best situated families that I know of: there are hundreds that have not a third part of the income that we have."[1]

By 1838, Rowbotham's income from loom rents, usually charged at 2s. 6d. per week and out of which he paid 10d. for a quill winder, averaged only 4d. per week because his looms were so often out of use through unemployment. A weaver's average earnings were then between 7s. and 10s. after deductions. How far this would stretch can be gauged from the budget of a man who may have been one of Rowbotham's journeymen at that time; a family man with a wife and three young children. This man took home 8s. per week from weaving a variety of silk goods. From this he paid 2s. in rent, his fuel cost 1s. and 11 lb. of candles 6d. Their weekly food list was as follows: 7 lbs. of meal, 8 lbs. of flour, 6 quarts of milk, 1 lb. of lard, 11 lb. of bacon, and 4d. worth of sugar. This used up the entire 8s. wage, but as the family liked to eat potatoes with their bacon, he managed to obtain these from a friend, possibly on some barter arrangement.

Garden produce helped many a weaver feed his family and gardening was a popular pastime in Macclesfield. In 1824 the millmen complained that the long hours they worked kept them from their gardens. Later, several weavers exhibited prize blooms in the annual flower shows for chrysanthemums and pinks, while others paraded their prize vegetables through town in the annual walks of friendly societies. Meat was rarely eaten: John West claimed in 1840 that families could hardly afford a pound of flesh meat a week and he knew of some who had not tasted it at all in a month. This was borne out by a *Morning Chronicle* reporter in 1849 and also by later national statistics, which, while making the average poor persons' consumption of meat 13.6 ounces per week, put Macclesfield weavers at the very bottom when listed by trade with only 3.25 ounces per person each week. Milk consumption, on the other hand, was much higher in Macclesfield than in other silk towns; at 41.5 fluid ounces per week compared to 11 in Coventry, 7.6 in Spitalfields and just 1.6 in Bethnal Green.[2]

This much greater use of milk reflected the local staple diet of oatmeal with milk that families, such as young Adam Rushton's, largely subsisted on. Breakfast for most weavers was invariably water porridge: the ingredients being oatmeal, water and a pinch of salt all boiled until thick. This was then poured into a large pan or dish which was placed in the middle of the table, where at each place setting would be a basin of milk and a wooden spoon. The master, his family and any domestic apprentices would dip the wooden spoons into the porridge and then into the milk basins before eating - and *"those who could bolt it hot got the most"*. Sometimes treacle was substituted for the milk. Oatcakes, made from similar ingredients to the porridge, but fermented overnight with sour dough and then baked, thinly spread on a 'bakston' - a brick fireplace with a circular iron top - were another staple food.

In adult life, Adam Rushton fared better than some silk workers. With his 15s. weekly wage as a warehouseman supplemented by another 5s. earned in teaching at the Useful Knowledge Society, he had money enough for clothing and books, and to deposit some in the Government Savings Bank at Park Green. Yet the poor journeyman weaver with 8s. per week had nothing left to clothe himself or his family, let alone save anything. Even undertaker John Prout, who by 1838 lived in a garret house at Bank Top with his wife and ten children, four of whom worked as weavers and two as piecers at the time, claimed to have no

Garret house at Bank Top - probably the home of John Prout c. 1840. (*MES*)

savings at all. In earlier times some weavers managed to save considerable sums of money though; one in 1829 claiming that in twenty years of working sixteen hours a day he had saved £250.

Others spent their earnings in a profligate manner. Heavy drinking was rife in Macclesfield, as indeed almost any other industrial town. Assistant Commissioner S. Keyser noticed this in October 1838 when he wrote, "Improvidence prevails among hand loom weavers in a great degree, a temporary improvement in the state of trade often leads to carelessness and somewhat dangerous excesses."[3]

Keyser also noted, "in idleness the beer shop offers an irresistible attraction"; although strangely, considering that he was in Macclesfield during Wakes week, he noticed less than a dozen drunks during all that time. Beer shops proliferated when the Beer Act of October 1830 allowed respectable householders to set themselves up at the cost of a £2 licence fee and sureties of £40: Nicholas Lynch being among several silk workers who did so. In 1849, an

Act of Parliament closed beer shops and public houses on Sunday mornings except to travellers, and this had, as Chief Constable William Harper claimed, *"a salutary effect to putting a stop to drunkenness and disorder that prevailed previous to its introduction."* Public houses also provided a valuable service in hosting meetings of clubs and societies, even those with political connections, as did the Bundle of Sticks at Watercotes. One other, the Reformer's Hotel in Sunderland Street, advertised in *Poor Man's Guardian* that its porter cost 6d per pint - 2d less than other Macclesfield hostelries.

Yet while drink held strong attractions for some, there were many others who spent their pennies and their few free hours, or the time spent 'playing' when unemployed, in less frivolous pursuits.

"Where the husband or father was sitting in the house (for want of employment) on a rickety chair, occasionally with a youngster on his knee, there was not the appearance of an ill tempered scowl or moroseness that I have often seen elsewhere under less penury and suffering. He would frequently be found with a well-thumbed book or newspaper, helping him to while away the time that must hang heavily on a man so situated - idle, not from choice..."[4]

High on the list of newspapers for the politically motivated would have been Cobbett's *Political Register*, *Poor Man's Guardian*, *Trades Journal* and many others, while Chartists would take Feargus O'Connor's *Northern Star*. Popular but inexpensive reading matter for those wishing to improve themselves was *Penny Magazine* published by the Mechanics Institutes and *Saturday Magazine* from the Society for Promoting Christian Knowledge, both beginning in 1836. John Prout said that during the silk slump after 1826 he knew of many weavers who had been forced to sell their book collections. He was probably speaking from personal experience.

Large numbers of weavers would have attended church or chapel on Sundays, with chapel, particularly Wesleyan Methodist or its secession movements, New Connexion and Primitive, much supported. As so many weavers were Irish by birth, Catholicism took some prominence. However, it is probable that most were indifferent to any religion or were sceptics at least: Reuben Bullock mocked the *"true Christianity"* of John Prout's employers during the 1832 strike; while Owenites like Timothy Falvey and Mr Lloyd Jones were entirely anti-religion. Few, if any, weavers, did their Sunday worshipping at the Mormon Tabernacle, as their actions at meeting in Statham Street in November 1857 demonstrated.

"Mr. William Boyle, a member of the Mormon fraternity, proceeded to lay before his "brethren" the claims of "Latter Day Saintism" and the charms of Salt Lake Valley, but seeing that the audience were making their way as fast as possible to the door, he prudently resumed his seat."[5]

For entertainment the weaver had several options other than the beershop or public house. Horse racing took place on a field near London Road until 1828, when a proper course was laid out on the Town Field and meetings held there twice yearly until 1853. Afterwards it became a public park. Football was played in the streets by some, being considered a particular nuisance in the Knutsford Road during 1814, but later evolving into club team games at more suitable venues. Some of the *"lowest orders"* followed dog fighting, while pigeon fancying was also popular. Other spectator sports included 'pedestrianism' [athletics], bowling and cricket. Bare knuckle 'prize fighting' was controversially staged in the Theatre Royal at the bottom of Mill Street during 1817, but usually, some of the leading actors of the day could be seen there for the price of a stalls ticket.

Clothing for men weavers invariably consisted of a cotton shirt and coloured neckerchief worn with a heavy fustian jackets and trousers. They were also identifiable, even when in the street, from wearing aprons. Few working men went bare-headed; if they could not afford a cap or hat, they made one out of folded paper. Their wives and daughters dressed more stylishly. Women who worked in the mills, where the work was said to be *"well fitted for females"* because they were able to wear nice clothes, were often favourably commented upon by strangers to the town. When a young *Morning Chronicle* reporter, Angus Bethune Reach, arrived in town in during the December of 1849 he found himself quite attracted by them; *"the girls were dressed rather to the style of milliners' apprentices than of ordinary female operatives"*, he wrote. One reason for this was provided by a young silk weaver he interviewed; *"they would have their backs very gay, though their bellies pinched for it"*, he told the reporter. In good times they were *"hardly distinguishable from the wives of small shopkeepers"*, as a *Manchester Guardian* reporter noted. Yet even in extremely hard times they made some effort to retain a neat appearance, even if their clothes were in rags. Of the many who attended a public meeting of silk operatives at the Town Hall in December 1862 it was said:

"a considerable number of females, whose hollow cheeks and emaciated frames beneath clean but tattered garments, told too plainly of the suffering they have had to endure."[6]

Five years later, both women and the manner in which they cared for their children received similar praise:

Garret houses at Arbourhay Street, Hurdsfield.   *(Macclesfield Environmental Services)*

Inside a Jacquard weaver's garret - the woman is doubling silk threads for use in a shuttle.

"The women are tidy and cleanly, even where their garments were worn and threadbare - their rags even look respectable; and the children are made the best of, - even when shoes and stockings were absent, their heads are well kempt, and a degree of liveliness and cheerfulness manifested as they run about, - although I fear there were scanty cupboards to appeal to after their frolic."[7]

However, Macclesfield's mill women generally made poor housewives due largely to lack of opportunity. During the 1842 strike Mrs Elizabeth Walker stated:

"A married woman's occupation ought to be the management of her own home. The man ought to be the bread provider, and the woman the bread distributor. But the scales had been sadly turned, women had to toil in factories from their earliest infancy..."[8]

The agitation to obtain shorter hours for them stemmed partly from the anguish felt by local men who not only envied them their jobs but resented, as John West stated, *"performing the household drudgery which is the proper province of the wife."*

A silk worker's home in hard times could still be, *"as a rule, clean and wholesome."* The street outside might be drab, unpaved and without drainage, and the houses of the back-to-back pattern arranged in terraces or courtyards. There would be earth privies and refuse pits or mounds nearby, all of which were rarely if ever cleaned or removed; while water was obtainable only from stand cocks, wells, mill ponds or rivers. Yet some homes had small gardens and the flowers or vegetables grown there would brighten the scene a little. Inside the two-up, three-down type of house with a loom shop reached by a ladder and trap door on the top floor, as occupied by a majority of outside weavers, the main lower room was used as a sitting room. Behind this was the kitchen, in which stood *"the eternal rocking chair by the fire."* On its walls were shelves with shiny cooking pots and rows of crockery, and a few prints as decoration. Suspended from many a kitchen ceiling was the 'oatcake rack,' a wooden frame interlaced with cords in which the family's supply of oatcakes were stored. Behind the kitchen would be the scullery where on Saturdays the weekly washing was done along with the scouring of stone-laid kitchen and scullery floors. Upstairs, the bedrooms might be sparsely furnished and the bedding would in hard times be among the first items to end up in the pawnshop.

Some better-off silk workers might rent a fully furnished home, as one did in the 1840s, in which after a period the furniture became the property of the tenant. A weekly payment of 7s. 6d. secured the house and about £12 worth of furniture. This included a sofa, chest of drawers, six cane chairs, a painted table, four pictures, a [looking] glass, fender and fire irons, a clock, a carpet, four chairs and two round tables, a painted dish, a tea kettle, a saucepan, three bedsteads, three chaff beds, bedding and warming pan, and "sundry other goods." David Rowbotham's journeyman on 8s. per week could never have lived in such a house, but it is possible that in moderately prosperous times, a well set up undertaker with a large family, such as Rowbotham himself, Thomas Cope or John Prout, may have lived in houses furnished and equipped in a comparable style.

The deadly disease Cholera hit Macclesfield in 1849; and among the several who died were two from the Bank Top area where John Prout and his family lived. Lack of adequate drainage and sewage disposal was one obvious cause and this was soon addressed by improvements under the 1848 Local Board of Health Act. From 1851, when a Local Board was set up, roads and courts were paved, streets given name plates and lamp lighting; drains and sewers were laid and the regular removal of household waste was brought into being. Other unwholesome aspects of the town were strictly regulated; common lodging houses and slum dwellings were compulsorily cleansed, unsafe houses were demolished and pig styes removed from back gardens. These much better conditions took many years to reach the majority of the population.

The local Board of Health also established the Public Baths and Wash houses in 1850, towards which local Radical MP John Williams contributed £500. For sums ranging from a penny to a shilling, people could use these facilities when those at home were inadequate or non-existent. Within the wash houses were heated cabinets for drying clothes and the destruction of lice, which were otherwise difficult to eradicate. Yet in spite of the advantages these presented to many poor people, there was a falling off in usage during the 1860's which eventually resulted in the wash houses being closed. The depression in the silk trade was blamed for this.

The possibility of sickness or even death were well to the fore in any silk worker's consciousness, and reminders were constantly about them. Life expectancy was short and many died young; Reuben Bullock's daughter Mercy, a harness knitter, died at the age of 30; John Prout's daughter Elizabeth, a silk weaver, at age 34. Infant mortality was very high, at 44% of all deaths in the town during 1842-48. John and Mary West lost their first child, a girl, during this period. Working mothers often farmed their babies out to child minders, who either dosed their charges on laudanum or carried them to the mill where the mother worked; as John West coyly indicated, *"brought to her at intervals to obtain those natural supplies of nourishment which it required..."*[9]

Poor health and disease among babies and children were commonplace. Adults suffered rheumatic and pulmonary ailments from damp living conditions while inadequate sanitation led to dysentery. With doctors charging up to 2s. a visit, the alternative most resorted to by working people was the town Dispensary in Mill Street, set up by local manufacturers and the town corporation in 1814, and where free treatment was available. However, to qualify the applicant had first to obtain a 'recommend' either from a sick club or a doctor. One man whose children were ill during the winter of 1847 spent a whole day knocking on doors without obtaining one. He was eventually given some medicine by a parish doctor, but as he was not on parish relief, there was only enough for one of his children, who died before the medicine took effect. Even with a 'recommend' the treatment was off-hand, with long waits for home visits to patients: in some cases the patient died waiting. Dr. Fleet, House Surgeon of the Dispensary for many years, was well-known for using leeches to bleed patients in almost all cases. Another alternative was the Barn Street barber shop of Tommy Neild, who also practised as a herbalist and alchemist.

Yet there were times when the cares of life could be forgotten for a few hours. The annual May fair, the June 'Barnaby' fair or the October 'Wakes' fair at Waters Green provided escapism for child and adult alike, with their amusements, side-shows and sweetmeat and toy vendors. On Wakes Monday the town's friendly societies formed up in processions with bands and music for their annual walks - and for members there would be a lunch to follow. The possibility of a dinner treat laid on by an employer, as did Messrs. Potts and Wright at the passing of the Reform Bill in 1832, seems to have been rare. Mr R.E. Hine of St. George's Street Mills was one who did; providing his workers with *"handsome entertainment"* at the Childers Inn, Brunswick Street, on the occasion of his marriage in March 1856. Later still, in October 1867, 400 of Brocklehurst's power loom weavers were invited to *"a substantial tea"* at their Waterloo Street mill. However, a feast which brought in the new year of 1854, did so in the finest style. It was at a large room in the upper story of the Chester Road Mill of Messrs. Harrop, Taylor, Pearson & Co., decorated throughout with evergreens, mistletoe and flowers, that the 200 or more people who worked there sat down for their *"treat"*. This consisted of rounds of beef, hams and other meats, currant cake and bread and butter, and was followed by games, a magic lantern show, an *"electrifying machine"*, entertainment by the Christ

Church School drum and fife band, and finally dancing to the music of a band from Newton Heath.

"The scene was one of the most exhilarating description...happiness beamed from every face and mirth and harmony reigned supreme. The whole of the operatives were very respectfully attired, and, to their credit be it said, not the slightest impropriety of conduct occurred to mar the pleasures of the evening."[10]

There were later occasions when this mill, under its benign manager Mr. Robinson Andrew, treated its workpeople to a feast; and when during the severe winter of 1857-58 some became unemployed, he provided them with £100 worth of beef and bread each week.

Overall, the silk workers of Macclesfield did remarkably well for themselves in the face of such miserably low pay and the extreme hardships which so often befell them. Angus Bethune Reach was moved by this contrast in their lives:

"One is inclined to wonder at the co-existence of, comparatively, so low a rate of wages, with the outward appearance of, comparatively, so fair a state of social comfort."[11]

References

1. Select Committee Report into the State of the Silk Trade 1831 - 32, Vol XIX, page 821.
2. Statistics for 1862 quoted in Hobsbawn, E.J., *Labouring Men* pp. 87, 96.
3. Hand loom Weavers: Reports from Commissioners 1840 Vol. XXII, page 493.
4. M.C. 16/11/1867.
5. M.C. 28/11/1857.
6. M.C. 13/12/1862.
7. M.C. 16/11/1867.
8. Macclesfield, Congleton & Stockport Chronicle, 20/8/1842.
9. M.C. 14/2/1846.
10. M.C. 7/1/1854.
11. M.C. 1/12/1849.

Chapter 11. Self Help

Without the umbrella of a modern state system to shield them from some of life's more violent squalls, Macclesfield's silk workers and others were largely dependent on what protection they themselves could provide. John Prout once said that,

"he did not believe there was a town in England where the spirit of independence was more deeply ingrained than in the inhabitants of Macclesfield."[1]

Within the town were several well-established local societies and clubs, and also branches of National and regionally organised friendly societies, all mutually owned, non-profit making and dedicated to dealing with the troubles that might befall a working man and his family. For the payment of a small weekly sum their members were insured against sickness, unemployment or death. Other societies aimed to house, feed and clothe them at fair prices, elevate them to political importance, or educate them for a better future.

One of the oldest and largest of any of Macclesfield's societies was the Peace and Union Society, a benefit society which dated from 1794 and had 900 members by 1850. It was commonly known by the name the 'Calvinist Club' because its meeting place was Townley Street Calvinist Chapel. The members' annual dinner treat, held during the October wakes week, usually took place in several public houses, but in 1837 they all dined together at the shambles behind the Town Hall. Three other early friendly societies made donations to the newly opened Large Sunday School in 1813; one, the Union, held meetings at the Golden Lion Inn. Later still came the Loyal Union Society, established in 1817 and which had 707 members by 1850.

Probably the earliest of the National friendly societies to open a branch in Macclesfield was the London Independent Order of Oddfellows, Loyal Hope Provincial Grand Lodge Number 1 of Cheshire District, which was established in the town in 1815. This had 80 persons on its books at the height of the slump in February 1826, when in one of their regular meetings at the Union Inn, the Dams, its distressed members were each awarded 8s. in assistance. By June 1847 there were 150 Lodge members who sat down to a celebration dinner at the Roe Buck Inn, Union Gateway; their regular gathering point for more serious occasions as well.

"The Lodge assembled at the house of Brother William May, the Roe Buck Inn, each member bearing the regalia of the order, and preceded by a band of music, which performed the Dead March in Saul, proceeded to the residence of their deceased brother, and thence followed [his] remains to the last abode."[2]

The next oldest Oddfellows' Lodge was the Morning Star, established in 1825. In June each year they celebrated their anniversary with a dinner for 100 or more at the Half Moon in Bridge Street. Other lodges followed in quick succession: the St. George's, the Rose of Sharon, the Good Samaritans, the Lily of the Vale Borough, the Loyal Waterloo, the Loyal Perseverance, the Queen Victoria, the Philanthropic, and the Victory Lodge; all formed between 1832 and 1840. One Oddfellows lodge that held its anniversary dinner at Derby Street in October 1848, the St. James Royal Oak Lodge, actually had a much longer pedigree:

"The Lodge is one of the oldest clubs in the town. It was formed as a benefit society in 1764 and eight years ago it joined the order in question."[3]

At Wakes Week in October 1836 two new branches of national friendly societies made their first appearances. The annual walk, a procession of members from each society marching behind their banner and led by a band, was lined throughout by crowds who particularly enjoyed the robes and regalia worn by newcomers, The Ancient Order of Druids. But then, eclipsing their impact on onlookers, came the Ancient Order of Free Gardeners, Rose of Sharon Lodge.

"Their regalia was set off with great taste, and had a most pleasing effect. Each member carried some emblem, or production of the gardens, amongst which we noticed a large cabbage and have since been informed that it weighed upwards of forty pounds, also some fine apples fourteen inches in circumference, two sticks of celery four feet high, pineapples, grapes, melons & c. A beautiful garland formed chiefly of roses and dahlias closed the procession."[4]

Their first Lodge room was at the Nags Head, but two years later they moved to the Castle Inn, Church Street, and were still there in 1877. By 1841, the annual Wakes walk was attended by four lodges of Ancient Free Gardeners. First in line was the Rose of Sharon Lodge, then the Laurel Grove, then Gooseberry, and drawing up the rear the Hawthorn Lodge. Each member wore their regalia and carried emblems along with the usual vegetables, fruits and flowers. Once more a *"monstrous cabbage"* excited wonder as did a huge turnip, and crowns and ornaments formed with dahlias were much admired.

The Ancient Order of Foresters were also represented in town. Court No. 582 celebrated its anniversary in June 1840 at the Waters Green Tavern, while

Druids Friendly
Society banner.
(MMT)

Below:
Foresters Friendly
Society funeral
card. *(MMT)*

during the previous June, Court No.
589 had held their anniversary dinner
at the Silk Mill Tavern.

"The evening was spent in great
harmony and conviviality. And on the
following evening the wives and
sweethearts of the brothers had a merry
tea-party to which dancing succeeded,
and was kept up with much spirit."[5]

The Ancient Order of Druids,
which seems to have disbanded some
time after their costume made such
an impact at the annual walks of
1836, were re-formed in October
1845 as No. 69 Lodge at the Druids
Arms in Pickford Street. They were

ANCIENT ORDER OF FORESTERS'

FRIENDLY SOCIETY.

Registered pursuant to 38th and 39th Vict., ch. 60.

—:O:—

CEREMONY

At the Funeral of a Member of the Order.

PRINTED FOR SPECIAL USE,

BY ORDER OF THE HIGH COURT MEETING.

—:O:—

1879.

Published and Sold by the Executive Council.

followed by a new lodge at Sutton in 1846, the Good Intent.

Some friendly societies were attached to local churches and chapels. Of these, the St. George's Church Friends Society seems to have been an early one, for they celebrated their first anniversary in June 1839, when it was reported that their numbers were "*steadily increasing.*" At the same time a tea party for scholars at the National School given by clergy, friends and patrons were setting up another:

"after tea, the plans of a Benefit society, of the children and teachers, about to be established for the relief in sickness was unfolded and explained very satisfactorily."[6]

At Wakes Week in 1842 were two similar societies; the Church of England Friendly Society and the Macclesfield Sunday School Friendly Society.

Women were also catered for separately. By 1842 there was a Wesleyan Female Club and a Roe Street Female Friendly Society. The Female Peace and Union Society, a branch of the men's society established in 1794, seems to have been formed in 1844, while another, the Methodist Female Union Society was "*old established*" at its anniversary and procession in 1847, when its funds were depleted because "*the mortality and sickness of the last year has been much above the average.*"

While friendly societies offered insurance against a variety of misfortunes, others were more specific in offering support. Several provided sickness benefit for the subscription of about a shilling per month, and others the cost of a funeral for a penny or halfpenny per week. The first recorded sickness society was the Manchester Sick List, which was operating in 1818. In 1842 there was also a Hurdsfield Sick List, with a membership totalling 361 people. Workers in some larger factories organised their own clubs as well; at Brocklehurst's there was the 'Funeral Box' to which weavers subscribed, the funds being held by clerks who paid out sums of £4 on the death of a weaver or his wife, and £1 for a child.

Burial societies may have been first started in Macclesfield about the year 1811, but the town's main and most popular burial society, termed the No.1 Burial Society, was formed in 1831. Within its first ten years it had 11,600 members on its books and paid out more than £3,000 for burials. The society was in some trouble by 1849 when *the Courier* reported upon the "*despotic*" powers of its governing body and disorderly meetings. These ructions originated when the cost of retaining a surgeon at a fee of £30 for six months reduced their funds to such an extent that members were requested to make extra contributions. A schism then developed and 6,000 of its 13,500 members had split away by 1854, after which the legal rights to own the funds were contested by the two groups at a court of chancery. This seems to have been resolved by November 1860, when the society had 13,000 members back on its books. In November 1857, owing to the trade depression in the town, the contributions of one penny per week were suspended for six weeks to cushion members who could not pay and prevent them falling out of benefit.

One local society provided for both ill health and death: this was the No. 2 Co-operative Burial and Sick Society, whose members celebrated its anniversary in June 1839 with an *"excellent dinner"* at the Fence Schoolroom provided by the White Lion, Hurdsfield. They seem to have been operating for ten years in 1841, when membership totalled 6,500. In dealing with sickness, medical aid cost the society £51 and another £5 was paid out for leeches in 1855. During that year, claims of accounting inefficiency were raised in a long speech by silk weaver William Barnett at their annual meeting, held at Townley Street. Then a schism developed the following year at the society's usual meeting place, the Childers Inn. Some members considered it too small and moved to the Roe Buck where they elected fresh officers. They then sought to obtain the society's funds through the magistrates court, but it was ruled that the Roe Buck meeting was not properly constituted and its officers improperly elected. Membership had fallen to 6,150 by 1860.

There was a No. 3 Burial Society, also known as the Good Samaritan, which was in existence by 1837 and had a membership of 3,500 four years later. The society was subject to fraud in 1837 when it paid out on the supposed death of a child who was very much alive. The 'bereaved' parents obtained the sum of £3.6s.10d. plus a ticket for free liquor valued at 4s.2d. from a total sum paid by the society of £3.12s.0d. The remaining shilling went to the officers of the society for *"refreshment."*

Burial societies came in for considerable criticism after allegations of encouraging infanticide and murder were laid against them in January 1841 by the Governor of the Macclesfield Union Workhouse - from which John Prout ably defended them [see Chapter 12]. Afterwards, the societies felt it necessary to guard against further charges. The No. 1 Society engaged the service of the surgeon in 1848 precisely to quash any rumours and to ensure that infanticide to obtain burial fees could not occur. Nevertheless, the suspicion remained in some minds and in 1860 a coroner at Knutsford stated that the burial club system tended to lessen parental affection and lead to *"permissive murder"* to obtain money. The President of the No 2 Society defended their record: with

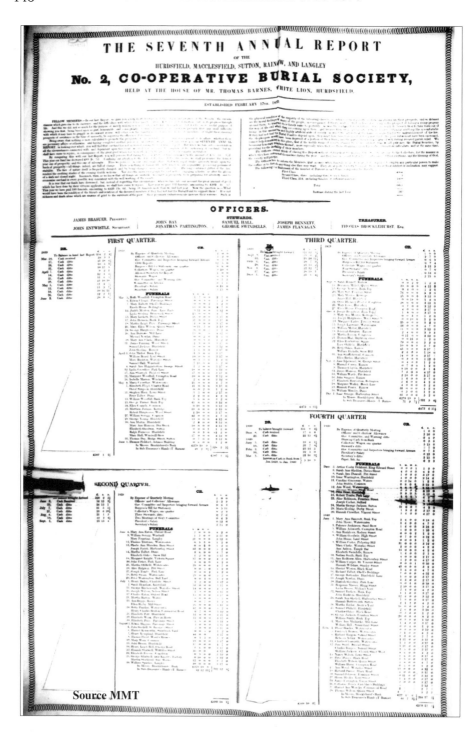

Source MMT

the death rate for the whole of Macclesfield's 29,645 population [1851] averaging 26 per thousand, the rate among the 19,000 members of all three societies was only 20 per thousand. That all but 10,000 of Macclesfield people were in a burial society, and the possibility that this remainder were in one of the friendly societies or other organisations, bears out John Prout's claim, made in 1837, that it was a disgrace not to belong to a sick club or burial society.

Other self help societies were devoted to building houses for their members. During the silk boom of 1822-5 several were formed, principally by weavers, and as many as 400 houses built by them. After 1826 most of the houses fell into other hands. One of these, the Macclesfield Friendly Building Society, had property in Crompton Road in 1829. The Victoria Building Society was formed in 1846 at Hurdsfield and at its first annual meeting, held at the Queens Arms there, the secretary reported that sixty shares had been taken up. He added: *"The object of this society is to enable the working man, who is not possessed of property, to build or purchase property and thus increase his political importance."*[7]

Another society, the No. 1 General Building Society, was probably long-established by 1859 when its membership total was upwards of 7,000.

The Co-operative movement spread into Cheshire during 1829. By January 1830 James Fitton, probably an ex-silk weaver of Mount Pleasant Square, was advertising his business as the *"2nd Co-operative Store, Macclesfield"*, where he was also an agent for John Doherty's unstamped publication, *United Trades Co-operative Journal*. Fitton was a retailer of beer, shopkeeper and dealer in groceries and sundries at Watercotes in 1834, but the term *"Co-operative"* had been dropped. Over twenty years later a more lasting co-operative venture was begun. In May 1855 a group of five silk weavers, all influenced by the writings of Robert Owen on co-operative societies, bought themselves a barrow full of wholesale goods then met to redistribute it amongst themselves in a small cottage in Exchange Street. They agreed to extend the experiment and encouraged by others, including William Barnett, rented a small shop in Sunderland Street for £15 a year. Soon afterwards the Rev. W.R.B. Arthy delivered a lecture at the Y.M.C.A. on co-operation, after which they had a great influx of new members. By 1860 the weekly sales amounted to £70 worth, in spite of the depression in trade. They then paid 5% on members' investments and a 1s. 4d. in the pound dividend; and with the surplus purchased two daily and two weekly newspapers. Ten years later they had four separate branches and were doing business of £12,000 per annum, from which £900 was

Co-operative store in Sunderland Street. *(MMT)*

returned in dividends. There was also a free library with upwards of 700 books on its shelves and which was supplied with daily and weekly newspapers, this open to the general public as well as members. Later still, Co-op members were offered regular Tea Meetings, lantern lectures and evening classes; and also an annual rail excursion to Liverpool on Barnaby Monday.

Self help in educational terms could begin at school if parents were so disposed or could afford it. Most weavers were unable to send their children to a day school though, not just because of the fees. David Rowbotham was one among many who lamented that poverty obliged him to set his children to work as soon as they were able, thus trapping them into following the trade of their father. They may have attended the classes in writing held on two nights a week at the National School, that he mentioned in 1838. But even when the 1844 Factory Act made half time education compulsory for eight to eleven year old factory hands, hard up parents, who had to pay 'school pence,' sent their children to *"the lowest* [and cheapest] *class of school which the law recognises."*

MACCLESFIELD SUNDAY SCHOOL.

The Large Sunday School c. 1820. *(MMT)*

Sunday schools provided another opportunity for working children to learn the 'Three R's,' and Macclesfield was well provided with them. The largest, the non-denominational school situated in Roe Street, could accommodate as many as 2,000 children at once. Most Sunday schools aimed to provide Christian teachings, basic literacy and numeracy skills, and hopefully to make the children *"good subjects and sincere citizens."* Yet some believed that teaching working people's children to read and write would make them dissatisfied with their station in life. John Doherty condemned one Macclesfield Sunday School where no reading and writing were taught, calling its leaders *"hypocrites covering enmity to our improvement ......under the sacred mantle of religion."* But improvement was rarely the overriding aim of these schools; much of their impetus came from the need to keep child-workers off the streets on the Sabbath, when their factory repressed spirits were unleashed and apt to break out in boisterous behaviour. Even then, one *Courier* correspondent was *"most upset"* by a wild outpouring of boys and girls from the Large Sunday School.

Yet this limited opportunity to receive some education, however inferior and ill-managed, or imposed on what could be free time, was gratefully taken up by many children. Adam Rushton wrote of his Sunday school writing classes at Higher Hurdsfield in the 1820s,

"And then came the glorious times of straight strokes, pothooks and ladles. How fascinating these elementary characters seemed.....Then more exhilarating still, came forth words, and sentences and even my own name, written in large strokes of my quill pen."[8]

Not all children were as eager; the Sunday schools had a high turnover and absentee rates, while some children *"deplorably rude, wicked and profane"*, did not attend at all.

Adult education, enabling working people to 'better themselves' was provided first through an evening 'Mutual Instruction Class' held at the Large Sunday School under the tutelage of Thomas Smith. He was joined in his teaching by a silk weaver, Thomas Kelly, in February 1827. Kelly taught scientific classes and while working at his loom during the daytime kept a slate and chalk beside him on which to jot down ideas for his lectures. By 1832 their classes covered a variety of subjects. Two years later, after a visit by John Brocklehurst, the two classes were amalgamated under his patronage. They aimed at those who were *"incessantly pursuing daily bread"*, intending to *"elevate the intellectual condition of the members"*. After an influx of members necessitated a move to Brunswick Street in 1835 they became the

'Society for Acquiring Useful Knowledge' with Brocklehurst as President. By 1837 they were running classes for writing and reading, arithmetic, grammar, drawing, geography, chemistry and music, and 70 persons were in regular attendance. But the Society was not welcomed by everyone:

Macclesfield Society for acquiring Useful Knowledge Exhibition.

THE Committee present their most sincere thanks to those Gentlemen who have so kindly volunteered to assist them in their present arduous undertaking, by the loan of many valuable Paintings, Models, Coins, and other Scientific and Ornamental Articles.

"it had to bear up against much bitter opposition on the part of many who could not believe that its operations, excluding religious instruction, could be of any use to its youthful members."[9]

In 1843 the Rev. J. Burnett of St. George's church felt obliged to speak up for it, saying that young men from his congregation who attended were not *"injured in their religious principles"* by their studies. Later, when female classes were begun, sewing was added to the list of subjects taught.

One of the first students at the Useful Knowledge Society was Adam Rushton, who among other subjects learned to weave silk on the Jacquard loom. During the late 1840's, when he earned 5s. per week as a teacher there, one long-serving teacher was *"honest, bluff, sturdy, plain-spoken"* John Wright [a warehouseman by trade who may have lived in Brook Street]. He taught shorthand and was *"a devout and enthusiastic worshipper of Byrom's system of stenography as improved by Mollineax"* [Thomas Mollineax of Chestergate]. Yet he also brought a Jacquard loom into the lecture room on one occasion and wove some superior figured silk goods, explaining the process to his students as he worked the treadles and sped the shuttle back and forth. Rushton's silk weaving expertise on the Jacquard loom was put to use when he set himself up in business as an undertaker with a garret of twenty looms in Pickford street during the 1840's. Later still he was a manufacturer for a few years in Buxton Road Mill.

Much earlier, Rushton had briefly attended the evening classes held twice weekly at the school and run by John Richards of Kerridge End, Rainow. The impetus for Rushton and two of his friends to go came from Richards speechmaking during the Feargus O'Connor rally in October 1838, which impressed them. But his school was less impressive, being situated in the largest room of his rather small house and furnished with old, rickety desks and forms. The bare, whitewashed walls were relieved only by a few unframed prints of ancient sages and reformers. Rushton did not record what Richards taught, only that he had made a study of the Utopias of the past.

By 1850 the Useful Knowledge Society was located in the old Parsonage at Park Green, where one year later, influenced by the Great Exhibition, the School of Art and Design was begun. This was followed in 1854 by a subscription reading room that not only provided newspapers and journals but also the most modern of communications, *"telegraphic intelligence"*, which was relayed three times a day. Depression in the silk trade did little to forward the Society in the latter part of the 1850's and during the next decade the subject range was reduced even though more scientific subjects were introduced. The School of Art and Design was poorly attended and few of the teachers were silk weavers by trade; in 1863 there were just six and a year later it was ten.

The Y.M.C.A., where the Rev. Arthy had lectured on co-operative principles, had opened its doors for the first time in 1856, enlisting 37 members by its second year. By 1865 it had 137 on its membership list. An entirely different clientele supported the evening classes begun at the Ragged and Industrial School at Turnock Street. This had opened in 1858 for orphaned and vagrant children, but started adult classes on two nights a week the following year. They were attended by *"young men who were more accustomed to amuse themselves by pigeon flying, dog fighting and other disreputable sports."* Day classes for street urchins and beggar boys, where they were taught to mend their own and others' clothes and clogs under the supervision of a skilled tailor, began at the Large Sunday School in the same year. The Working Men's Total Abstinence and Mutual Improvement Society set up class rooms in Pickford Street during 1862, where the lectures were mostly on temperance topics. Their membership rose to 190 within two years, but had decreased to 150 by 1866, when, as the Secretary explained, some were *"unable to resist the fearful temptation"* and resumed drinking alcoholic liquor.

In 1859, the widely promoted book *Self-Help*, by Samuel Smiles, showed how some pre-eminent Victorians had achieved success in spite of lowly birth or misfortune. There were many more, less successful and untrumpeted, but nonetheless worthy practitioners in Macclesfield. Through their own efforts, or in concert with others, they did succeed in raising themselves above the apathy, ignorance and sheer self-destructive capabilities that so many of their contemporaries suffered from.

References
1. M.C. 10/6/1837.
2. M.C. 17/11/1832.
3. M.C. 7/10/1848.
4. M.C. 8/10/1846.
5. M.C. 29/6/1839.
6. ibid.
7. M.C. 28/11/1846.
8. Rushton Adam, *My Life as Farmer's Boy, Factory Lad, Teacher and Preacher,* 1909.
9. Nicholson J.O. *Macclesfield Past Present and Future,* 1866.

Chapter 12. The Union Workhouse

Before the Poor Law Amendment Act of 1834, most of Macclesfield's poor were provided for by a system of outdoor relief in money payment. The able bodied were put to work doing paid labour; men usually breaking stones for the highways, sweeping the streets or carrying coal to the workhouse, while children were 'apprenticed' to silk mills. Anyone really destitute would be housed within the poorhouse in Commercial Road, which had room for 220 inmates but was generally so overcrowded that immorality and rowdyism were daily occurrences. The Poor Law's most harsh aspect was the Act of Settlement, dating from the reign of Charles II, which allowed any parish to expel a person not born there and who was likely to become a burden on local poor rates. In one local instance, Richard Leather, an elderly unemployed weaver in poor health, was forced to walk to Knutsford, his place of settlement, to obtain money for the burial of one of his children. Returning, he first collapsed at Chelford and died on reaching Macclesfield. Others resented the compulsion attached to receipt of poor relief. A workman named Cosgrove who went to Macclesfield Races when he should have been breaking stone on the highway, said when up before magistrates:

"Punish me as you wish, just like a soldier, aye you may flog me through the town, if that will do you any good. I am sorry I had ever anything to do with abolishing the slave trade, when I am a slave myself." [i]

In normal circumstances, the system locally was barely adequate, but in the tremendous slump which occurred after 1825 it was unable to cope with the huge numbers of unemployed. The cost of maintaining the poor of Macclesfield alone escalated from £3,837 in 1824 to £8,670 in 1830 and continued to rise. In October 1826, worries about paying increasingly higher poor rates prompted *the Courier* to suggest that overseers of the poor applied to the proprietors of the new canal building project, to see if they could obtain the contract for cutting the section through Macclesfield, Sutton and Hurdsfield. This seems to have been successful and a contract entered into, for it was calculated that once work on the canal was begun it would bring £500 per week to the town.

The crisis in poor relief was also a national problem, one that the Government addressed soon after the 1832 Reform Bill had changed its composition. The Poor Law Amendment Act of 1834 brought more than fifteen thousand different parishes to merge into a much more manageable number of Poor Law Unions. Under these, all outdoor relief for the able-bodied was ended and their only option was to enter the workhouse, where rigid discipline and harsh, Spartan conditions were intentionally provided to ensure that applicants were only those who were absolutely desperate. It was aimed to be economical, rational and moral - and the sexes, even married couples, were strictly segregated. Yet while the old system was flexible enough to vary considerably in accordance with local needs; the new system - inappropriate for the industrialised towns and cities of the north - was applied rigidly throughout the whole country.

The Macclesfield Union was formed in September 1836 and immediately rumours began about the building of a new workhouse. One day in April 1837 the Rev. J.R. Browne of Prestbury, a member of the Board of Guardians, was driving towards Macclesfield when he saw some twenty or thirty men in a field. He stopped and asked what they were about. They asked him in return if this was to be the site of the new *"Bastille."* When he told them it was, they said they would pull it down. Hostility to the new workhouse preceded its arrival and was shared by thousands of others in the town and surrounding districts.

Browne was Chairman at a meeting against the new Act held in the Town Hall on the 10th May, when the place was filled to overflowing. In spite of being on the Board of Guardians he made a virulent attack on *"that most cruel and oppressive law"* which would have a serious impact on any man applying for relief:

"He goes to them - these Poor Law Commissioners; what then? These vultures clench him in their talons, and take him to prison (hear, hear) - for, call it what they like, dress it up as they please, the poor house is nothing but a prison. (hear, hear)" [2]

Browne reserved his most angry remarks for the Act's bastardy clause, which lay all the blame for illegitimacy on the woman.

Eventually the meeting grew so large it had to be adjourned to Park Green, being escorted down Mill Street by bands playing music, men carrying emblems and so-called specimens of a work house diet, together with an effigy of the Governor of the new workhouse. At Park Green between 8-10,000 people had gathered to hear the speakers, among whom were William Butterworth, William Parker, Timothy Falvey and John Prout. Falvey read a resolution opposing the Act and its bastardy clause in particular:

"While criminality attached to the poor in such cases, the bastard sons of royalty could go into the fashionable world." (cries of "Well done Timothy. That's a good point.")" [3]

His resolution was seconded by John Prout. Throughout their speechmaking the weather was awful, for it rained and hailed throughout, yet without dispersing the crowds. Eventually though, the meeting was adjourned back to the Town Hall.

Back inside the Hall, the eloquent Mr Lloyd Jones re-opened the proceedings, after which it was silk weaver William Forrest's turn. Having been married by the Rev. Browne only three years before, he said he would rather *"dance the gallows harlequin"* than be separated from his wife in the workhouse. The meeting's Secretary, John Prout, then scathingly attacked the Town Council and magistrates for their non-appearance at the meeting. But they did not need their support, he said, and he was proud that the voice of Macclesfield people would be heard without sectarian feeling, adding:

"He had written all the documents sent to Parliament on the distress of the silk trade, and stood before a committee of the house of Commons to be examined on that subject when those men to whom he alluded [the Town Council] had shrunk from notice (cheers)."[4]

The middle classes were also condemned by Prout and others who accused them of neglecting the trust that the 1832 reforms had awarded them. After Prout read out their Parliamentary petitions and signatures were obtained, another speaker proposed sending a petition to the Board of Guardians, asking them to dissolve the Macclesfield Union and suspend the building of the workhouse. Amid cries of *"Pull it down"* and *"Burn it down"* this was also agreed upon. When the meeting closed and dispersed from the Town Hall, the effigy of the Governor of the workhouse was burned in the Market Place.

Their petition received nearly 10,000 signatories. Copies were sent to the House of Lords by way of the Bishop of Exeter and to the Commons through John Brocklehurst MP. John Prout also sent a letter to the Macclesfield Board of Guardians requesting that they receive the Anti-New Poor Law Committee's deputation, which was to include himself, Reuben Bullock and William Parker. The Board agreed to meet them within the hour, but this was impossible as the weavers were working, so a special meeting was arranged. Meanwhile, the Rev. Browne was hauled over the coals by the rest of the Board for his part in the Town Hall meeting and had to expressly disassociate himself from the cries of *"Pull it down,"* and *"Burn it down,"* made about the workhouse.

The Board of Guardians met the forty strong deputation led by John Prout at the Town Hall in the first week of June. From the outset, the Board's

Chairman insisted it was illegal for the two sides to discuss the Poor Laws. He was dissuaded from closing the meeting altogether and persuaded to hear what Prout had to say by the Rev. Browne, who told him *"they were bound to hear him."* As spokesman for the deputation, Prout, restrained from discussing the Act, then re-capitulated their objections to it. Their first was of the *"tyrannical"* nature of the powers invested in the Poor Law Commissioners. But their greatest objection was that the Act was totally incapable of being carried into effect in manufacturing districts, where any temporary recession in trade made in-door relief impossible for such huge numbers of unemployed people. He had obtained returns of all those seeking poor relief in the quarter from 1st April to 23rd May, when 412 men, 674 women and 1,169 children under 16 had applied. With the addition of a further 1,000 of Macclesfield's out-door poor living elsewhere, who under the law would become inmates of the town's new workhouse, plus those already living in the old one, the total numbers added up to 2,465. No one building could house such numbers he added.   Another objection was to the bastardy clause, which Prout said *"encouraged a spirit of libertinism and demoralisation."* He then dropped a broad hint that someone on the Board had reason to feel shame from *"a fact that delicacy forbids in an open court"*, refraining from going further only because *the Courier's* reporter was present. The meeting closed when the deputation were told that the Guardians had no powers to dissolve the Union.

Prior to their meeting, Prout had sent a letter on the 24th May to the Chairman of the Macclesfield Union, the Rev. Edward Stanley, one-time Vicar of Alderley but recently made Bishop of Norwich. In requesting his support he wrote of *"a system of oppression at variance with the professions of liberality and disgraceful to the political pretensions of the age - subjecting the poor to a cruel and oppressive treatment and leading to a violation of the laws of God."*[5]

The reply from the Bishop's residence at Alderley Rectory on the 27th was not the least bit supportive. He claimed the Act was *"most enlightened"* and that under the old law that *"manly and honest spirit of independence had been nearly annihilated."* The letter ended with a barb aimed at Prout. The law has been, he wrote *"the object of many prejudiced, designing and interested persons, by misrepresentation and exaggeration to vilify and oppose..."*[6]

The Bishop's support for the New Poor Law was fully condemned by John West. When it was announced that West was to speak on the New Poor Law at the Grapes Tavern, Sutton, the Bishop indicated his desire to hear him and was taken there by John May, a local J.P. West's performance was impressive; *"a more complete denunciation of the outdoor relief system has seldom been heard"*, wrote May, much later. The Bishop would have replied to West, but was prevented from so doing by a ruffian and was very glad to depart from the tavern unharmed. He also invoked some Biblical wrath from the Chartist Rev., Joseph Rayner Stephens, one of the north-west's leading antagonists to the New Poor Law, at the O'Connor rally in 1838. The Bishop had *"aided and abetted"* the new law, he thundered *"the Bishopric was his reward for that damnable deed of an infernal wolf. I impeach him publicly for that damnable deed. He is an infidel Bishop, a son of Belial, as being a son of Hell."* [7]

In the meantime, residents of Hurdsfield had met at the Fence School, where proposals to withdraw from Macclesfield Poor Law Union were discussed. Among those supporting the motion were William Parker and William Butterworth; with Butterworth expressing his view, *"He would rather see the inhabitants of Hurdsfield shot dead in the street than shut up in the Bastille."* [8] However, the Union remained intact: the *"Bastille"* was inexorably coming to Macclesfield.

One of John Prout's statements before the Board of Guardians referred to the numerous benefit societies in the town; it was, he said *"a disgrace if any man was not in a Sick Society to be relieved in a time of need."* He also praised the Burial Societies which provided insurance for a death, some of these being well over thirty years old. It was these that were attacked by the Governor of the Workhouse in January 1841; in a letter to *the Courier* he made the claim:

"Burial Societies, in the case of illegitimate children in particular, was the cause of immorality, in the first place on the part of the parents, and of slow murder at least -Every illegitimate child which came to the workhouse was enrolled in a Burial Society."[9]

John Prout sprang to the defence of this, a well-supported working peoples' institution in Macclesfield. First he queried whether it was not the poor law itself which encouraged infanticide and whether the obstacles placed in the way of a mother obtaining support from the father encouraged illicit intercourse. Then he added, concerning the cheese-pairing efficiency of the workhouse regime:

"But are there no evils in the present workhouse system? Can we calmly take a view of the wants of nature being regulated by measure and weight? and the poor diet being reduced to such an extent that the paupers leavings of thick porridge must be heated up until they are disposed of?"[10]

Finally, he presented a challenge:

"If the Governor of the Workhouse can bring one instance of slow murder, or immorality caused by the Burial Societies of Macclesfield, let it be published now, and, if he cannot by facts support his opinion he must remain a convicted calumnist."[11]

There seems to have been no reply to his letter.

The new Macclesfield Union workhouse in Prestbury Lane was completed in 1845. It could accommodate 500 inmates. John Prout's and the Anti-New Poor Law Committee's fears about the its capacity and the Board of Guardians' penny-pinching ways had been well founded. By February and March 1855 terribly wintry conditions coupled with very high unemployment due to war in the Crimea had brought extreme suffering to many people in Macclesfield. Soup kitchens were giving out 150 gallons daily, at a penny a quart with a small loaf of bread. Hundreds of tons of coal had been donated and these were intended to be distributed in 2 cwt. portions to the most needy 1,800 families. However, as the canal was frozen solid no coal barges could get to the town wharf. *The Courier* reported on the 17th February:

"The Union workhouse contains at the present time a larger number of inmates than at any period since its erection and the appeals for out-of-door relief to the Board of Guardians on Thursday last were unusually numerous."[12]

A deputation from the relief committee consulted with the Board to get them to grant more outdoor-relief, which they could now do under an Order of 1844. They were already employing weavers in a quarry at 1s. 6d. per day; which one of the deputation said was *"as bad as sending them to work in the trenches in the Crimea."* The Board ought to find work fit for weavers, said the Rev. Edward Weighall, vicar of Hurdsfield and one of the deputation, adding that there were many cases of distress where, due to the stringency of the law, lots of people would have starved if it had not been for private benevolence. The Board expressed their aim to provide £400 for the soup kitchen - if some legal means was obtainable.

One week later, when the soup kitchen was in low funds, Rev. Weighall reported that the Board had not obtained this legal means. The Board explained that there was nothing to prevent them giving out soup and bread, but it would have to be done under the supervision of their relieving officers. They would investigate the wants and earnings of each applicant, after which they added; *"the 2,000 cases of which Mr Weighall had spoken would dwindle down very materially."*

The high unemployment continued throughout the latter 1850's. A disease of silk worms and floods in southern France meant that raw silk from Europe was in short supply, pushing up the price of raw silk from Bengal and China to

West Park Hospital formerly Macclesfield Union Workhouse. *(David Broadhurst)*

levels where British demand for silk goods fell away. The soup kitchen became a regular feature of life throughout the winter months, particularly in 1857-58. In late October 1857, just as the soup kitchen opened, unemployed silk weavers petitioned the Board of Guardians:

"We the unemployed in public meeting assembled, take the liberty to solicit your assistance in helping us to a little out-door relief during out present distress. If this is denied we must break up our homes and be a continual burden on the parish, and, considering the low state of wages and the uncertainty of employment, we shall not be able to regain them. Many in the lowest stages of privation do not wish to come under the Vagrant Act by begging tickets for soup, and are now in the most extreme state of destitution and consequently now solicit your assistance to save life."[13]

The Guardians retorted that they would grant outdoor relief *"in all proper cases"*, when the able-bodied would be put to work breaking stones. The weavers then asked if the work provided could be more suitable for men of their trade, such as light agricultural work or picking oakum in their own homes. They also decided to send a memorial to London the ask the Commissioners there if the rule which bound the Guardians to providing outdoor relief only after this 'Labour Test' could be rescinded, but the local Board refused to add their support to it. The reply from London indicated that their request would receive consideration, but little changed.

An operative's home in hard times, c 1860.   (From the Illustrated London News)

In the meantime it was left to private benefactors and charitable people to provide for the vast majority of the poverty stricken. One gentleman soup ticket distributor was shocked:

"He had witnessed such scenes as he never expected to see, and he was so much hurt when he found that the assistance he was enabled to afford fell far short of what was required even for temporary relief."[14]

Almost 3,000 families were visited daily and provided with soup, bread, milk and packets of tea, all from charitable fundholders other than the Poor Law Guardians. Many destitute people remained isolated and untouched by either provider of relief though, for certain slum districts were neglected by the soup kitchen committee and those who lived in the tidiest looking houses were likely to be overlooked. Some were refused soup tickets on account of extravagance, as were a man who kept pigeons costing him 3/4d per week in food and another whose liking for a glass of ale was so well known that he was told that he should have looked after his money when he had it.

The Board of Guardians' provision of outdoor relief was eventually expanded. Men could either break stone in quarries or be employed in raising the road level from Upton to Prestbury and widening the road to Whirley; hard physical work that the more sedentary weaver was ill-equipped for. One silk weaver sent by the Board to Boughey Lane worked from 7am until dusk and was paid 4s. per week for himself, his wife and their child. By January 1858 there were over 2,200 persons, mostly children, working on outdoor relief. When the start of these roadworks was announced by John West at a Statham Street meeting of the unemployed in December 1857, he had explained, *"the work would not be heavy work"*, whereupon a person on the platform beside him added, *"Nor yet heavy wages"*. At this, the audience collapsed with laughter; but there was little to provide humour in such desperate times.

While outdoor relief was provided in the shape of hard labour to a majority of applicants, there were others who were incapable of such work and who required a medical certificate to obtain an exemption. But the certificates were not always accepted. Edwin Adams, a weaver in bad health who had a wife and child, was sent to break stone in spite of possessing one such certificate. The work was so hard for him that he later joined two other weavers on a walk to Chester, intending to join the militia there. They had no money at all between them and along the route were arrested for begging in Northwich. Each man was sentenced to fourteen days imprisonment at Knutsford - and to be fed on bread and water only. At a meeting of the unemployed, a vote of censure was passed on the Northwich magistrates, who, John West said, were *"destitute of Christian charity."*

A picture of the destitution suffered by Macclesfield's poor was provided by a *Manchester Guardian* reporter that December:

"Day after day the long shambles which form the road to the soup kitchen of Macclesfield are traversed by a train of women and children, many of them evidently of a class certainly not wont to seek its bread from charity: women who, in better times might be hardly distinguishable from the wives of small shopkeepers: and children who do not seem habituated to squalor, or the yet more degrading effects [of] the charitable. "But for the soup kitchen," many of them say, "we must have died of hunger."[15]

But hunger was not the only suffering felt by such people, as the Committee for the Relief of the Poor reported:

"Many distressing reports were furnished by the district visitors the lamentable want of clothing and bedding; cases were known where not a single article of covering (sheet, blanket or coverlet) was to be found in the house - all had gone to purchase food; and the poor inmates had only straw to lay down upon; parents and children huddling together at night to retain as much animal warmth as possible by such means."[16]

The extreme poverty endured by so many over the winter of 1857-58 was repeated throughout 1862 and on into 1863, for by that time yet another Government inspired free trade Act had further undermined Macclesfield's competitiveness in the production of silk, with predictable results. At new year 1863, 2,525 people were in receipt of Parochial relief while another 3,000, many representing large families, applied to the local charity. They provided bedding, flannel, calico, linsey petticoats and clogs to 1800 applicants; with blankets rationed to one per family for sharing, *"father and mother enjoying it one portion of the night, and then transferring it to the children for the remainder."* As before, the charity bore the greater burden of poor relief while the local Board of Guardians stuck rigidly to their rule book.

At the pawnbroker's shop. (From the Illustrated London News)

References
1. M.C. 29/7/1826.
2. M.C. 13/5/1837.
3. ibid.
4. M.C. 13/5/1837.
5. M.C. 3/6/1837.
6. ibid.
7. M.C. 6/10/1838.
8. M.C. 3/6/1837.
9. M.C. 23/1/1841.
10. ibid.
11. ibid.
12. M.C. 17/2/1855.
13. M.C. 31/10/1857.
14. M.C. 14/11/1857.
15. M.C. 12/12/1857.
16. M.C. 9/1/1858.

Chapter 13. The Macclesfield Board of Trade

Writing under the pen name *"Scipio"* in August 1827, John Prout explained that the silk weavers' petition to Parliament to obtain legislation for the regulation of wages was to include a kind of arbitration procedure; a combined meeting of equal numbers representing both manufacturers and weavers which would from time to time fix prices for weaving. These prices would be binding on both parties and could only be altered when *"the exigencies of the trade"* required it. In due course this procedure was adopted - twenty-two years after it was first proposed.

The impetus came after strike action by the weavers in February 1849. Several thousands assembled at Park Green and with two bands playing and lots of flags waving went on an orderly procession around town, handing out a new list of prices at each manufacturers. But although the list was accepted almost unanimously, some manufacturers were underpaying before a week had passed by. The strike then resumed. After another fortnight of bickering, the Committee called a public meeting where both sides agreed to adopt the manufacturers' suggestion and set up a local Board of Trade. This was to be based on a French example, The Consiel de Prud Hommes at the silk town of Lyons. It was to consist of 12 delegates each from weavers and manufacturers and to be financed by levies on both employer and employee. Samuel Higginbotham, a local solicitor, Superintendent of the Large Sunday School and *"a disinterested person"*, was appointed as Chairman. Within days they were in conference at the Angel Inn. Within a week the Board of Trade had drawn up a new list, which was to be binding on manufacturers and backdated by two weeks.

After a further month, one manufacturer, Smith's of Parsonage Street, refused to pay by the new list; but a turn out of his weavers and a visit by Board of Trade delegates soon resolved the issue. From then onwards the Board managed to regulate affairs between men and masters with apparent success and no strikes for almost two years, although growing resentment simmered beneath the surface. This burst out in the last two months of 1850, when a third of the outdoor weavers and a large portion of indoor weavers were unemployed. First it was discovered that Smith's weavers were again working underprice, this time willingly. John West exclaimed bitterly:

"that after all our labour and expenses in getting the price, they returned "like a dog to his vomit," being more in love with the title of Knobstick than honourable men to the trade."[1]

Then, early in November the weavers convened to discuss a suggestion by a deputation from Brocklehurst's that a temporary lowering of prices on certain articles currently woven outside of Macclesfield might have the effect of bringing the work back into town. John West, the Chairman, ensured its rejection and said that the deputation, which included Nicholas Lynch and Thomas Cope, were *"viewed with distrust by the trade"*. At this Lynch and the others were openly hostile to the Board of Trade itself. Lynch wrote to *the Courier:*

"I should like to know how our Board can justify adhering to a list which causes the weaving to leave the town? An empty list without employment is only a bag of moonshine."[2]

The problem with the Board, they felt, was not the manufacturers nor the Chairman - who West called the *"most honest man in Cheshire"* - it was rather the composition of the weavers' delegates who sat on it. When the Board next met in late November, Lynch and another Brocklehurst inside weaver proposed altering its constitution so that the weavers' portion comprised six undertakers and six journeymen; their reasoning being that the change would favour outside weavers, who were more likely to make concessions to prevent work leaving the town. West, who had only recently made the transition from journeyman to undertaker, was against this, maintaining that the interests of all weavers were alike. He ensured that the Board was kept in its original format.

By mid 1851 the Board was under more serious threat; six manufacturers who were against it had made private contracts with their undertakers and others were not contributing their levies. Even manufacturers who supported the Board thought that their delegates ought to be in the majority, for at almost every division the weavers solidly opposed them and the deciding vote was left to the Chairman. The weavers were disillusioned by the activities of manufacturers who sat on the Board but sent work into the country and paid their Macclesfield weavers under the list price. At a Board meeting in September 1851, William Barnett said of John Brocklehurst; *"He sits on the Board and he, of all men, does the most to violate its regulations"*. Manufacturers agreed, saying, *"How can you expect us to go along with the Board when Brocklehurst does not pay the list prices?"* They were disgusted at seeing his delegate, mill manager Joseph Mann, sitting there when he had no intention of paying the prices he actually voted for. Their Chairman, Samuel Higginbotham, threatened not to continue if the Board's decisions were no longer respected. The continuation of the Board itself was only granted grudging approval for its continuation at a meeting by manufacturers to decide the issue held later that September.

In the meantime the weavers' almost unified demand for the full list prices had slipped, even from one of its most vociferous supporters. A letter to *the Courier* from John West in November requested the Board of Trade to make a temporary reduction in the list prices for certain goods where manufacturers thought the price was too high. A reduction would bind them to keep the work in town, he claimed. West had finally come round to thinking as had John Prout in March 1847 and was in full agreement with the stance taken by Nicholas Lynch, Thomas Cope and other Brocklehurst's delegates' the previous November. But the Board rejected West's argument. At this, a sizeable faction of Brocklehurst's outside weavers soon took matters into their own hands.

In December 1851, the Board's Secretary, Charles McDonnell, wrote to Brocklehurst's requesting them to pay the list prices and collect outstanding levies from their outside weavers. When no levies were forthcoming by January, the Board threatened that Brocklehurst's weavers would be asked to strike until the regulations were complied with. The levies were then collected, but some men refused to pay and six contrived to get enormous sums docked from their wages in payment, in one case 2s. out of a week's wages of 5s.4d. They then drew money in the form of a 'sub' to take out a summons against Brocklehurst for docking such large sums from their pay packets, all it seems with the collusion of their employer. Their purpose was to *"disparage and vilify"* the Board of Trade in Court.

By early March the Board, much criticised by Joseph Mann on behalf of his employers in the Town Hall Court, had ceased to exist. At the annual meeting of manufacturers to elect representatives for it, only seven turned up and they voted for its discontinuation. The weavers' section of the Board then called a meeting at Waters Green, where they demanded the immediate dismissal of four of the six outside weavers who had brought the summons and called upon other Brocklehurst's weavers to strike until they were. Almost all of their inside weavers then turned out. In response, Brocklehurst's put placards around the town to state that the four men were *"respectable and industrious."* This, as far as other weavers were concerned, proved the collusion between them and their employer. The strike began at the end of April with each male striker being paid 7s.6d. per week, financed by a levy of 1s. 6d. per loom on working weavers.

A few of Brocklehurst's weavers did not join the strike and a novel form of intimidation was practised. One of these men, John Laird, left the factory in Hurdsfield one mid-day to walk to his home at Stoney's Buildings, Watercotes, for his dinner. As he did so a lad carrying a board stepped in behind him. The board had a placard fixed to it which stated *"Look Here! John Laird is still at work in Brocklehurst's; inside."* When Laird got to Sunderland Street, stones were thrown at him. On his return from dinner there was a large crowd gathered at Park Green and among them three more such boards with other men's names upon them. He tried to seize the board with his name but was stopped by the crowd and beaten. Two men were later charged with intimidation; one of them being George Bailey, the President of the now defunct Board of Trade. But the intimidation was not just one-sided; it was claimed that Brocklehurst's had *"bagged"* [sacked] women silk winders who were the wives or sisters of strikers.

Bailey next presided over a huge assembly of over 2,000 weavers at Waters Green. He should have been in gaol but was out on bail after a sentence of one month's imprisonment at the Town Hall Court for intimidation. The solicitor defending him, Mr Norris of Chestergate, managed on appeal to have the case taken to a higher court at Knutsford. Addressing the crowds, Bailey said that Brocklehurst's had manufactured the evidence against him and exhorted the weavers to stand firm. He announced that subscriptions for the strike fund had come from men and women in all trades and even children gave their pennies, so much so that strike pay was now 8s. for men and 5s. for women. The meeting closed with three cheers for Mr Norris *"the poor man's advocate."*

A further gathering at the same venue in the first week of May was informed by Bailey that a few men had returned to work, but contributions were still coming in and they could hold out for as long as twelve months. He referred disparagingly to John West; *"a great Chartist"*, one who had armed himself with a home-made pike for the 12th August [1839 'Grand National Holiday'] but who was now working underprice. When West stood before the meeting he was ill-received, for he spoke out against the strike. There was a political motive behind it, he told them; Tory agents and well-known knobsticks had engineered it to discredit John Williams MP and throw him out in the coming elections. But the popularity, even adulation, that he had received for so long as a weavers advocate and political activist had evaporated. When he complained about aspersions being cast upon his character and reminded the crowd *"He had worked for them for twenty-three years as no man in Macclesfield had ever worked,"* a voice shouted out *"And you've been well paid for it."* This incensed the crowd further and he was eventually shouted down by cries about the payments he was supposed to have received. *"Knock him down,"* and *"Pull him off the cart,"* was urged by some. Charles McDonnell refuted West's political charges and said the conspiracy was entirely by Brocklehurst's outside-weavers who wished to break up the Board. After much further bickering, the meeting ended, having voted to continue the strike.

Meanwhile, deputations from the weavers attended Brocklehurst's to negotiate with his manager, Joseph Mann. At first, Mann made it quite plain that until their weavers returned to work and the demand for the discharge of the four weavers was withdrawn, there would be no discussions. After four days of quibbling the weavers resolved to return to work unconditionally and give Brocklehurst's the opportunity to pay the list prices. Before they could do so, Mann withdrew his offer of discussions and Henry Brocklehurst, a son of Thomas Brocklehurst, told them they could only return to work if they paid the full cost of loom rents for the duration of the strike and any expenses the firm had incurred in publishing placards. At this the strike resumed. On the 22nd May Brocklehurst's published a letter in *the Courier* which stated they were *"maintaining our authority as employers"* by imposing certain conditions before the men could return, such as *"acknowledging their misconduct"* and paying the loom rents for the strike period. It continued however;

"taking into consideration the bad state of the trade, and the deprivations of those who have been misled, we ordered that the loom rent which has accumulated against them to be remitted."[3]

The strike was finished by early June, its aim unrealised. Gradually, Brocklehurst's weavers went back on their master's terms. At a Park Green meeting held before their return, ex-secretary of the Board of Trade, Charles McDonnell, read out two letters from the National Trades Association enquiring into the workings of their Board with a view of petitioning Parliament for the formation of a national network with statutory powers. He said Macclesfield was honoured to have been the model for local boards, which were now supported by so many MPs. The throng of weavers then voted to request manufacturers to re-convene the Board of Trade. But they were no longer interested.

It is also unlikely that John Brocklehurst would have been among the ardent advocates for a nation-wide network of local boards of trade, but he was

Average wages of silk workers and significant events 1790-1870.

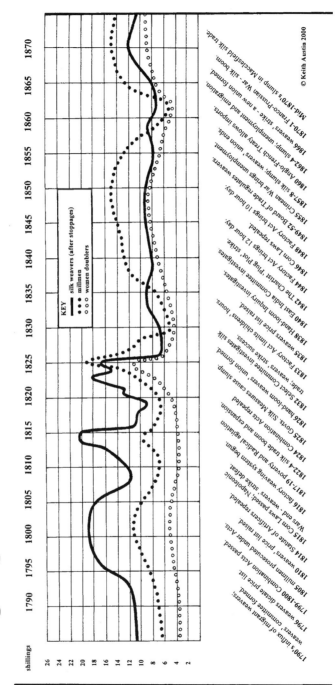

© Keith Austin 2000

KEY

━━━ silk weavers (after stoppages)
••• millmen
ooo women doublers

1790's influx of migrant weavers; weavers' committee formed.

1799-1800 millmen prosecuted under price list.

1805 Combination Acts passed.

1810 weavers' price list raised.

1814 Statute of Artificers repealed.

1815 Corn Laws passed; Napoleonic War's end - weavers' strike defeat.

1816 factory weaving system begun.

1817-19 poverty and Radical agitation

1822-4 silk trade boom and expansion.

1824 Combination Acts repealed.

1825 Govts. Silk Measures cause slump.

1826 hand-loom weavers' union formed.

1832 Select Committee investigates silk trade; weavers' union formed.

1833 Factory Committee investigates silk.

1835 weavers' price list limits 'hours'.

1838 hand-loom Inquiry list raised.

1840 East India Committee investigates.

1842 The Chartist 'Plug Plot' strike.

1844 Corn Laws repealed.

1846 Factory Act brings 12 hour day.

1848 Factory Act brings 10 hour day.

1849-52 Board of Trade regulates weavers.

1857-8 silk slump; weavers' unemployment.

1860 Anglo-French Treaty allows imports.

1862-4 slump; unemployment; union ends.

1866 weavers' strike - a new union formed.

1870-1 Franco-Prussian War - silk boom.

Mid-1870's slump in Macclesfield silk trade.

re-elected as one of Macclesfield's two MPs in July 1852. Prior to the election, the Courier published a letter from *"A Silk Weaver"* about the other MP, John Williams, and his broken promises. He was *"a wind-bag, a word-monger, a pie-crust promiser"*, the disappointed ex-supporter raged. Despite his call not to support Williams, the election was fought with the utmost hostility shown by working men to both Brocklehurst and the Tory, Edward Egerton. As Egerton's narrow lead over Williams at the polls increased daily, that hostility turned to extreme violence. Mounting the hustings on the final day, Egerton was greeted by a barrage of stones, brickbats, bottles and horseshoes - and then a twelve inch long, horn-handled dagger which was thrown from amidst the crowd. It pierced the side of the wagon on which he stood. In return, special constables armed with staves *"too frequent in use"*, managed to badly injure five men. The outcome was defeat for Williams by a margin of 62 votes, this in some minds corroborating John West's claims that the whole affair of the Brocklehurst's strike was a Tory conspiracy engineered to unseat Macclesfield's Radical MP.

The conclusion of that strike began a long period of further decline in wages. Towards the end of 1853 McDonnell told weavers gathered at Waters Green that manufacturers were paying 33% under the list of prices:

"why if the wages of the whole of the weavers could be averaged for the last twelve months, he was ashamed to say that the little girls who piece at the engines would laugh at them; they were getting better wages than the weavers."[4]

But not only did weavers earn less than mill-workers - man, woman or child even; the skilled-worker status they once enjoyed had largely dissipated too. Another weaver remarked:

"As things were now, the finger of scorn was pointed at weavers; no trade was so degraded as theirs. If a stranger enquired who such or such a person was, if he belonged to the trade, the contemptuous answer was "Oh, he's only a weaver." [5]

References
1. M.C. 16/11/1850.
2. M.C. 9/11/1850.
3. M.C. 22/5/1852.
4. M.C. 17/9/1853.
5. ibid.

Park Green, late 19th century. *(MMT)*

Punch cartoon - The effects of a strike. *(MMT)*

Chapter 14. New Beginnings

After the break up of the Board of Trade, the weavers' Central Committee gradually lost all influence as shop after shop broke off all ties with it and negotiated separate deals with their employers. As a result, weavers faced more cuts in the prices paid for woven goods. High unemployment during 1854 drove wages lower still and the severe winter which spread over into 1855 only increased their misery.

Added to the difficulty of obtaining fair prices for their work was the manner in which justice was meted out during disputes. In September 1855 six power loom weavers, one of whom was George Bailey, were charged before Macclesfield magistrate William Brocklehurst, under the Act of 1767, with leaving work in their looms and absenting themselves during a strike. They had turned out to support one of their number whom their employer, Thomas Birchenough, had insisted should put two colours into handkerchiefs for the same price as one. Acting for the defendants was William Prowting Roberts, a full-time trade union lawyer, a one-time Chartist and the scourge of magistrates and colliery owners in

William Brocklehurst, 1784-1859. *(MMT)*

Lancashire and the north during the 1840s. Word that he was coming was enough to have his collier clients released from gaol immediately and if not, his able use of a writ of Habeas Corpus invariably had them acquitted.

Roberts first argued that the case should never have been pursued, for the Act was passed long before the power loom was invented and was aimed principally at home workers. He added;

"Why, Good God, what would become of the working men if they did not co-operate together? What would become of their wages if they did not act together and unite in supporting a fellow workman when he demanded a fair price for his labour?" [1]

He then turned his attention to the magistrates, claiming he had heard that any silk master with £500 could become a magistrate - *"if this was so, might God help the operative weavers"*. A heated argument then ensued between Roberts and Brocklehurst, who said he was not a silk master [but he was a brother of J & T Brocklehurst], adding, *"You insinuate that, because the magistrates of the bench are silk masters, justice would not be done."*

"I insinuate that you are a silk master, or you would not interrupt me," Roberts replied.

Continuing, he then stated that the six men were all resolutely prepared to go to gaol, for they would not submit to having work imposed upon them for which they were not paid. It was their *"sacred duty to protect the rights of labour"*, he said, telling the magistrate that by enforcing such working practices they were *"parties to the fraud."* He left no-one in doubt of what he thought of the local magistracy and concluded his summing up;

"In my mind Mr. Birchenough is a grossly dishonest man, and I say it though he may one day be elevated to the judicial bench to administer the law he has so grossly infringed." [2]

Birchenough then offered to withdraw the charges and pay the price for two colours in the handkerchiefs if the six weavers would pay the court costs and loom rents for the duration of the strike. This they refused and were still prepared for imprisonment. More argument ensued, but in spite of their able defence lawyer, known as the trades unions' 'Attorney General,' the case was finally settled with the weavers still having to pay 10s. each in court costs but no loom rent.

Three years later, Birchenough and Roberts crossed swords once more in a similar dispute over paying loom rents for the duration of a strike; when intense local interest in the case had the court room filled to overflowing. The case was finally settled out of court by Roberts, acting for the defendants, and Mr Norris of Chestergate, acting for Birchenough. The Master and Servant Act under which these and countless other weavers had been charged over many years was only finally abolished in 1875.

A large pool of unemployed weavers undermined any strong resistance to pay cuts. By January 1857 several manufacturers were said to be paying as much as 50% below others for certain goods, often because undertakers would take the work at almost any price. Some demanded the restoration of the Board of Trade, or at least to re-unionise the weavers themselves, *"who are at present very much disunited"*. At a crowded Town Hall meeting George Bailey even tried to arouse all weavers, inside and out, to work only between the hours of seven in the morning and six in the evening, almost as Reuben Bullock had advocated in his pamphlet *On Mending the Times* back in 1833. He pointed to the better wages and full employment of mill workers whose hours of work were regulated. It was a proposal that was greeted with mixed laughter and applause by the gathering, and then total hostility by John West, who said it was *"nonsensical"* and called Bailey a *"mountebank"*. West, the one-time ardent supporter of the Board of Trade, was now totally against its re-establishment, claiming its greatest defect was that most of the decisions had been left to the casting vote of the chairman. The meeting rejected Bailey's idea but carried a motion by Joseph Hooley; to have delegates from both inside and outside weavers of every shop attend a further meeting to choose a new committee.

If there was a committee to come from this, its activities went unreported in *the Courier's* pages. Instead it was Hooley who much later that year chaired other quite different meetings; of unemployed silk weavers intent on obtaining relief from the local Board of Guardians during the severe slump which befell them over the winter of 1857-58. When next they assembled to discuss their trade, it was in October 1859 at the Town Hall, where the subject was a Bill recently introduced into Parliament by a Mr McKinnon MP for the formation of Equitable Councils of Conciliation between workmen and their employers. This was in effect the same arrangement as the Macclesfield Board of Trade but with legal standing - a list of prices would be legally binding on both sides.

The discussion about McKinnon's Bill had almost immediate effect among the weavers. Soon afterwards they met at the Joiners Arms in Paradise Street to discuss the code of rules issued for the guidance of those wishing to form such an association. These were adopted, a committee was elected to conduct the association's affairs and a levy of 3d. per loom was ordered to fund it. The committee took office on the 22nd October and had soon formed a new union, *The Friendly Society of Broad Silk Weavers of Macclesfield*. At the Town Hall in early December the union's new rules were then read and accepted unanimously. Both the union secretary and John West assured them all that there would be no obstacle to outside weavers joining, as it was essential that inside prices were paid to all.

But the optimism of this time was soon in decline, as was the new union.

A late January 1860 meeting at the Town Hall seems to have been the last public airing of its views, when they expressed unanimous approval for McKinnon's Bill. In the event, the Bill came to nothing but another Act of Parliament was to cause yet more grief to Macclesfield's silk workers. This, the Anglo-French Treaty introduced by Free Trade advocate Richard Cobden, allowed unrestricted imports of French silks into Britain. Strangely, considering the dire consequences to Macclesfield silk workers, they seem to have made little unified protest.

Mayor of Macclesfield, Jeremiah Clarke, was in total support of the new treaty that December, but warned the town's workers that its benefits depended on their *"willingness to compete"* and not to enter into strikes. On the weavers' behalf, *"Weaver Boy"* of Chester Road, complained in a letter to *the Courier* that Mayor Clarke had thrown the responsibility for the success of the Anglo-French Treaty on the working man and that his previous predictions about earlier Acts had *"most signally proved fallacious"*.

"See what depreciation of mill and other property since the unpolitic measures of 1826; see how the profits of employers have dwindled away; see how the comforts of the work-people have been curtailed; and themselves reduced to wretchedness, want, and pauperism; see the squalid appearance of our poor people as they pass along the streets - and then ask, where are the boasted advantages we were told would flow to us by Huskisson, Cobden and Bright when those changes were brought about?"[3]

"Weaver Boy" also noted that none of the Mayor's investments were in Macclesfield and concluded the his reference to strikes was a forewarning of attempts to reduce wages.

The truth of this was made apparent within two years. In December 1862, silk weavers at a Town Hall meeting were asked to provide exact written statements about their previous six months wages for the committee to place before the County in the hope of obtaining some relief for their distress. The silk trade had been in complete stagnation since 1857, when only a third of the town's 4,600 weavers had work. Now, although there were four weavers in work for every three then, their wages were reduced so that four earned what three had previously. Joseph Hooley gave an instance of one street where 102 people lived in fourteen outside weavers houses. The loom shops above them contained 35 looms but only eleven of them had been at work in the past two years. Average wages for the weavers there fell short of 5s. per week. Corroborating this scenario was John West, who had canvassed several large employers in the town and found that wages of inside weavers ranged from 7s.

6d. to 12s. before the payment of loom rents; and one firm with 100 looms had only 30 of them weaving.

Others reported similarly to the Mayor at the Town Hall. He was told by local gentlemen of the distress that existed in the Borough on the 13th December 1862: namely that of its 12,000 silk operatives, there were 1,950 still in employment while another 4,687 were on part-time and the remaining 5,272 were unemployed. The average wages of each employed worker was 5s. per week. Over 2,500 were on parish relief and another 600 received private charity. As conditions in town once more plummeted and thousands were in receipt of food, bedding, clothing and clogs, some silk weavers sought another, quite dramatic solution - emigration to America.

This was probably the ultimate act of self help by Macclesfield's silk weavers: helping some of their fellows to leave the town in a body and set off for a new life in North America. Emigration had occurred before this date; two weavers, one from Hurdsfield and one from Mottram, had gone off to America in 1829, while William Butterworth, one of the 1832 strike leaders, had set off for Schyler, Illinois in September 1841. During the mid 1840s a member of the Ryle family had started manufacturing silk at Paterson, New Jersey, and was later joined by many emigrants from Macclesfield in what became a flourishing business there. In May 1851 a party of 20 emigrants left town bound for Port Lyttleton in New Zealand, and they were to join another 50 who had gone before them to the Canterbury Settlement. One of the settlers was William Gosling, latterly of Jordangate but living in Port Lyttleton when he wrote to *the Courier* in February 1852. He complained of silk weavers *"always expiating on the beauties of the silk trade...The most useless gabbing fellows in this place; - I am ashamed of my native town."*

The wave of emigration that was precipitated by the French Tariff of 1860 was done under the auspices of the Macclesfield Silk Weavers Emigration Society. In its initial month of June to July of 1863, 87 members, all *"hale, strong, young men"*, enrolled before the books were closed. Of these, 47 volunteers were balloted for the first ten places and were all set to leave England on board the *Georgio*, bound for Canada on the 18th August 1863. Funds had been raised to help the emigrants; £7.14s. 0d. being collected from one sermon alone given at Park Green Chapel. The Society had hoped to obtain a government supplementary grant of £2 per head to assist in payment of the emigrants' passages. But before the first emigrants could sail, this was ruled out by a Committee at the Mansion House, London, as the grant was only payable for cotton workers. This upset the arrangements and the *Georgio* sailed without the Macclesfield emigrants. But the Society was then helped by the *"extraordinary exertions and the kind assistance of several gentlemen"* so that they could book passages on the screw steamer *Olympus* to New York and from there to Toronto by rail.

On the day of their departure, late that August, the emigrants first met at the Society's meeting rooms in Mill Street and then went down to Park Green. There, John West had a few words to say;

"the emigrants did not leave their country through choice, but of necessity, their country had forsaken them, not they their country; their Rulers through the system of policy, had taken their trade from them and bestowed it on the foreigner; there was nothing left for them, but for a large portion of every year to lead a pauper's life, or in the hospitality of our Colonies seek that protection and remuneration for their labour which has been denied them here; with manly independence they preferred the latter, though they would never forget their native land, nor the good old town where in bygone times they had spent so many happy years."[4]

A procession was then formed with banners to the fore, followed by the band, the emigrants and their family and friends, then the Committee, and finally a vast crowd of well-wishing people. As the band struck up with such lively tunes as *"Cheer Boy's Cheer"*, the long procession trailed up Mill Street, through the Market Place and down Jordangate until arriving at Hibel Road railway station. Still more people were waiting there, bringing the total numbers up to around 2,000. Throughout the procession and at the station there was no *"noisy bluster"*, as everyone seemed overawed by the importance of the occasion and the need to honour the emigrants. These were the most cheerful of all. Their train left the station at 7.45am.

The Emigration society was wound up in January 1864, but a few more emigrants awaited the word to sail for North America. These were mostly the wives and children of those who had left the previous August; and their turn came in June 1864. Once again large numbers of people gathered at Hibel Road railway station to see them off and wish them well. This time there were four married men, twenty women and eight children. Several were being sent out 'passage paid' by Levi Malkin, a manufacturer of Fence Street, Hurdsfield, who was acting on behalf of the Hartford Carpet Company of Connecticut, and in whose service they were expected to obtain work on their arrival.

Most emigrants ended up in other parts of the United States, particularly Paterson, New Jersey. One, once a *"skilled weaver of rich goods"*, was by July 1864 working as a track layer on the railway at Rich Valley, California.

John Stubbs was long dead by 1865, yet his efforts in the cause of a wider franchise, from the post-Napoleonic Radical period through to the era of Chartism, were not forgotten. A gathering of non-electors at the Market Place that June were reminded of his dedication by their chairman. They were

assembled to support the Liberal candidate, David Chadwick, who was to stand against the Tory MP, Edward Egerton, in the forthcoming election. The speakers included John West, Joseph Hooley and Nicholas Lynch, who was addressing his first meeting in seven years. Hooley pointed to the limited voting rights of the town's population: because of property depreciation, he said, 170 individuals whose homes were now valued at less than the annual £10 rent

David Chadwick and supporters on the hustings beside the Town Hall during the 1865 election. *(Doug Pickford)*

threshold had lost their right to vote. [only 18% of Macclesfield's adult males had the vote, compared to a national average of 47%] Politically, Chadwick was said to be in favour of extending the franchise and of ballot voting. Yet Lynch was more concerned to highlight Chadwick's association with the Globe Cotton Spinning Company of Lower Heyes mill and its new cotton weaving enterprise. It was a flourishing trade and would bring Manchester prices and more employment into town, he enthused.

David Chadwick laid the foundation stone for a new weaving shed at Lower Heyes that July. It was said to be the largest in the world. A procession of thousands of working people, led by the company directors and attended by bands playing and much waving of flags and banners, left Park Green for the mill at 6.30p.m., after the working day was ended. As church bells rang out they first followed a circuitous route along Mill Lane, Cross Street, High Street and Park Street, to return to Park Green. Then they set off once more, this time via Mill Street, the Market Place, Jordangate and Hibel Road to Lower Heyes. All around town were slogans painted on walls: *"The dawn of better days for Macclesfield"* or *"Work versus Charity"*. The stone that Chadwick laid was inscribed with the information that 80,000 spindles and 1,450 looms would be housed within the shed; and he claimed that the Globe Cotton Spinning Company had £200,000 in capital. Nicholas Lynch had said that Chadwick was its principal shareholder; but *the Courier*, hostile to Egerton's election rival, scathingly stated that he owned a mere twentieth part.

The newspaper's fears were unfounded, for Egerton defeated Chadwick in the July 1865 election. Chadwick's supporters, disappointed that he was therefore unable to lend his voice to the Commons debates on reforming the franchise, soon turned to the Reform League, a London-based organisation pressing for manhood suffrage. But when the Reform League's mass demonstration in Hyde Park turned to riot after the defeat of Lord John Russell's Reform Bill in June 1866, Macclesfield's response was muted. Announced by posters declaring *"Demonstration"* and inviting the working classes to show that they were not indifferent to the League's cause, a mere 300 people attended the peaceful procession which with bands playing and banners waving marched through the town to Park Green. There they supported John West's proposal to send a memorial to Queen Victoria. It asked her to dismiss her advisers and *"call to her council such statesmen as will secure to the country a full and comprehensive measure of Parliamentary reform."*

That long overdue reform was partly forthcoming early in 1867, when Disraeli's Bill enfranchised the urban working man but ignored ballot voting. David Chadwick thus benefited from both the wider franchise and the usual treating of electors when he was returned as one of two Liberal Macclesfield M.P.s in 1868 - the other being William Coare Brocklehurst, son of ex-MP John Brocklehurst. Yet Chadwick's claims to be a sympathiser with Macclesfield's working people and advocate of trade unionism - even that, were he a member himself, he would support any strike - was soon to sound as hollow as the *"better days for Macclesfield"* claim. Workers striking for higher wages at the Globe Cotton Spinning Co.'s mill in March 1868 were told by Chadwick not to return until they had rejected their union and were ready to work at their old wage rates. Worse was to follow: wages were reduced in spite of a two week long strike at the mill in December 1877 and two years later, with the cotton trade seriously depressed, a lock out of their 1,000 employees drove wages lower still.

The silk weaver's trade union was re-formed, as the Macclesfield Silk Weaver's Trade and Friendly Society, after a spontaneous five weeks long strike during July and August 1866 over *"an accumulation of wrongs"*. They originated that February, when a deputation from the town's 300 or more Persian and sarsnet weavers tried to get manufacturers to pay by a revised list of prices. Their wages were less than 7s. per week and they aimed at a 2s. 6d. increase. Most manufacturers refused to acknowledge any such list and some would not even see the deputation. Meetings between delegates from both sides followed, at which the Mayor presided, and to these were soon added delegates from the silk handkerchief, scarf and fancy trade weavers. But when the Mayor gave his casting vote to the weavers over prices paid for chintz, the manufacturers terminated the proceedings forthwith.

Exasperated, the weavers finally insisted that from July their hours of work would be limited to ten per day for inside weavers and lights out at 8p.m. for outside weavers - as similar to the suggestions of Reuben Bullock and George Bailey in previous years - and that if the 1849 list was not complied with a strike would ensue. When manufacturers refused the strike began; with the strikers numbering 1,174 and their strike fund totalling £62. Fortunately, the weather that summer was hot and many obtained alternative work from sympathetic farmers in the surrounding districts, having first been issued with cards certifying they were *"Macclesfield weavers out on strike"*. By mid-August the strike was over, with almost all manufacturers agreeing to abide by the 1849 list. Returning to work, the weavers still had a £30 residue from their strike fund and this was shared out between the 22 shops that took part.

Joseph Chapman had played a leading role in organising the strike and in October became the new union's paid executive, the first ever in Macclesfield. Simultaneously, a permanent committee room was established at the Co-operative store in Pickford Street. Chapman also acted concurrently as Secretary to the No.1 Power Loom Silk Weavers Association, formed in Macclesfield one year previously to represent about 300 such weavers. A hand loom silk weaver himself, Chapman originated in East Anglia, where he worked as an agricultural labourer from the age of seven. Two years later his family moved to Wigan and he obtained employment in cotton mills. A later move to

Middlewich, where the family fell upon hard times, brought him into contact with a local curate. When this curate took office as the Rev. C.N. O'Pratt at Macclesfield, he encouraged Joseph Chapman to join him. After some years in silk mills, washing silk or stripping reels, he was apprenticed to a weaver around 1840. Later, during the wholesale unemployment after 1857, he travelled widely, returning to town in the early 1860s. Yet with only a meagre parish school education behind him, Chapman soon showed himself to be among the most able of union leaders.

His first real test was in June 1867, when the new union came into conflict with the Board of Guardians. The Board, having consulted manufacturers and then interviewed delegates from the weaver's union, *"as if they were poor people applying for relief"*, concluded that any weaving work being sent out of Macclesfield was entirely the fault of the union and their *"fixing of arbitrary prices."* They suggested a three year period free of price lists and arbitration to settle disputes. This the union rejected, having tried arbitration before without success. The Board of Guardians then threatened to refuse all claims for relief from unemployed weavers who were union members, declaring them responsible for their own distress. Correspondence between Chapman and various Board members through the pages of *the Courier*, whose editor firmly supported the Guardians, became more heated and personally abusive each week. In one letter Chapman poked fun at an overweight Guardian and in return was labelled *"an eel of the first rate"* by another. However, it was Chapman who that December seems to have had the last word on this lengthy issue, appealing to the town's shopkeepers and traders: *"if a man earns a bare subsistence he cannot be a customer to the draper, tailor or silk manufacturer."*

Such wars of words, waged in *the Courier's* letter pages, were Chapman's speciality. These, often bitter, disputes with manufacturers and town councillors made him several enemies, but he also gained the respect of others. When one Alderman, the butt of Chapman's caustic wit on several occasions, took the opportunity of a Town Hall dinner party to criticise his antagonist, manufacturer William Corns rebuked the Alderman, saying that Chapman was:

"a man whose extreme talent would always be brought to bear to advise them [the weavers] rightly from their point of view, a man whose watchful eye was ever alert, a man who could tell at once the career of almost every manufacturer, and was ready to give an account of every thing on paper - black or white. That was not the man to be put down by a slight or sneer." [5]

In his own words, Chapman was a *"firebrand Chairman"*, but otherwise his tenure of office, from 1866 to 1879, was almost a replay of the years 1824-60. First there was a boom period while the Franco-Prussian War lasted, during which manufacturers enticed all sorts of people into their weaving sheds; elderly women, soldiers, shopmen, carpenters, clerks, painters or labourers. Undertakers too followed suit, teaching youngsters to weave in a few months, as many as four at a time in a garret of six looms. The union tried to stop this but was unsuccessful and as a result vast quantities of silk were spoiled. Soon afterwards fashions changed and silk goods made in Coventry superseded those from Macclesfield in public taste. The slump that resulted was exacerbated by periodic winters of severe conditions for the many unemployed. Then there was the ever-lasting controversy over the price list coupled with the perennial problem of manufacturers sending work out into the country, in which Brocklehurst's, who would no longer acknowledge the union, again played a key role.

Much later, following a lock-out by manufacturers in February 1878, arbitration was re-attempted with the establishment of the short-lived and unworkable Macclesfield Handloom Silk Trade Board, comprising delegates from both manufacturers and weavers. Eventually, having stuck out for and defended the list of prices ardently for many years, Chapman, like John Prout and Nicholas Lynch in the 1840's, and then John West in the 1850's, decided that price reductions were better than losing the work altogether. But when he advised a meeting of 2,300 weavers to do so, his opinion was rejected and he subsequently resigned his office. His final speech epitomised much of what had occurred over the years since 1826.

"We are surrounded by treachery; there is no power or unity. In almost every shop in Macclesfield the weavers are sneaking about and taking the bread out of their brothers' mouths. (a voice: "We want the union.") What? Union! There is no Union. Dissension has crept in, and I tell you it is impossible to rally the forces." [6]

A new union was formed in January 1880. Its first task was to organise the emigration of weavers.

References
1. M.C. 9/8/1855.
2. ibid.
3. M.C. 22/12/1860.

4. M.C. 29/8/1863.
5. M.C. 10/11/1877
6. M.C. 26/7/1879.

Above: Hurdsfield House, home of John Brocklehurst.
Below: 'Backs' at Arbourhay Street. *(MES)*

Chapter 15. Postscript

Owd time is a troublesome codger,
Keeps nudging us on to decay.
Crying out, "You're nobbut a lodger,
Get ready for going away."[1]

John Prout had moved house from Bank Top to Water Street by 1851. By then, four of his ten children, including the three eldest boys, had left home - the second son, John, also a silk weaver, married and living at Black Road. Left with him and Elizabeth, his wife, were four girls employed as silk weavers, a boy silk piecer and the youngest, a schoolgirl. It was at Water Street that John Prout died of apoplexy [a stroke] on the 27th March 1853, having been paralysed for four days. A brief paragraph in *the Courier* on 2nd April 1853 provided a few words of obituary:

"He was well known as a ready scribe to many of his fellow workers requiring memorials or petitions to be indited, an occupation that he preferred to the toil of his loom. He was engaged in the compilation of a pamphlet entitled a "Practical View of the Silk Trade" that attracted some notice about five and twenty years ago."

In that 1829 pamphlet, Prout had explained his penmanship in a completely different light;

"Accustomed to "handle the shuttle" errors of the pen will be liberally considered: circumstances and the times have alone driven me to the use of the latter."[2]

Whether John Prout did favour working his loom to writing a letter, a petition or a pamphlet can only be guessed at, but one certainty was that *"the times"* had changed little since then and poverty would dog the hand loom silk weavers for many years to come.

By 1853 some of Prout's contemporaries in weavers' affairs were either already dead or soon to be so. John Wright and John Stubbs had preceded Prout to the grave by two years and Samuel Simister was to follow on soon afterwards, leaving his Beech Lane home, and a wife and three sons, for his final resting place at Christ Church in January 1854 at the age of 47. None of the three men were still employed in the silk trade at the time they died, for Wright and Stubbs were beersellers while Simister, more tastefully, called himself a *"victualler"*. John Wright had changed from silk steward to beerseller before 1841 and after his death, in February 1851, his wife, Ann, took over the licence of their Roe Street shop. Similarly, John Stubbs, *"who on several occasions took a prominent part in this town in favour of the political agitations of his time"*, and who died on the 12th November 1851, had been selling beer for more than a decade. It was left to his wife, Rebecca, to continue beer sales at the family home in Back Wallgate.

Others, by then quite elderly, had abandoned silk weaving for different trades. David Rowbotham, 67 years old in 1851, had left a garret house in Arbourhay Street to become the Superintendent of the Baths and Wash Houses, at which place his wife, Elizabeth, was Matron and one of his sons the stoker. They lived in the attached house which fronted on to Davenport Street. Likewise, Reuben Bullock, at 76 years of age and a widower, had departed from Roe Street and by 1851 was a coal agent at Peel Street, Sutton. His two daughters, Mary and Mercy, both silk workers, resided with him.

Some others, although still weaving silk were no longer active participants in politics or trade unionism. William Parker, having moved from an Arbourhay Street garret house to Lord Street by 1841, seems to have taken no further part in either Chartism or weavers' affairs after the 'Grand National Holiday' riots of 1839. By 1851, aged 54, both he and his 18 year old son worked as silk weavers while his wife, Mary, kept house at their home in Park Lane. William Forrest was a regular at weavers' meetings only until the late 1840's. He was still weaving silk at the age of 54, living at Watercotes with his wife, Hannah, a silk winder, in 1851.

Others remained active in trade and political issues for many years to come. William Barnett, a bachelor, shared lodgings in Charles Street with William Adam, the *"leveller"* arbitrator of the late 1820s period in 1851. Barnett was still supporting the weavers' union in 1859 when aged 62 and was active in the No. 2 Co-operative Burial and Sick Society. Thomas Cope, whose six children were raised in a garret house in Fountain Street that he occupied from at least 1825, was still there with his wife Mary and four children, all silk weavers, in 1851. Ten years later, his eldest son, James, had taken on the house, but Thomas Cope was still around to take part in the Parliamentary reform movement of the mid 1860s at the age of about 75. George Bailey, who may also have lived in Fountain Street in 1861, would have spoken at a weavers' meeting in July 1877, but was prevented from voicing his opinions as he was no longer a union member. He seems to have died in August 1879, aged 63. Longer-lived was the schoolteacher and Radical, John Richards, whose small house and schoolroom was at Kerridge End, Rainow. By the late 1870s, then in his eighties, his once tall, stout figure was bent over with rheumatism and his ruddy complexion topped with white hair. A life-long bachelor, he was often seen, wearing his old-fashioned and scrupulously cared for clothes, walking the three miles from Rainow to Macclesfield to change his library books.

The two most notable Irish born silk weavers, Nicholas Lynch and John West, survived until around 1880 and beyond. They each had a liking for drink. In Nicholas Lynch's case, his beershop proprietorship in the mid 1830's may have triggered this thirst. Much later, his prowess when on union business became legend. A delegate at a Sunderland Street meeting in August 1866 related the following, probably much exaggerated, tale:

"The meeting would recollect Nick Lynch - he always called him "Old Nick" because he "sold" the weavers so often (a laugh). Well "Old Nick and Co. were deputed to take the matter in hand [reductions in prices at Brocklehurst's], they adjourned to the Wheat Sheaf in Waterloo St. and what did the meeting think "Old Nick and Co." chalked up against the trade? £30! ("Oh, Oh.") He did not know how much they consumed in the way of eatables but he knew that sausages in Hurdsfield went up a penny a pound. (Much laughter and a voice "They had several barrels of oysters")"[3]

Lynch's home was in Brunswick Street by 1842; and both he, his Irish born silk weaver wife Mary and their son Joseph were still there in 1851, when Joseph, aged 23, was employed as a portrait printer - probably by Thomas Bullock the photographer, who lived nearby. Nicholas Lynch, like his fellow 1832 strike leader and later arch-rival John West, was still active in the agitation for Parliamentary reform in the 1860's, but seems to have dropped out of union business well before then. His awful fate is all the more poignant for having been such an active participant in the local and national movements of his time. In May 1878, police and poor law guardians, called out by neighbours, forced an entry into a house at Pitt Street, Sutton. On the outside the house looked uninhabited; inside presented "such a state of filth and desolation as beggars all description", with empty medicine and spirits bottles laying everywhere, and the stench appalling. Nicholas Lynch, then a 77 year old widower, was found lying on a flock mattress, "in a wretched state of destitution and filth....entirely nude and suffering from debility". His 50 year old son Joseph, described as an artist, lived there with him and like him was a heavy drinker, so much so that he was suffering from delirium tremens. There was very little furniture in the house, no food and all their clothes except the trousers worn by Joseph had been pawned. Both men were taken to the Workhouse. Neither were still there by 1881, presumably having died.

Fate was kinder to John West. After his Chartist years he joined the local campaign to create a free public park and recreation ground on the Town Field; became a vociferous supporter of Poland's struggle against Russia during the early 1860's, and like Lynch was active in the Parliamentary reform movement that enfranchised urban working men in 1867. He continued working as a silk weaver but during his latter years lost his wife, Mary, and became dependent on strong drink. His son John, an iron moulder by trade and married with four young children, had taken him into his home at 155, Great King Street by 1881. In November 1881, a letter to *the Courier* from one-time national Chartist leader George Julian Harney, then in Boston, America, drew attention to West's poverty and suggested financial help. *The Courier* endorsed Harney's plea, adding that not long before he had unexpectedly arrived at a Town Hall meeting on the subject of atrocities in Bulgaria, *"and with his old fire and eloquence, turned the feelings of the meeting by his incisive speech against the policy of Russia."* A few months later, as West's 70th birthday approached, a local J.P., John May, wrote to *the Courier* requesting assistance for West in his decline and praised his past achievements;

"In his most eloquent and stirring speeches there was an admixture of wit and humour so characteristic of the country man.... Few of our public local men have escaped West's criticisms, I have shared as many as most; they were always independent - always honest."[4]

After this he was in receipt of support from May and others, including, despite West's long term antagonism to the family business, William Coare Brocklehurst M.P., the son of John Brocklehurst. West's one-time accusation that such manufacturers built up vast fortunes on the labour of weavers was aptly illustrated in August 1870 when John Brocklehurst died, aged 80, leaving an estate valued at £800,000. His brother Thomas also died that year and left £600,000. John West, who in 1832 had refused the opportunity to become a barrister in order to fight for what he believed in, died in poverty on the 15th January 1887, aged 75.

West's one time opponent over Free Trade, the more urbane Timothy Falvey, fared better than most of Macclesfield's silk weavers in later life. As a widely known and popular speaker, whose hearty laughter at his own jokes endeared him to audiences, his enthusiasm for the Liberal-Free Trade cause made him many friends in Southampton on his first visit in 1844. After the Corn Laws were finally repealed, he was in 1848 offered the editorship of the *Hampshire Independent*, a leading Liberal newspaper, in which he continued to battle against the injustices of the times. In this fight he maintained his efforts

Timothy Falvey, 1813-1889.
(Southampton Archive Services)

on the platform for both Southampton's Parliamentary and municipal elections, gaining for himself a local victory in the St. Lawrence ward. He also held office as the Government Distributor of Stamps for Southampton from 1851-65; was Deputy President of the local Board of Guardians; a governor of two schools; a member of the Polytechnic Institution, and a well-known Freemason and philanthropist. Falvey's penmanship was also put to use on behalf of his newly-adopted Southampton; for he wrote and presented the Town's address to Louis Kossuth, the Hungarian refugee, in 1851, and another to the Italian patriot, Joseph Garibaldi, in 1864 - of which both Lord Palmerston and *the Times* newspaper expressed high approval.

In his personal life Falvey was not so fortunate, for his Irish born wife died in 1864 and he outlived his daughters, both of whom died young. He was it seems, a soft touch where the poor were concerned, mildly derided by some acquaintances as *"Poor old Tim"* when he too readily subscribed to their appeals. In this respect he did not forget his Irish relatives and generously sent them parcels of clothing or money. Although he retired from the *Hampshire Independent* in August 1869, he continued in his public duties as representative for St. Lawrence ward on the Town Council until the day he died, *"one of the best known - if not the best known - public men in Southampton."* After attending a meeting on a cold, damp day early in October 1889, he caught a chill and died on Wednesday the 9th, aged 76. He was engaged in writing a history of a *"Period of Sixty Years"* at the time and as he lay ill told a friend that he hoped to be spared long enough to complete it. Had he done so, what more might be told of events during his time in Macclesfield?

Adam Rushton did leave an invaluable account of his years. Having survived the "crushing slavery" of a silk mill, become a warehousemen and evening class teacher, and later worked as both an undertaker and a manufacturer, he eventually took office as a minister in the Unitarian church.

By 1881 he had retired and lived with his wife, Irene, at 108 Great King Street. There, he had sufficient funds to employ a domestic servant and time enough to write his memoirs, published under the title *My Life as Farmer's boy, Factory lad, Teacher and Preacher* in 1909.

References

1. Finney, Isaac, *Glimpses of Macclesfield in ye Olden Days*, 1873.
2. Prout, John, *A Practical View of the Silk Trade*, 1829.
3. M.C. 11/8/1866.
4. M.C. 22/1/1887.

Adam Rushton in later life.

Macclesfield Sunday School early 19th century. *(MMT)*

Bibliography

Aspinall A. *The Early English Trades Unions.* 1949.
Broadhurst David, *Parkside Hospital, Macclesfield 1871-1996.* Pub. Churnet Valley 1997.
Bullock Reuben, *On Mending the Times,* 1833.
Chaloner W.H. *Mrs Trollope and the Early English Factory System; Victorian Studies Vol. IV*
                                                                                        No.2 Dec 1960
Cheshire Directory, 1857.
Collins, Louanne and Stevenson, Moira, *Silk: Sarnets, Satins, Steels and Stripes.* 1995.
Corry John, *History of Macclesfield,* 1817.
Davies Stella, *A History of Macclesfield.* 1961.
Earles John, *Streets and Houses of Old Macclesfield.* 1915.
Employment of Women in the Silk Trade, 1893-4, Vol.XXXVII, 1894.
Engels Frederick, *The Condition of the Working Class in Britain,* 1845.
Factory Inspectors Evidence on the Workings of the Factory acts, 1840.
Finney Isaac, *Glimpses of Macclesfield in ye Olden Days,* 1873.
Hammond, J.L. and B, *The Skilled Labourer 1760 - 1832,* 1936.
Hampshire Independent, 12/10/1889.
Hand Loom Weavers: Reports from Assistant Commissioners, Vol. XXIII, 1840.
Inspectors of Factories Reports, 1835-1860.
Inspector of Factories Reports, 1862.
Journals of the House of Commons, Vol. LXXIII, 1818.
Kirby R.G. and Musson A.E. *The Voice of the People. John Doherty 1798-1854 Trade Unionist,*
                                                Radical and Factory Reformer. 1975.
Longden George, *Life and Labour in Victorian Macclesfield,* 1983.
Macclesfield Courier 1811-1880.
Macclesfield, Stockport and Congleton Chronicle 1842.
Malmgreen Gail, *Economy and Culture in an Industrialising Town: Macclesfield, Cheshire,*
                                1750-1839. Indiana State University Phd. Thesis, 1981.
McGilchrist John, *Life of Richard Cobden,* 1865.
National Census Returns for Macclesfield, 1841,1851 and 1861.
Nicholson J.O. *Macclesfield Past, Present and Future,* handwritten essay, 1866.
Persons Summoned for Offences against the Factory Act between 19th December 1835 and
                                                1st May 1836, Vol. XLV, 1836.
Pigot's Directory of Macclesfield 1834.
Pigot and Slaters Directory of Macclesfield 1841.
Poor Man's Guardian 1832-35.
Prout John, *A Practical view of the Silk Trade,* 1829.
Report of Factory Inspectors to Local Government Board, 1873.
Reports of the Select Committee to Inquire into the Law Respecting Artisans, Machinery,
                                Combinations of Workmen, Etc., 1824.
Rules and Orders to be observed by the Silk weavers of Macclesfield. 1826.
Rushton Adam, *My Life as Farmer's Boy, Factory Lad, Teacher and Preacher,* 1909.
Second Report of Children in Factories, 1833.
Second Report of Commisioners on Child Labour, Vol. XXI, 1833.
Second Report of Select Committee on Ribbon weavers of Coventry and Leek and the Silk
                                Weavers of Macclesfield. 1818.
Select Committee on Hand Loom Weavers Report, Vol. XIII, 1835.
Select Committee Report on Masters and Operatives, Vol. XIII I, 1856.
Select Committee Report into the State of the Silk Trade 1831-32, Vol. XIX I, 1831-32.
Southern Reformer, 7/8/1880.
Thompson E.P. *The Making of the English working Class,* 1979.
Trollope F.E. *Frances Trollope: Her Life and Literary work from George III to Victoria,* 2 Vols. 1895
Trollope T.A. *What I Remember,* Vol. II 1883.
United Trades Co-operative Journal, Jan. to Oct. 1830.
Vareys Directory of Macclesfield 1825.
Voice of the People, Jan. to Aug. 1831.
Ward J.T. *The Factory movement 1830-1855.* 1962
Webb, S and B. *The History of Trade Unionism,* 1920.

Index